◼ Contents

T3-BHM-592

Lawn and Residential Landscape Pest Control

A Guide for Maintenance Gardeners

PESTICIDE
APPLICATION
COMPENDIUM
8

Lawn and Residential Landscape Pest Control

A Guide for Maintenance Gardeners

Susan Cohen
Senior Writer
University of California Statewide IPM Program, Davis

Mary Louise Flint
Associate Director, Urban and Community IPM
University of California Statewide IPM Program, Davis

Extension Entomologist
University of California, Davis

Nila Hines
Graduate Student Researcher
University of California Statewide IPM Program, Davis

UNIVERSITY OF CALIFORNIA
STATEWIDE INTEGRATED PEST MANAGEMENT PROGRAM
AGRICULTURE AND NATURAL RESOURCES
PUBLICATION 3510
2009

To order or obtain ANR publications and other products, visit the ANR Communication Services online catalog at **http://anrcatalog.ucdavis.edu** or phone 1-800-994-8849. You can also place orders by mail or FAX, or request a printed catalog of our products from

University of California
Agriculture and Natural Resources
Communication Services
6701 San Pablo Avenue, 2nd Floor
Oakland, California 94608-1239

Telephone 1-800-994-8849
(510) 642-2431
FAX (510) 643-5470
E-mail: danrcs@ucdavis.edu

Publication 3510
ISBN-13: 978-1-60107-560-4
Library of Congress Control Number: 2009900078

Funding for this manual was provided in part through an agreement between the California Department of Pesticide Regulation and The Regents of the University of California, Agreement Number 05-0093C, and through the Extension Service, U.S. Department of Agriculture, under Special Project Section 3(d), Pesticide Safety Education Program.

To simplify information, trade names of products have been used. No endorsement of named or illustrated products is intended, nor is criticism implied of similar products that are not mentioned or illustrated.

 This publication has been peer reviewed for technical accuracy by University of California scientists and other qualified professionals. This review process was managed by the ANR Associate Editor, Agricultural Pest Management.

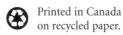 Printed in Canada
on recycled paper.

2m-pr-5/09-SB/NS

■ Acknowledgments

This manual was produced by the University of California Statewide Integrated Pest Management Program through a Memorandum of Understanding between the University of California and the California Department of Pesticide Regulation.

TECHNICAL ADVISORY COMMITTEE

The following group of academic, regulatory, and field experts were key advisers and contributors for knowledge expectations, style, and content and helped identify information sources and contributors.

Bethallyn Black, University of California Cooperative Extension, Contra Costa County

Phil Boise, Urban/Ag Ecology Consulting Services, Gaviota

Adolfo Gallo, California Department of Pesticide Regulation, Sacramento

George Kaiser, Landscape Management Services, Mountain View

Jeff Phillips, Monsanto, Elk Grove

Mac Takeda, California Department of Pesticide Regulation, Sacramento

Kathleen Thuner, San Diego County Agricultural Commissioner

Cheryl Wilen, University of California Cooperative Extension, San Diego County and University of California Statewide IPM Program

PRODUCTION

Design and Production Coordination: Seventeenth Street Studios

Photographs: Jack Kelly Clark and Michael Poe, except as noted

Drawings: Seventeenth Street Studios

Editing: Stephen Barnett

SPECIAL THANKS

The following people provided ideas, information, and suggestions or reviewed one or more of the many manuscript drafts.

J. Betourne, City of Davis

B. Black, University of California Cooperative Extension, Contra Costa County

P. Boise, Urban/Ag Ecology Consulting Services, Gaviota

D. Burger, Department of Plant Sciences, University of California, Davis

C. Carr, San Diego County Agricultural Commissioner's Office

S. Dreistadt, University of California Statewide IPM Program

C. Elmore, Department of Plant Sciences, University of California, Davis

A. Gallo, California Department of Pesticide Regulation, Sacramento

D. Giraud, University of California Cooperative Extension, Humboldt County

R. Hansen, Suisun Valley Fruit Growers, Suisun Valley

D. Haver, University of California Cooperative Extension, Orange County

M. Juhler, Yolo County Planning and Public Works Department, Woodland

J. Karlik, University of California Cooperative Extension, Kern County

P. Kjos, Shasta County Agricultural Commissioner's Office

R. Landon, Yolo County Agricultural Commissioner

M. LeStrange, University of California Cooperative Extension, Tulare County

L. Leondis, San Diego County Agricultural Commissioner's Office

J. Letterman, Professional Applicators

Professional Association, Salinas

T. LoCoco, Recreation and Parks Department, City of Santa Rosa

V. Matonis, Parks, Recreation and Community Services Department, Redwood City

F. McCutcheon, San Diego County Agricultural Commissioner's Office

R. Melnicoe, University of California Office of Pesticide Information and Coordination, Davis

M. Moore, San Diego County Agricultural Commissioner's Office

M. Moratorio, University of California Cooperative Extension, Solano and Yolo Counties

T. Olsen, San Diego County Agricultural Commissioner's Office

G. Patzkowski, Facilities, Operations and Maintenance, University of California, Davis

M. Pepple, California Department of Pesticide Regulation, Sacramento

E. Perry, University of California Cooperative Extension, Stanislaus County

D. Pinto, Davis, CA

M. Scally, Professional Gardening Services, Woodland

J. Strand, University of California Statewide IPM Program

M. Takeda, California Department of Pesticide Regulation, Sacramento

K. Thuner, San Diego County Agricultural Commissioner

M. Werner, Landscape Manager, Gualala

C. Wilen, University of California Cooperative Extension, San Diego County, and University of California Statewide IPM Program

■ How to Use this Book

WHAT IS A MAINTENANCE GARDENER?

Maintenance gardener pest control businesses primarily perform cultural tasks, such as mowing lawns, and they maintain landscaped areas. Although they also perform pest control, applying pesticides is only incidental to their primary business of maintaining landscapes.

This book is one volume of the University of California's Pesticide Application Compendium, a series of books for pesticide applicators in specific settings. Our purpose in publishing this book is to help maintenance gardeners use pesticides safely and study for licensing exams. The book will also be an important resource for home gardeners and others who control pests in their landscapes. In addition to explaining how to use pesticides, it tells how to prevent accidents and avoid injuries and environmental problems, and if they occur, how to take the right action to maximize safety.

The proper handling of pesticides involves many special skills and responsibilities. It is important that you know the hazards of pesticides so you can avoid them. You must know the laws and regulations that relate to the use, transport, storage, and disposal of pesticides. If you have employees, you must know the requirements for their safety and training. Use of pesticides by maintenance gardeners requires licensing by a state agency.

As a maintenance gardener you will have many tools available for maintaining landscapes and managing the pests that affect the areas you take care of. Pesticides are one of the tools you may use. Many pest problems can also be solved with nonchemical methods. However, when you do use a pesticide, it is very important that you know how to use it safely and legally and in a way that will effectively reduce the target pest.

Maintenance gardeners who use pesticides must be licensed by the State of California. If you already have the maintenance gardener pest control license, this book is a useful reference tool for the knowledge and skills you use in your work. If you are a maintenance gardener who is not licensed, this book will help you prepare; it is the California Department of Pesticide Regulation's (DPR) official study guide.

USING THE REVIEW QUESTIONS

At the end of each chapter are several review questions to test your grasp of the information presented in that chapter. These questions are written in a similar format as the questions on the DPR maintenance gardener pest control examination, so they provide a good practice tool. Begin your study by reading a chapter and then read the review questions at the end of that chapter. Make a note of any subject material you do not fully understand. Check your answers against the correct answers at the end of the book. If you missed any of the questions, go back and reread the sections of the book that cover the information. Also review the illustrations and their captions.

KNOWLEDGE EXPECTATIONS

At the beginning of each chapter is a list of knowledge expectations that cover all the information you are expected to know for the maintenance gardener pest control examination. The knowledge expectations have also been placed within the chapter where the information you need to know is located. Study these lists before and after you read each chapter and be sure to learn the material that is addressed by each knowledge expectation.

Lawn and Residential Landscape Pest Control

A Guide for Maintenance Gardeners

1 Pesticide Laws and Regulations

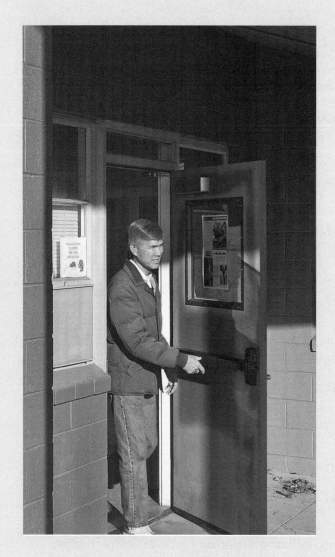

Pesticide applicators must follow all pesticide use laws and regulations. This chapter explains the most important laws and regulations for persons who perform pest control as an incidental part of their business of maintaining landscapes.

1. Know the roles of the Department of Pesticide Regulation and the county agricultural commissioner, and how to work with their offices.

2. Know the kind of pest control you may perform and where you are allowed to apply pesticides if you have a

    - Maintenance Gardener Pest Control Business License
    - Category Q or B Applicator License

3. Know the renewal requirements for the Maintenance Gardener Pest Control Business License, the Qualified Applicator Certificate, and the Qualified Applicator License.

4. Know the requirements for pesticide use record keeping and use reporting.

5. Know the pesticide application notification requirements.

6. Know the requirement to use only registered pesticide products that include the intended use site on the label.

7. Know the different sections of the label, be able to locate them, and be able to find specific information.

8. Know how to properly store pesticides and application equipment.

9. Know how to properly transport pesticides.

10. Know how to legally and properly dispose of excess pesticides and empty pesticide containers.

11. Know worker safety requirements, including providing pesticide safety training for handler employees and emergency medical care for all employees.

12. Be aware of personal protective equipment requirements and know the ones that apply to your pest control activities.

P ESTICIDE APPLICATORS must follow all pesticide use laws and regulations. This chapter explains the most important laws and regulations for persons who perform pest control as an incidental part of their business of maintaining landscapes. Doing incidental pest control at locations where your primary business is maintaining landscapes is allowed only if you have the proper business and applicator licenses issued by the California Department of Pesticide Regulation (DPR). This chapter discusses the various requirements that apply to the Category Q maintenance gardener pest control business, including the supervision by a qualified applicator; use reports and records; reading and following pesticide labels; storage, transportation, and disposal of pesticides; and pesticide worker safety requirements for employers and employees. If you have questions about regulatory or legal requirements for pesticide use, your county agricultural commissioner can help guide you and provide you with answers.

Figure 1-1. Federal, state, and county governments regulate pesticides. The county agricultural commissioner enforces the rules, even in cities and towns.

■ Who Regulates Pesticides?

Federal, state, and local agencies control the manufacture, sale, transport, storage, and use of pesticides (Figure 1-1). At the national level, the U.S. Environmental Protection Agency (EPA) is the primary

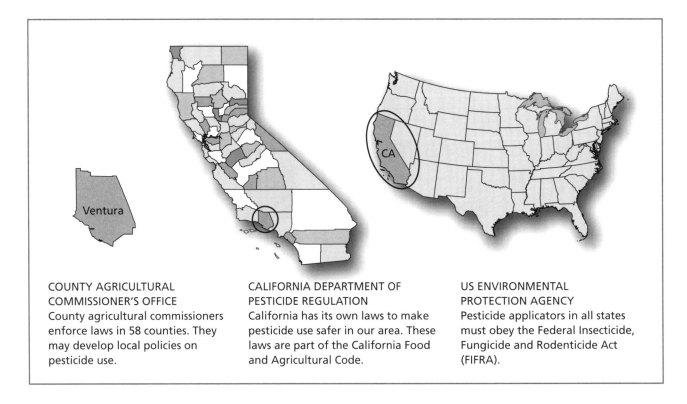

COUNTY AGRICULTURAL COMMISSIONER'S OFFICE
County agricultural commissioners enforce laws in 58 counties. They may develop local policies on pesticide use.

CALIFORNIA DEPARTMENT OF PESTICIDE REGULATION
California has its own laws to make pesticide use safer in our area. These laws are part of the California Food and Agricultural Code.

US ENVIRONMENTAL PROTECTION AGENCY
Pesticide applicators in all states must obey the Federal Insecticide, Fungicide and Rodenticide Act (FIFRA).

agency regulating pesticides. At the state level, DPR is the lead agency that is responsible for the enforcement of all the pesticide laws and regulations. County agricultural commissioners (CACs) enforce pesticide laws and regulations at the local level in each county. California pesticide laws are part of the California Food and Agricultural Code. These laws are made by the state legislature and signed by the Governor. Regulations are the more detailed working rules that explain how the laws will be implemented. For a more detailed explanation of pesticide laws and regulations, review DPR's *Laws and Regulations Study Guide.* You can download this free publication from the DPR Web site (**www.cdpr.ca.gov**), or you can purchase it from DPR.

1. Know the roles of the Department of Pesticide Regulation and the county agricultural commissioner, and how to work with their offices.

Get to Know Your County Agricultural Commissioner

The county agricultural commissioner's office (Figure 1-2) is the pesticide applicator's primary source of information regarding the legal and proper use of pesticides. Before starting a maintenance gardener business or getting licensed or qualified, it is a good idea to become acquainted with the county agricultural commissioner's office in each county where you will be working. Agricultural commissioners can provide you with information about upcoming nearby Qualified Applicator Certificate (QAC) or Qualified Applicator License (QAL) examinations, licensing information, requirements, and study materials. Also, once you have a Maintenance Gardener Business License, before starting work you must register the business each year and with each of the agricultural commissioners' offices in the counties where you apply pesticides. To find your local (county) agricultural commissioner, look in a telephone directory under County Government Offices.

Figure 1-2. Visit the agricultural commissioner's office to find out how to get licensed. They can give you information to help you use pesticides safely and legally.

Each agricultural commissioner is charged with protecting agriculture, the environment, consumers, and public health in the county. Although they are called "agricultural" commissioner, they are responsible for overseeing the safety of pesticide applications in all settings, including nonagricultural situations such as landscapes. As part of their responsibilities to enforce pesticide laws in the county, inspectors from the county agricultural commissioner's office may periodically watch your pesticide applications, inspect your storage facilities and pest control equipment,

and audit (review) your pesticide records for applications and employee training.

The county agricultural commissioner's office is your local reporting agency for issues involving pesticide use. You are required to file a monthly pesticide use report (Figure 1-3) with the county agricultural commissioner where you apply pesticides. Turn them in even for months when no pesticides were applied. Also, pesticide spills and accidents must be immediately reported to the county agricultural commissioner.

Figure 1-3. Submit pesticide use reports monthly to the county agricultural commissioner's office in each county where you work.

STATE OF CALIFORNIA

MONTHLY SUMMARY PESTICIDE USE REPORT

DEPARTMENT OF PESTICIDE REGULATION
ENFORCEMENT BRANCH

PR-ENF-060 (REV. 9/07)

INSTRUCTIONS FOR COMPLETING THIS FORM ARE INDICATED BELOW AND ON THE REVERSE SIDE

OPERATOR (FIRM NAME)		ADDRESS		CITY		ZIP CODE	PHONE NUMBER
OPERATOR ID/PERMIT NUMBER	LICENSE NUMBER		COUNTY WHERE APPLIED	COUNTY NUMBER	MONTH/YEAR OF USE		TOTAL NUMBER OF APPLICATIONS

1. Complete Columns A, B, C, and D for *All Users*
2. Complete Column E by using one of the following codes:
   Code 10 - Structural Pest Control...includes any pest control work performed within or on buildings and other structures.
   Code 30 - Landscape Maintenance Pest Control.............includes any pest control work performed on landscape plantings around residences or other buildings, golf courses, parks, cemeteries, etc.
   Code 40 - Right-of-Way Pest Control..............................includes any pest control work performed along roadsides, power lines, median strips, ditch banks, and similar sites.
   Code 50 - Public Health Pest Control..............................includes any pest control work performed by or under contract with State or local public health or vector control agencies.
   Code 80 - Vertebrate Pest Control...................................includes any vertebrate pest control work performed by public agencies or work under the supervision of the State or county agricultural commissioner.
   Code 91 - Commodity Fumigation (Nonfood/Nonfeed).....includes fumigation of nonfood/nonfeed commodities such as pallets, dunnage, furniture, burlap bags, etc.
   Code 100 - Regulatory Pest Control.................................includes any pest control work performed by public employees or contractors in the control of regulated pests.
3. Complete Columns F and G, if use *does not* fit one of the above codes

A	B	C	D	E	F	G
MANUFACTURER AND NAME OF PRODUCT APPLIED	EPA/CALIFORNIA REGISTRATION NUMBER FROM LABEL INCLUDE ALPHA CODE	TOTAL PRODUCT USED (Check One Unit of Measure)	NUMBER OF APPLICATIONS	CODE	COMMODITY OR SITE TREATED	ACRES/UNITS TREATED
		☐ ☐ ☐ ☐ ☐ LB OZ PT QT GA				
		☐ ☐ ☐ ☐ ☐ LB OZ PT QT GA				
		☐ ☐ ☐ ☐ ☐ LB OZ PT QT GA				
		☐ ☐ ☐ ☐ ☐ LB OZ PT QT GA				
		☐ ☐ ☐ ☐ ☐ LB OZ PT QT GA				
		☐ ☐ ☐ ☐ ☐ LB OZ PT QT GA				
		☐ ☐ ☐ ☐ ☐ LB OZ PT QT GA				
		☐ ☐ ☐ ☐ ☐ LB OZ PT QT GA				
		☐ ☐ ☐ ☐ ☐ LB OZ PT QT GA				
		☐ ☐ ☐ ☐ ☐ LB OZ PT QT GA				

REPORT PREPARED BY _____   DATE _____

When pesticide laws or regulations are violated, the county agricultural commissioner determines the enforcement action, which may include a fine of up to $5,000. More serious pesticide violations may be prosecuted through the district attorney's office. To be safe, find out how to follow all laws so a county agricultural commissioner does not take enforcement action against you.

Your agricultural commissioner's office is a good resource for information about pesticides and pest issues. If you have a pest you need identified, take it to the agricultural commissioner's office or UC Cooperative Extension (UCCE) office in your county. The county agricultural commissioner's office may also be able to help you find continuing education classes required to maintain your QAC and may provide pesticide safety training. County agricultural commissioner offices should be your first source of information when you are not certain about pesticide laws and regulations. They can give you guidance about proper application methods, pest control equipment, and transportation, storage, and disposal of pesticides. Take advantage of your agricultural commissioner's staff; many of their services are free.

■ Maintenance Gardener Pest Control Business Licensing; Applicator Certification; Pesticide Record Keeping, Use Reporting, and Notification

MAINTENANCE GARDENER PEST CONTROL BUSINESS LICENSE

DPR requires that any person who carries out pest control for hire (which includes advertising, soliciting, or operating as a pest control business) must be licensed as a pest control business. The qualified person for the pest control business must be certified as a qualified applicator. If your business is primarily controlling pests in landscape locations, the qualified person will need a Qualified Applicator License in the Landscape Maintenance Pest Control category (category B). However, if your business is primarily maintenance of ornamental and turf plantings at residences, businesses, or commercial parks and uses pesticides only incidentally at those sites, you need a person with a Qualified Applicator Certificate in Maintenance Gardener Pest Control (category Q) and a Maintenance Gardener Pest Control Business License (Table 1-1).

2. Know the kind of pest control you may perform and where you are allowed to apply pesticides if you have a

- *Maintenance Gardener Pest Control Business License*
- *Category Q or B Applicator License*

Table 1-1. Types of Licenses. Use this table to determine what type of license you need.

TYPES OF LICENSES		
	LANDSCAPE MAINTENANCE PEST CONTROL	**MAINTENANCE GARDENER PEST CONTROL**
Type of pest control to be performed	All types of landscape maintenance pest control.	Incidental pest control as part of maintenance gardening work.
Types of pesticides used	Restricted-use and general-use pesticides.	General-use pesticides only.
Nature of work	Pest control activity is a major part of service offered.	Work is primarily maintenance of landscapes; pest control is only incidental.
To get a license for the business	Submit application to DPR with the following information: • Qualified person (QAC or QAL): name, QAC or QAL number, expiration date. • Financial responsibility covering chemical liability. • Worker's compensation insurance information (if business has employees). • Corporation or Fictitious Business Name Statement. • Fee. • Your signature.	

The Category Q (maintenance) license is more restricted in scope than the Category B (landscape) license. As a result, Category Q has a reduced continuing education requirement for maintaining the applicator license or certification. The Q fees are less than those of B. The Q category

- does not allow you to apply pesticides as a primary part of your job
- is valid only when working for a licensed maintenance gardener pest control business
- limits the types of jobs you can do
- does not allow the use of California restricted materials or federally restricted-use pesticides

SCOPE OF WORK AND SETTINGS

The primary business of maintenance gardeners is mowing and edging lawns; maintaining residential yards or other turf plantings;

removing weeds; pruning shrubs, bushes, or trees; and planting. Pest control is incidental. The landscaped areas can be located indoors or outdoors, surrounding structures, or in commercial parks. (A commercial park is a site with commercial establishments such as offices, restaurants, stores, or other businesses.) You can work in public areas such as parks, golf courses, and cemeteries, and other similar areas as well as in private areas, such as residences.

CATEGORY B: LANDSCAPE MAINTENANCE PEST CONTROL

Licensed pest control businesses engaged in the Landscape Maintenance Pest Control Category are legally authorized to perform pest control in landscaped areas. Pest control is their primary business but they can also perform landscape maintenance (gardening) work if they wish. The category B license is *not* for businesses that primarily *maintain* landscaped areas by performing cultural tasks such as mowing, fertilizing, planting, and general cleanup.

CATEGORY Q: MAINTENANCE GARDENER PEST CONTROL

Maintenance gardener pest control businesses primarily perform cultural tasks, such as mowing lawns, and they maintain landscaped areas. They also perform pest control, which includes the occasional use of pesticides, but applying pesticides is only incidental to the primary business of maintaining landscaping. This book is the DPR-approved study guide for the category Q maintenance gardener examination.

Applying for the Maintenance Gardener Pest Control Business License

A person applying for a Maintenance Gardener Pest Control Business License must submit to DPR a complete application and fee. The application, made up of various forms, must identify the certified commercial applicator (who holds a QAC in category Q) who will supervise the incidental pest control work (application of pesticides) performed by the company. The maintenance gardener business must also provide certain information including the following:

- proof of financial responsibility covering chemical liabilities

- proof of worker's compensation insurance

- document verifying the type of business such as corporation, fictitious business name, etc.

3. Know the renewal require-
ments for the Maintenance
Gardener Pest Control Business
License, the Qualified Appli-
cator Certificate, and the Quali-
fied Applicator License.

The application must also be signed by the applicant. Businesses must immediately notify DPR in writing of any changes in business name, address, qualified person (holder of the QAC), insurance, or any other item on the business license application.

Renewing the Maintenance Gardener Pest Control Business License. Maintenance Gardener Pest Control Business License holders must renew their licenses every two years by submitting the required DPR form and fee. They must also register in each county in which they will work, each year.

CERTIFIED DPR COMMERCIAL APPLICATOR

Both landscape maintenance (category B) and maintenance gardener (category Q) businesses require a qualified person in the business to be a certified commercial DPR applicator (hold a QAC or QAL). This cides) performed by the company. The qualified person is usually the business owner, an officer of the business, or an employee. Anyone who performs pest control (using pesticides) for the company must either be a certified commercial applicator or, while performing pest control, be supervised by a certified commercial applicator.

To become a certified commercial applicator you must first complete and submit an application and pay a fee to DPR, then pass the appropriate DPR examination. For the category Q (maintenance gardening) QAC, you must pass the examination that covers pesticide use laws, regulations, and basic principles and pest control in the maintenance gardening setting.

Renewing the Qualified Applicator Certificate or Qualified Applicator License. Commercial applicators must renew their QAC or QAL every two years (last names starting with letters A–L renew in even-numbered years, and M–Z renew in odd-numbered years). The person holding only a category Q QAC is required to attend eight hours of DPR-approved continuing education (CE) classes (Figure 1-4). A minimum of two hours of CE must be on pesticide laws and regulations. Other classes may cover information on pesticide laws and regulations, pesticides, and pest management techniques. The CE must be obtained during the valid period of the QAC or QAL in order to renew for the next two-year period; if CE is not obtained during this period, the test must be retaken.

Figure 1-4. QACs must attend eight hours of DPR-approved continuing education classes every two years to renew their licenses. Two of these hours must be about laws and regulations.

Category B licensees must have 20 hours of CE every two years, with a minimum of four hours on laws and regulations relating to pesticides. Category Q licensees must have eight hours of CE every two years, with a minimum of two hours on laws and regulations relating to pesticides. DPR does not keep track of the CE classes you take. You are responsible for maintaining the documentation of approved classes you have attended.

Colleges and universities, professional organizations, and private companies offer DPR-approved CE courses. Lists of approved courses are posted on the DPR Web site at **www.cdpr.ca.gov/docs/license/classes.htm**. Keep records of the classes you take so you can submit the list with your renewal. Keep CE records for three years. Include the name of the instructor or sponsoring organization, title of class, location, the class's DPR identification code (meeting code) number, and the number of hours of credit (broken down into "laws and regulations" and "other"). Many courses offer a certificate of course completion that will contain this information.

PESTICIDE USE RECORDS

Maintenance gardener pest control businesses must keep records (Figure 1-5) of all pesticides used for two years. The records must be readily available for inspection if requested by the county agricultural commissioner or DPR. Records must include the following information:

4. Know the requirements for pesticide use record keeping and use reporting.

- date of application
- name of the operator of the property treated (this can be the homeowners' association, owner or manager)

- location of property treated (address or description of location)
- site treated (location of plants treated on property)
- total units treated at the site (for example, number of square feet)
- identity of the pesticide, including the EPA or California pesticide product registration number
- amount of pesticide used (for example, number of ounces or pounds)

MONTHLY PESTICIDE USE REPORTS

Maintenance gardener pest control businesses must submit monthly pesticide use reports to the county agricultural commissioner and keep copies of these reports for two years. Obtain the DPR Monthly Summary Pesticide Use Report (see Figure 1-3) from your county agricultural commissioner or from the DPR Web site (**www.cdpr. ca.gov**). Fill it out and submit it to the county agricultural commissioner's office in the county where you applied pesticides by the 10th of the following month. If no pesticides are applied during a month, submit a monthly pesticide use report indicating "no pesticides were applied." The county agricultural commissioner's office will help you fill out the form the first time you must make a report. Many county agricultural commissioners' offices allow you to submit your reports online. Contact your county agricultural commissioner for more information.

The Maintenance Gardener Pest Control Business License and the Qualified Applicator License or Certificate may be refused, revoked, or suspended by DPR if any false or fraudulent pesticide use reports are submitted.

Figure 1-5. Keep records of your pesticide use for two years. Include the following information.

PROPERTY OWNER OR MANAGER	DATE APPLIED	LOCATION	PLANT OR SITE	SIZE OF TREATED AREA OR NUMBER OF TREATED PLANTS	AMOUNT OF PESTICIDE	PESTICIDE NAME	EPA REGISTRATION NUMBER FROM LABEL

PESTICIDE APPLICATION NOTIFICATION REQUIREMENTS

You must get consent and notify property owners or managers before applying pesticides to the property. The notification (Figure 1-6) must be in a format the customer can understand. This notice must include the common or brand name of the pesticide(s), the date of the application, and any label or regulatory precautions that should be taken. Notification is especially important so that appropriate protective measures can be taken for infants, the elderly, and those who are chemically sensitive; also, people with pets will need time to make arrangements, if necessary. It is a good idea to put up signs in the treatment area (Figure 1-7) (but only with permission from the property operator) if the location is one that people or pets may use.

5. Know the pesticide application notification requirements.

Figure 1-6. The homeowner or property manager must consent before you use pesticides. Be sure residents know any safety precautions that they must take. Here is an example of a notification form that you could use.

PESTICIDE APPLICATION NOTIFICATION

Pest to be controlled: _____

Pesticides to be used (active ingredients): _____

Area to be treated: _____

Date to be treated: _____

Please keep children and pets out of the treatment area for at least _____ hours.

PLEASE NOTE ANY SPECIAL INSTRUCTIONS HERE:

_____

_____

FOR MORE INFORMATION, CONTACT:

Name of applicator: _____

Business name: _____

Telephone: _____

For further information about pesticides, contact the county agricultural commissioner.

If you believe you may be experiencing poisoning symptoms, contact your doctor or poison control center at 1-800-222-1222.

Figure 1-7. Posting treated areas with signs is a good idea. Make sure the property manager or owner agrees to have the signs. Explain that you will take them down. Remove the signs when it is safe to enter the treated area.

■ The Pesticide Label

6. Know the requirement to use only registered pesticide products that include the intended use site on the label.

Pesticide label information must be read, understood, and followed. Labels are the primary and most important source of information for protecting the applicator, nontarget organisms, and the environment. They help you use the product as effectively as possible. Pesticide labels (Figure 1-8) are legal documents; it is a violation of law to use any pesticide in violation of the label instructions. The label must always be at the use site. If you have put the pesticide into a properly labeled service container, you will still need a copy of the full label at the use site.

DO NOT USE PESTICIDES IN CONFLICT WITH THE LABEL

Before you buy a pesticide or decide to use a particular product, read the label to be sure the pesticide is allowed for your intended use. The label will list the allowed sites for application and any other requirements for storage, handling, or use. For instance, do not apply a pesticide labeled "only for turf" on an ornamental plant unless the plant is also listed on the label. Do not apply pesticides labeled only for ornamental plants on food plants like apple or citrus trees or vegetable gardens.

The law requires that you follow the label directions. This means that you must use pesticides in a manner consistent with their labeling and you must not use them in a manner inconsistent with their labeling. Label directions are not advisory; rather, they are requirements. If you think you might not be able to follow the label directions or do not understand them, consult with the county agricultural commissioner before applying the pesticide. It is against the law to not follow the label directions.

CIRCUMSTANCES WHEN YOU DO NOT NEED TO FOLLOW THE LABEL EXACTLY (DEVIATIONS)

Federal and state regulations allow you to sometimes use the pesticide product in a way that is different from the label directions but only when this will make the application safer. This is referred to as "deviating" from the label. California regulations allow only the following six deviations from following the label directions:

1. applying less pesticide

2. applying a lower concentration of pesticide

3. applying the pesticide less often

4. applying the pesticide on another pest as long as the application site is listed on the label and the label does not prohibit the use

5. using a different method of application and the label does not prohibit the method and you can meet all other label requirements

6. mixing in another pesticide or a fertilizer and the label does not prohibit combining

Figure 1-8. You may apply pesticides only to the sites listed on the pesticide label. The label may also tell you to keep the pesticide away from other sites. Before you buy a pesticide, read the label to be sure the site you wish to treat is included.

TURFLON* ESTER

Controls Broadleaf Weeds And Bermudagrass In Ornamental Turf

General Information
(READ CAREFULLY BEFORE USING)

TURFLON ESTER herbicide is recommended for the control of actively growing annual and perennial broadleaf weeds and bermudagrass in perennial bluegrass, perennial ryegrass or tall fescue turf.
DO NOT apply to bahiagrass, bentgrass, bermudagrass, centipedegrass, St. Augustinegrass or zoysiagrass, unless turf injury can be tolerated.

Manufactured For:

MONTEREY
LAWN AND GARDEN PRODUCTS, INC.
P. O. Box 35000 • Fresno, CA 93745
(559) 499-2100
www.montereylawngarden.com

0 22179 10105 0
NET CONTENTS: 1 PINT/473.16 mL
0397/0298(02)

7. *Know the different sections of the label, be able to locate them, and be able to find specific information.*

PARTS OF THE PESTICIDE LABEL

The pesticide label (Figure 1-9) can be confusing. However, you must read and understand all of its contents before making a pesticide application. Once you learn how to locate the standard sections of a pesticide label, it will be easier for you to find important specific information on any pesticide label. Labels differ greatly as to how they are written and arranged, but they always have the information discussed here.

1. **Brand Name of Product.** Products have brand, chemical, and common names. Pesticides with similar brand names may not be the same product. The brand or trade name is the name the manufacturer gives the product and uses for marketing. Know how to find the active ingredient on the label and distinguish it from the brand name. (See Chapter 2 for more information on what an active ingredient is and why this is important.) For example, the herbicide glyphosate goes by many names, including Advanced Garden Power-force, Weed and Grass Killer, Round-up, and others. Another example is the insecticide acephate, which has the names Orthene, Dexol Systemic Plant Care, Isotox, and others.

2. **Formulation** information is usually shown on the label. First, you will need to know whether the product is liquid or solid. If it is a liquid, you will want to know whether it is an emulsifiable concentrate, a flowable, or some other liquid formulation. If it is a solid, it could be a granule, a dust, or a wettable powder. You must know whether the product is supposed to be mixed with water (diluted) before it is used.

3. **Ingredients** are listed on pesticide labels as a percentage of active and other (or inert) ingredients, by weight. **Active Ingredients** identifies the chemical or common names of the pesticide and the percentage (%) in the packaged pesticide product. The active ingredients are the chemicals that control the pest(s) listed on the label. Applicators and all pesticide users should know the amount (percentage) of active ingredient that they apply. Liquids will indicate pounds per gallon

Figure 1-9. Know how to find the different parts of a pesticide label. Be sure to read the entire label, including brochures attached to the container. If you aren't sure you understand the label, get help.

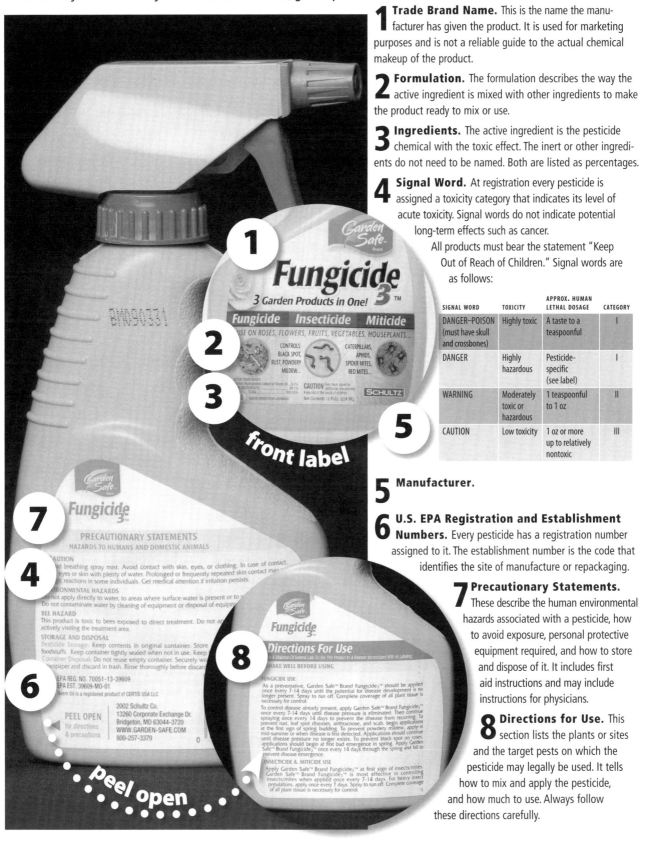

1 Trade Brand Name. This is the name the manufacturer has given the product. It is used for marketing purposes and is not a reliable guide to the actual chemical makeup of the product.

2 Formulation. The formulation describes the way the active ingredient is mixed with other ingredients to make the product ready to mix or use.

3 Ingredients. The active ingredient is the pesticide chemical with the toxic effect. The inert or other ingredients do not need to be named. Both are listed as percentages.

4 Signal Word. At registration every pesticide is assigned a toxicity category that indicates its level of acute toxicity. Signal words do not indicate potential long-term effects such as cancer.

All products must bear the statement "Keep Out of Reach of Children." Signal words are as follows:

SIGNAL WORD	TOXICITY	APPROX. HUMAN LETHAL DOSAGE	CATEGORY
DANGER–POISON (must have skull and crossbones)	Highly toxic	A taste to a teaspoonful	I
DANGER	Highly hazardous	Pesticide-specific (see label)	I
WARNING	Moderately toxic or hazardous	1 teaspoonful to 1 oz	II
CAUTION	Low toxicity	1 oz or more up to relatively nontoxic	III

5 Manufacturer.

6 U.S. EPA Registration and Establishment Numbers. Every pesticide has a registration number assigned to it. The establishment number is the code that identifies the site of manufacture or repackaging.

7 Precautionary Statements. These describe the human environmental hazards associated with a pesticide, how to avoid exposure, personal protective equipment required, and how to store and dispose of it. It includes first aid instructions and may include instructions for physicians.

8 Directions for Use. This section lists the plants or sites and the target pests on which the pesticide may legally be used. It tells how to mix and apply the pesticide, and how much to use. Always follow these directions carefully.

of the active ingredient. **Other (or inert) Ingredients** tells you the percentage of other ingredients in the product that are not for the control of the pest but carry the pesticide or dissolve the active ingredients. The other ingredients may be toxic, flammable, or pose other safety or environmental problems. Some, however, are harmless, such as clay.

4. **Signal Word and Symbol.** On the label you will always find "Keep Out of the Reach of Children" and one of the following **signal words:** CAUTION, WARNING, or DANGER. Some products also include the word POISON; if the word POISON is included, the product will have a skull and crossbones symbol. The signal word indicates the pesticide's potential immediate hazard level to humans or the environment. DANGER means that the pesticide is highly toxic, WARNING indicates moderate toxicity, and CAUTION means low toxicity. When a pesticide is registered by the federal government, each pesticide product is assigned to a toxicity category based on the level of hazard. The signal word manufacturers must use on their labels is a guide to you, the user, as to the immediate toxicity (or danger) of the product.

5. **Manufacturer's Name and Address** are always shown on the product label. Use this information if you need to contact the manufacturer for any reason.

6. **EPA Registration Number** is unique for each product. All pesticide products sold in the United States must be registered with the EPA. Some products will have only a California registration number (for example, adjuvants require California registration). The registration number shows the product has been reviewed and approved by the EPA. The EPA registration number identifies the actual mix in the container. If there is a pesticide injury or illness, the EPA registration number is very important to identify the actual product that was the cause and to get the best medical treatment. The California EPA (Cal/EPA) also registers (approves) the product before it is legal to use in California. Be very careful of any Internet or magazine purchases since all pesticides you use must be registered by Cal/EPA and EPA. EPA establishment number identifies the site of manufacture or repackaging.

7. **Precautionary Statements** can have three parts: (a) hazards to humans and domestic animals, (b) environmental hazards, and (c) physical and chemical hazards. This section is very important because it explains how to avoid problems and provides safety information.

- **Human and pet hazards** tells why the pesticide is hazardous. This section lists adverse effects that may occur if people or pets become exposed. It describes the type of protective equipment to wear while handling pesticides and when mixing and applying the product. This section also gives information on ways to prevent exposure to people or pets.

- **Environmental hazards** explains whether the product is potentially toxic to nontarget organisms such as wildlife, fish, birds, endangered plants, honey bees, or other animals. This section also may mention the risks of using the pesticide near wetlands or other water resources. This section teaches you how to use the product and avoid environmental damage. Find extra information here on how to protect fish, water systems, and the environment. This section is especially important to the maintenance gardener if there are fish ponds near treated landscape settings.

- **Physical or chemical hazards** explains pesticide hazards such as the flammability of the product or possible problems that can occur when the product is mixed with other chemicals.

    Storage and disposal information and what to do with unused product and empty containers also appear on this part of the label. Some pesticides may become ineffective if improperly stored or stored for a long time. Improper storage may even cause explosions or fires.

    First aid information describes the actions required if someone swallows or breathes the pesticide, or if it gets on their skin or in their eyes. Labels may contain a section labeled **note to physicians** that provides doctors with specific medical information. Some labels also have a **statement of practical treatment** with emergency information. This section tells you what to do to decontaminate someone who has become exposed to the pesticide, and it also tells you when to get medical attention. For first aid information you can also call the phone number on the label; these are often toll-free numbers.

8. **Directions for Use** is an important part of the label. It is a violation of the law if you do not follow these instructions. This section includes the target pests, plants, animals, or other sites where you can use the pesticide. Here is where you will find special restrictions that you must observe. This section of the label tells you how and when to apply the pesticide, how much to use, how to mix it up, and where to use the product. Sometimes product manufacturers include a booklet on the container that outlines how to use it. Read this before use. For questions, some labels provide a toll-free telephone number to the manufacturer.

■ Pesticide Storage, Transportation, and Disposal

PROPER STORAGE OF PESTICIDE CONTAINERS AND EQUIPMENT

8. Know how to properly store pesticides and application equipment.

On any property that you control, including your business office or home, you are responsible for all containers and equipment that hold or have held pesticides. To prevent potential injury to people who should not be in contact with these containers and equipment, you must store the pesticide containers and equipment in a locked enclosure (Figure 1-10). During times when pesticides are not locked up, you must designate a responsible person to maintain control over the pesticide containers and application equipment. If the pesticides are not locked up and are in an area where people may go, the responsible person must be able to see the pesticide at all times and keep people away.

To organize your storage space to reduce potential hazards, do not store pesticides and fertilizers together because these products may chemically react with each other and cause a fire. Review and follow the labels of all pesticides and fertilizers to determine which products may or may not be stored together. Do not store pesticides near food, feed, seed, or near personal protective equipment (PPE) because of the possibility of contamination. Keep containers off the ground to reduce their exposure to moisture. Regularly inspect containers for leaks or damage.

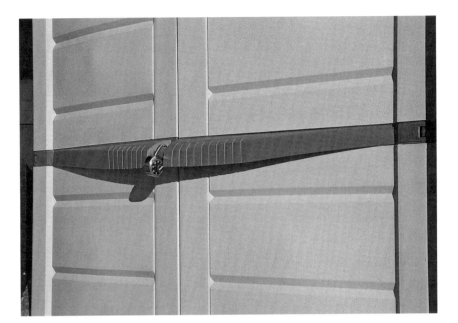

Figure 1-10. Store pesticide containers and equipment in a locked place. Post warning signs if pesticides with signal words "DANGER" or "WARNING" are stored there.

Post Warning Signs

Always keep pesticide storage areas locked. Warning signs must be posted all around the storage area when it holds pesticide containers with the signal word DANGER or WARNING. Repeat warning signs in an alternate language if there is a risk that people who do not read English may approach the pesticide storage area.

Service Containers

A service container is any tank or other container that you use to hold, transport, or store pesticides, except the one in which the pesticide was originally sold (Figure 1-11). Service containers must be labeled with all of the following:

- name and address of the person or business responsible for the container

- identity of the pesticide in the container (common name is OK)

- signal word (DANGER, WARNING, or CAUTION) from the original label

Illegal Containers

It is illegal to place or store pesticides in any type of container that is commonly used for food, drink, or any other household products (Figure 1-12). This is to help prevent accidental pesticide poisonings or injuries, especially to children.

Figure 1-11. Service container labeling. Backpack sprayer tanks and other service containers must be labeled with the name of the responsible person, pesticide name and signal word.

ABC Maintenance Gardening
123 Main St
Anytown, CA 91111

GLYPHOSATE 41%

CAUTION

Figure 1-12. Prevent accidental poisoning! Always store pesticides in proper containers. Never store pesticides in food or drink containers.

TRANSPORTING PESTICIDES

Pesticides must never be transported in the same vehicle compartment as people, food, or animal feed. You must secure pesticide containers in the vehicle during transportation in a way that prevents spills. An enclosed secure locker is an excellent way to transport pesticides in a pickup truck. Protect pesticide containers made of paper, cardboard, or similar material from moisture when they are transported in an open bed, for instance by placing them in a covered compartment or sealed plastic bin. Secure pesticide containers (Figure 1-13) so they or their contents will not blow or bounce out of the truck bed. Be sure that any pesticides in service containers (including spray tanks) have required service container labeling.

9. Know how to properly transport pesticides.

CONTAINER RINSING REQUIREMENTS

When you empty a liquid pesticide product container, you must immediately rinse and drain it following specific procedures before disposing of it. Rinse at the time of use; do not save empty containers for rinsing and draining later. Make the rinsing process part of the mixing process so that the rinsate (rinse water) becomes part of the applied mixture.

10. Know how to legally and properly dispose of excess pesticides and empty pesticide containers.

Figure 1-13. When transporting pesticides, keep them in a secure part of the vehicle. Secure containers so they cannot move. Do not carry them in passenger areas.

Choose a safe site, away from people and where spills can be easily and quickly cleaned up. It is helpful to place small containers into a secondary tub in case there are spills. Allow the container to drain for 30 seconds after you empty it. To rinse, take the steps shown in Sidebar 1.1 on the next page. Be sure to wear the personal protective equipment required for mixing the pesticide as described on the pesticide label. (See Chapter 5 for more information on personal protective equipment.)

An exception to the rinsing requirement applies to pesticide products that are packaged as ready-to-use pesticides (for example, certain home-use products). Ready-to-use containers do not need to be rinsed, but once empty, they can be wrapped up and put into the trash can.

Always drain the rinse solution into the mix tank for application to the treatment site. If you are unable to apply the rinse solution to the application site, you must find another appropriate site where it can be applied or else dispose of it at a local hazardous waste collection site. Do not put it into storm drains or down sewers!

PESTICIDE AND CONTAINER DISPOSAL

An empty, triple-rinsed, clean pesticide container with home-use labeling can be disposed of in the trash can. Tighten all lids or closures on containers securely. If you have punched a hole in the bottom, let the inside of the container dry out completely before placing it in the trash. Before disposing of property rinsed empty pesticide containers not labeled for home use, first check with the county agricultural commissioner for local regulations. Some counties require an inspection of empty, clean containers before you dispose of them at the local approved disposal site (landfill or dump). Disposal sites that accept pesticides and empty pesticide containers must comply with many state and local environmental laws.

If you have leftover mixed or diluted pesticide product in the container, there are special handling requirements that you must know. Contact your county agricultural commissioner for more information. Do not pour leftover pesticide down storm drains or into toilets, sinks, or other drains. Do not combine different leftover pesticides! The best way to dispose of diluted pesticide is to apply it according to label directions. If you cannot find a legal way to use it up, you must make arrangements for transport to a hazardous waste disposal site

SIDEBAR 1.1—RINSING AND DRAINING LIQUID PESTICIDE CONTAINERS

Empty containers of concentrated pesticides used by maintenance gardeners must be rinsed at the time they are emptied. If possible, combine the rinsing process with the mixing process when you mix up a batch of pesticide for application. Always wear PPE and put rinse water back into the tank and apply it to the site.

STEPS FOR RINSING AND DRAINING LIQUID PESTICIDE CONTAINERS

1. Drain the last drops from the pesticide container into the mix tank.

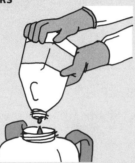

2. Add water to the pesticide container.

3. Replace lid and shake or swirl to rinse all inner surfaces.

4. Drain rinse solution into mix tank.

5. Repeat steps 2, 3, and 4 at least two more times and until the rinsate is clear.

6. Punch a hole in the bottom of the triple-rinsed container so it cannot be reused.

7. Apply the mix at an appropriate site.

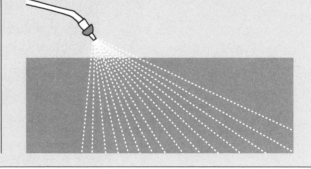

Figure 1-14. If you have leftover pesticides that you cannot use at a site described on the label, dispose of them at a hazardous materials disposal location.

or participate in a local program for recycling or disposing of unwanted pesticides (Figure 1-14).

If you need to dispose of leftover pesticides, it is best if they are in the original fully labeled containers. Undiluted home-use pesticides in their original containers can be disposed of at a household hazardous waste center. Contact your agricultural commissioner for information on how to best dispose of pesticides.

■ Pesticide Worker Safety Requirements: What Employers and Employees Should Know

11. Know worker safety requirements, including providing pesticide safety training for handler employees and emergency medical care for all employees.

The owner of a maintenance gardener pest control business must assure that all employees are trained in pesticide safety before they handle pesticides and annually after that. If a new type of product is brought in during the year, training is required prior to use. Handling pesticides includes the mixing, loading, applying, storing, and transporting of them, for any purpose. (If employee handlers possess a valid QAC or QAL, the training is not required. Make a copy of employee certificates for your records.)

The employer should review employee training records to assure that training has covered all pesticides they may handle. Employers must review work practices to make sure the workplace is safe and that all legal requirements are met. Employees must always work with safety in mind. The employer must provide all of the required PPE and other safety equipment to all employees who handle pesticides and assure that employees properly use the PPE and other safety equipment. It is the legal responsibility of the employer to assure that employees follow good safety practices.

WRITTEN PESTICIDE TRAINING PROGRAM

Employers must have a written pesticide safety training program for employees who handle pesticides, and these employees must receive training at least annually. The employer must assure that each employee completes the pesticide handler safety training before handling any pesticide. Whenever new pesticides are used, the employer must update the training to cover them. Training must be repeated at least annually after that.

The employer must document in writing the extent of the initial and annual pesticide safety training (Figure 1-15). Documentation must include the names of all pesticides, the topics covered, the training resources used (videos, books, pamphlets, labels), and the names of all employees trained. The training record for each employee must include the date, the topics covered, and the job assigned to each person. Each individual's training record must be signed by the employee, dated, and kept for two years at the workplace. All employee training records must be readily available for inspection by the county agricultural commissioner.

Employers are not required to train their employees who possess a valid commercial applicator certification (QAL or QAC). If a new noncertified employee has a current training record showing proof that prior training met all of the requirements, including all of the pesticides and use situations of maintenance gardener pest control, retraining is not a requirement for the current year. Keep a copy of the prior training record.

The written training record must describe the materials used for training. These training materials include pesticide study guides, pesticide labels, DPR's Pesticide Safety Information Series (PSIS) leaflets, pesticide Material Safety Data Sheets (MSDSs), pesticide training videotapes, and any other information that is used in the training. Training must cover all of the topics listed in Figure 1-16, and employees must understand and be able to respond to questions.

**Figure 1-15. Employees must be trained each year about the pesticides they use.
Keep a written training record for each employee.**

SAMPLE PESTICIDE TRAINING RECORD

Employer Name: _____ Employee Name: _____

Employee's Pest Control Job Duties: _____

Trainer's Name: _____ Date of Training: _____

Trainer's Qualifications: ☐ QAL/QAC   ☐ PCA

TOPICS COVERED

_____

_____

_____

TRAINING MATERIALS

Name of videos, pamphlets, or other training materials, and a brief description:

1. _____

2. _____

3. _____

Pesticide Label Used in Training: MSDS Used in Training:

1. _____   1. _____

2. _____   2. _____

3. _____   3. _____

DPR Pesticide Safety Information Series (PSIS) leaflets used:

1. _____

2. _____

3. _____

Employee Signature: _____ Date:_____

Figure 1-16. Employers must cover all of the topics on this checklist when training workers on pesticide safety.

PESTICIDE HANDLER TRAINING CHECKLIST

☐ Pesticide label: Format and meaning of information, such as precautionary statements about human health hazards

☐ Hazards of pesticides, including acute and chronic effects, delayed effects, and sensitization, as identified in pesticide product labeling, Material Safety Data Sheets, or Pesticide Safety Information Series leaflets

☐ Routes by which pesticides can enter the body

☐ Signs and symptoms of overexposure

☐ Emergency first aid for pesticide overexposure

☐ How to obtain emergency medical care

☐ Routine and emergency decontamination procedures, including

    ☐ spill cleanup

    ☐ the need to thoroughly shower with soap and warm water after the exposure period

☐ Personal protective equipment: Limitations

☐ Personal protective equipment: Appropriate use and sanitation

☐ Heat illness: Prevention, recognition, and first aid

☐ Safety requirements and procedures for handling, transporting, storing, and disposing of pesticides

☐ Environmental concerns such as drift, runoff, and wildlife hazards

☐ Warnings to not take home pesticides or pesticide containers

☐ Pesticide safety requirements, including information in Material Safety Data Sheets and DPR Pesticide Safety Information Series leaflets

☐ The location of the written Hazard Communication Information for Employees

☐ Handling Pesticides (DPR Pesticide Safety Information Series leaflet N-8); other DPR Pesticide Safety Information Series leaflets; and Material Safety Data Sheets

☐ The employee's rights, including the right

    ☐ to personally receive information about pesticides to which he or she may be exposed

    ☐ for his or her physician or employee representative to receive information about pesticides to which he or she may be exposed

    ☐ to be protected against retaliatory action due to the exercise of any of his or her rights

REQUIREMENTS FOR EMERGENCY MEDICAL CARE

You must plan ahead for emergency medical care for your employees and be sure that everyone knows the name and location of the facility (clinic or hospital emergency room) to go to in the case of pesticide illness. Post the name, address, and telephone number where anyone can find them at a designated work site (Figure 1-17). If there is no designated work site, you must post the information in the work vehicle.

Take the employee immediately to a medical care facility or hospital emergency room if there are reasonable grounds to suspect exposure to pesticides or if any symptoms of pesticide illness or injury are showing (see Chapter 4). The employer is responsible for arranging for transportation. Do not tell employees to find their own way to get to medical care! It's against the law and is also dangerous.

Symptoms of pesticide illness or injury may include

- headache
- weakness
- dizziness
- blurred vision
- breathing difficulties
- skin or eye irritation
- nausea
- abdominal cramps
- sweating
- tightness of chest

Figure 1-17. Emergency contact information must be posted at the work site.

EMERGENCY PHONE NUMBERS FOR PESTICIDE APPLICATION

For any emergency, call 9-1-1.

EMERGENCY MEDICAL CARE FACILITY:

Name: _____

Location (address): _____

Telephone: _____

For questions regarding pesticides and human health:
Poison Control Center, 1-800-8-POISON (1-800-876-4766)

For help with spills, fires, and accidents involving hazardous chemicals:
CHEMTREC, 1-800-424-9300

For medical and consumer information on pesticides:
National Pesticide Information Center, 1-800-858-7378

For questions on pesticide disposal, how to deal with misapplications, obtaining a license, and more:
County Agricultural Commissioner: _____

PERSONAL PROTECTIVE EQUIPMENT (PPE) AND SAFE WORKING CONDITIONS

Every person who handles pesticides should know the importance of wearing and correctly using personal protective equipment (PPE) (Figure 1-18) and which PPE is required (by the label directions or regulations). The employer must provide the required PPE and assure that it is properly worn, cleaned, and maintained. Do a daily inspection and replacement when necessary. PPE should be cleaned daily, kept in good repair, and stored in a clean, pesticide-free, specially designated place or locker when it is not in use. PPE is not to be taken home from work or kept where pesticides are stored.

When the pesticide label specifies certain PPE, the employer must provide it to their handler employees and assure that it is used according to the requirements in the label use directions. In addition, the employer must assure that employees are provided with and use the PPE during handling activities specified in the regulations. For example, a label may require eye protection only when mixing the concentrate. However, California regulations require employee handlers to use eye protection and chemical-resistant gloves for virtually all handling activities, with few exceptions.

You are required to provide enough water, soap, and clean towels for thorough washing of hands and face at the place where the employees end their pesticide exposure work and where they remove their PPE. There must also be a place for employees to change clothes and safely store any personal clothing away from pesticides. Keep all personal protective equipment safe and in good repair. Watch for the potential of heat illnesses and take measures to prevent them. For example, don't allow employees to apply pesticides when it is too hot to safely wear the required PPE.

Be sure there is adequate light to be able to read the label and work safely. If there is inadequate natural light at the mixing and loading site you must provide adequate artificial light.

Coveralls

Coveralls are one- or two-piece garments of closely woven fabric that cover the entire body except for the head, hands, and feet. Employers are responsible for providing clean coveralls each day to each employee who handles any pesticide with the signal word DANGER or WARNING. Employers also must assure that employees wear the clean coveralls and at the end of the workday remove them and wash

12. Be aware of personal protective equipment requirements and know the ones that apply to your pest control activities.

Figure 1-18. Use personal protective equipment (PPE) when handling pesticides or pesticide application equipment. Eye protection and gloves are always required. PPE may also include coveralls, protective headwear, and chemical-resistant boots.

- Read the label to find out what PPE is required.

- Wear eye protection.

- Wear gloves when opening containers.

- Wear PPE when mixing.

- Wear PPE when cleaning equipment.

up. A clean extra pair of coveralls must be available in case of contamination. Don't allow anyone to take coveralls home; however, if employees do not return to a headquarters at the end of the workday, they can remove their coveralls and store them in a sealable container on the truck for later return to the employer for laundering.

You are responsible for the laundering of your employees' coveralls. You must inform the person or firm doing the laundry that pesticide clothing should be laundered separately. If you establish written procedures and employees follow these procedures, you may wish to develop a written agreement with them to separately and correctly launder the coveralls they use. Be sure to always tell employees to remove, store, and launder pesticide application clothing separately from other clothing and to wear gloves when loading the washing machine.

Eye Protection

Employers must provide proper eye protection (goggles, face shield, or safety glasses with brow and temple protection) and assure that employee handlers use it whenever required by the label and when doing any of the following activities:

- mixing pesticides
- adjusting, cleaning, or repairing application equipment that contains pesticides
- applying pesticides by hand except if
  - applying vertebrate pest control baits
  - applying solid fumigants to vertebrate burrows
  - baiting insect monitoring traps
  - applying noninsecticidal lures

Protective Gloves

Employers must provide appropriate pesticide-handling gloves made of rubber, neoprene, or other chemical-resistant material and assure that handler employees use them whenever required by the label and when doing any of the following activities:

- mixing or loading pesticides
- adjusting, cleaning, or repairing contaminated mixing, loading, or application equipment
- hand-applying pesticides
- using hand-held equipment (except when using equipment that prevents hand contact with rodenticide bait or contaminated equipment)

Whenever gloves are required, each workday the employer must provide new gloves or previously used clean gloves. Gloves must be in good condition, have no rips or cracks, and if previously used, be thoroughly washed inside and outside with soap and water and dried.

Footwear

Employers must provide to handler employees and assure that they use chemical-resistant footwear when the pesticide label requires it. When the label requires chemical-resistant footwear, the employer must assure that employees wear one of the following types:

- chemical-resistant shoes
- chemical-resistant boots
- chemical-resistant coverings over boots or shoes

Headgear

Employers must provide and assure the use of chemical-resistant headgear when the pesticide label requires it. Employers must assure that employees wear a chemical-resistant hood or a chemical-resistant hat with a wide brim if that is what the label requires.

LABEL REQUIREMENTS

Pesticide labels require PPE for certain handling activities that apply to anyone handling the pesticide, including the employer. In addition, California regulations contain stricter PPE requirements for employees performing certain pesticide-handling activities. Many of the PPE requirements noted here apply to pesticide safety protections employers must assure for their employees. Everyone who handles a pesticide must always use the PPE that is required by the pesticide label's directions.

■ Chapter 1 Review Questions

1. The county agricultural commissioner
   - ☐ a. is responsible for local enforcement of pesticide laws and regulations
   - ☐ b. can charge fines
   - ☐ c. is a good resource for information about pest control issues
   - ☐ d. all of the above

2. If you hold a valid Maintenance Gardener Pest Control Business License, you must also have (Note: There are two correct answers.)
   - ☐ a. a restricted materials permit
   - ☐ b. proof of financial responsibility
   - ☐ c. approval from the city where you will apply pesticides to buildings
   - ☐ d. an Applicator Certificate in category Q or B

3. To renew your Qualified Applicator Certificate (category Q), you must have completed
   - ☐ a. 40 hours of continuing education
   - ☐ b. 20 hours of continuing education
   - ☐ c. 8 hours of continuing education
   - ☐ d. a written exam

4. Your pesticide use records and use reports must be able to be inspected by the
   - ☐ a. county health department
   - ☐ b. California Department of Food and Agriculture
   - ☐ c. Regional Water Quality Control Board
   - ☐ d. county agricultural commissioner

5. Pesticide application notification can help by
   - ☐ a. warning residents that a pesticide has been applied so they can avoid recently treated areas
   - ☐ b. warning parents not to allow babies to crawl in recently treated areas
   - ☐ c. assuring that clients are aware of all pesticides recently applied in yards
   - ☐ d. all of the above

6. If the intended use site is not shown on the pesticide label, the pesticide may be used only
   - ☐ a. in California
   - ☐ b. in the United States
   - ☐ c. if you have a license
   - ☐ d. never

7. Pesticide label information is key to applicator safety. Which information is not found on a pesticide label?
   - ☐ a. the manufacturer's latest discount for bulk purchases
   - ☐ b. specific safety information for handlers
   - ☐ c. what to do in the case of a fire in a pesticide storage area
   - ☐ d. the name and amount of the active ingredient

8. Pesticides must be stored
   - ☐ a. with application and safety equipment
   - ☐ b. near garage exits so they are easy to locate
   - ☐ c. in locked enclosures
   - ☐ d. outside

9. A service container should be labeled with which of the following information?
   - ☐ a. product name
   - ☐ b. signal word
   - ☐ c. responsible party
   - ☐ d. all of the above

10. Never transport pesticides in passenger vehicles unless they are
   - ☐ a. to be used by a commercial applicator
   - ☐ b. out of reach of children
   - ☐ c. in a nonpassenger part of the vehicle
   - ☐ d. mixed with fertilizers

11. Half-full pesticide containers can be disposed of
   - ☐ a. at certain household hazardous waste sites
   - ☐ b. down storm drains
   - ☐ c. by the applicator only
   - ☐ d. by mixing with other leftover pesticides

12. Worker safety requirements include
   - ☐ a. providing pesticide safety training for handler employees
   - ☐ b. arranging for emergency medical care
   - ☐ c. providing all necessary safety equipment and training in its use
   - ☐ d. all of the above

(Answer sheet is on pages 206–207.)

Pests and Problem Diagnosis

Every landscape contains a great variety of plants and animals. Very few of these organisms are pests. Many different kinds of organisms, often hidden in the landscape, play vital roles in keeping landscape plants healthy. Correctly identifying pests is important for choosing the right management tools.

1. Know that plants may be injured or stressed by inadequate or improper cultural practices, environmental conditions such as drought and nutritional deficiency, and chemical injury such as air pollutants and spray drift.

2. Know what questions to ask to find out whether a problem is caused by a pest or nonliving factors such as poor management practices or chemical toxicities.

3. List and describe groups of organisms that are common pests (insects, mites, weeds, vertebrate pests, fungi, bacteria, and viruses) and the damage they cause to landscape plants.

4. Be able to recognize and distinguish the following invertebrate pest groups: aphids, whiteflies, mites, scales, caterpillars, snails and slugs, lawn grubs, ants, and mealybugs.

5. Distinguish damage caused by insects with sucking mouthparts from damage done by insects with chewing mouthparts.

6. Describe the developmental stages of insects with complete and incomplete metamorphosis.

7. Know the difference between broadleaf, grass, and sedge weeds.

8. Describe the life cycle of annual and perennial weeds.

9. Describe how vegetative reproductive structures of perennial weeds, such as rhizomes, bulbs, and stolons, make them difficult to control.

10. Know that many diseases caused by plant pathogens must be diagnosed by an expert.

11. Be able to recognize powdery mildew and the conditions that favor it.

12. Describe symptoms and conditions associated with root and crown diseases.

13. Know where to go to seek information about pest identification.

EVERY LANDSCAPE contains a great variety of plants and animals. Very few of these organisms are pests. Many different kinds of organisms, often hidden in the landscape, play vital roles in keeping landscape plants healthy. Beneficial roles might include controlling pests, breaking down organic matter, or pollinating plants. Other organisms have both negative and positive impacts, and some are pests. Landscape pests include any organism that damages plants, causes other problems in the landscape, or is unwanted by the owner of the landscape. In addition to pests, plant injury may also occur as a result of poor management practices such as improper irrigation, pruning, fertilizing, or contact with toxic chemicals including herbicides or mineral excess. This chapter will help you identify causes of plant damage in the landscapes you manage.

■ Damage Caused by Factors Other than Pests

When people see a damaged tree, shrub, or lawn, they often assume it has been injured by some living pest such as an insect, fungus, or rodent. However, in addition to pests, landscape plants also can be damaged by misuse of equipment, overwatering, chemicals, or other nonliving factors. Injuries caused by nonliving factors, also called abiotic disorders, are very common in the landscape, often causing more damage than pests (which are living, or biotic, factors) (Figure 2-1).

1. Know that plants may be injured or stressed by inadequate or improper cultural practices, environmental conditions such as drought and nutritional deficiency, and chemical injury such as air pollutants and spray drift.

Figure 2-1. Not all plant damage is due to pests. Salty irrigation water caused the tips of these clematis leaves to die.

The following are the most common non-living (abiotic) factors that damage plants in landscapes:

- overwatering
- underwatering
- nutrient and mineral deficiencies
- nutrient and mineral excess such as over fertilizing
- pesticide (especially herbicide) injury
- mechanical injury
- excess sun exposure
- too much shade
- site or plant selection or wrong plant for site
- extremes in temperature
- wind
- air pollution

Abiotic factors and pest organisms may be present at the same time, often working in combination to damage plants, sometimes making it difficult to determine the exact cause of the problem. Making a proper diagnosis of a plant problem is the first step in managing landscape pests and disorders (Table 2-1, Figure 2-2).

TIPS FOR DISTINGUISHING CAUSES OF DAMAGE		
	PEST-CAUSED	**ABIOTIC-CAUSED**
What do you see?	Signs of a living pest including insects, excrement, or fungi.	No organisms consistently found with the damage.
How does it spread?	Signs of damage move progressively through the plant, usually starting out with slight damage in one part of the plant but spreading through the plant and causing more serious damage in a matter of days or weeks.	Damage symptoms develop suddenly and do not spread through a plant or to other plants over time.
Which plants are affected?	Most insects and plant pathogens cause injury only to one or a few closely related species. Unrelated nearby plants not affected.	Plants of several species in a planting area may be affected. Abiotic disorders not limited to specific plant species.

Table 2-1. Tips for Distinguishing Causes of Damage. Look for the differences between pest-caused and abiotic-caused (non-living-caused) damage.

2. *Know what questions to ask to find out whether a problem is caused by a pest or non-living factors such as poor management practices or chemical toxicities.*

Figure 2-2. Plant damage caused by abiotic (nonliving) factors can look like pest damage.

ABIOTIC DAMAGE   **SIMILAR PEST DAMAGE**

Leaf color changes

Iron deficiency in gardenia.

Rose leafhopper feeding damage on a rose leaf.

Leaf curling or distortion

Curling of leaves from 2,4-D herbicides on sycamore (right).

Curling of leaves caused by black cherry aphid.

Branch dieback

Branch dieback on ash caused by insufficient water.

Branch dieback caused by bacterial canker disease.

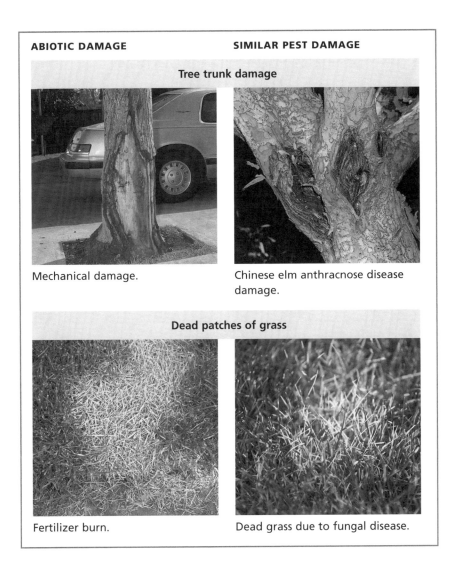

ABIOTIC DAMAGE   **SIMILAR PEST DAMAGE**

Tree trunk damage

Mechanical damage.

Chinese elm anthracnose disease damage.

Dead patches of grass

Fertilizer burn.

Dead grass due to fungal disease.

Damage symptoms caused by pests and abiotic disorders often look similar, especially to the untrained eye. Diagnosing problems usually involves detective work and investigation to obtain adequate information and clues. You must be certain that the damage you see is actually due to a pest and not some other cause. In some cases, you may see an insect on a damaged plant, but the insect is not causing the damage. Misidentification could cause you or your client to make poor management decisions, prevent you from solving the problem, and cost money. More information about identifying and managing nonpest (abiotic) plant problems can be found in the book *Abiotic Disorders of Landscape Plants* listed at the end of Chapter 3.

3. List and describe groups of organisms that are common pests (insects, mites, weeds, vertebrate pests, fungi, bacteria, and viruses) and the damage they cause to landscape plants.

Figure 2-3. Common groups of pests found in California landscapes.

■ Pest Identification and Biology: Common Pests Found in California

Proper identification of pests is essential for successful pest management so you can choose the correct control tools. Common pests (Figure 2-3) include invertebrates such as insects, mites, and snails and slugs; unwanted plants (weeds); microorganisms (plant pathogens) such as fungi, bacteria, and viruses that cause plant disease; and vertebrate pests such as gophers, moles, deer, and ground squirrels. Take pests or damaged plants you cannot identify to your county agricultural commissioner's office or county UC Cooperative Extension office. They can help you identify them or show you how to submit samples for analysis.

PEST GROUP	EXAMPLE ORGANISMS	DAMAGE
Plant pathogens	Microorganisms, including fungi, bacteria, and viruses.	Grow on or in plants and may cause disease symptoms such as leaf spots, powdery fungal growth, cankers, wilting, or plant distortion. Reduce the growth and health of a plant and may eventually kill it.
Invertebrates	Animals without backbones, especially insects, mites, and snails and slugs.	May feed on any plant part, reducing plant growth and health. May produce holes, discolorations, or distorted growth on plants. Some kill plants.
Vertebrates	Animals with backbones, especially gophers, ground squirrels, moles, and other rodents,	Damage plants through their feeding. May dig holes in turf, damage irrigation lines, and kill young trees.
Weeds	Any unwanted plant, including dandelions, bermudagrass, and nutsedges,	Compete with desirable plants for water, nutrients, and light. Reduce the visual beauty of the landscape.

INVERTEBRATE PESTS

Invertebrates are animals without backbones. Invertebrate pests are commonly found living on and around ornamental plants and trees in landscapes. Some of the most common invertebrate pests include aphids, whiteflies, scales, caterpillars, ants, snails and slugs, mites, mealybugs, and lawn grubs, as shown on pages 44 and 45.

Damage Caused by Invertebrates

Most invertebrate pests damage plants through their feeding activities. The type of feeding damage depends on the pest's mouthparts (Figure 2-4). Insects and related pests generally have chewing mouthparts or sucking mouthparts. The most common invertebrates with chewing mouthparts include beetles, caterpillars, grasshoppers, earwigs, snails, and slugs. The most common pests with sucking mouthparts include aphids, scales, whiteflies, psyllids, true bugs, and leafhoppers. When insects with sucking mouthparts such as aphids excrete honeydew (Sidebar 2.1), it can lead to plant problems such as sooty mold and messy surfaces.

Figure 2-5 shows photographs of some common invertebrate pests and describes the damage each pest can cause.

4. Be able to recognize and distinguish the following invertebrate pest groups: aphids, whiteflies, mites, scales, caterpillars, snails and slugs, lawn grubs, ants, and mealybugs.

5. Distinguish damage caused by insects with sucking mouthparts from damage done by insects with chewing mouthparts.

Figure 2-4. Chewing and sucking mouthparts.

INSECTS WITH CHEWING MOUTHPARTS

- beetles
- caterpillars
- grasshoppers
- earwigs

Insects with chewing mouthparts make distinct holes in fruit, leaves, flowers, or stems.

chewed leaf section

grasshopper

INSECTS WITH SUCKING MOUTHPARTS

- aphids   • scales
- leafhoppers   • true bugs
- mealybugs   • whiteflies
- psyllids

Insects with sucking mouthparts cause plant parts to discolor, distort, or drop. They do not make holes in leaves.

yellowing of leaves

honeydew

ash whitefly

Figure 2-5. Common invertebrate pests and typical damage caused.

COMMON INVERTEBRATE PESTS AND TYPICAL DAMAGE CAUSED

Aphids are small, pear-shaped, soft-bodied insects with long, slender mouthparts that pierce stems, leaves, and other tender plant parts to suck out plant fluids. They excrete sticky honeydew and may cause leaves to curl or distort.

Caterpillars are immature forms of butterflies, moths, and sawflies. They feed on all types of succulent plant parts, including leaves, buds, flowers, and shoots, and can substantially defoliate a plant. A few species bore into stems, branches, or trunks of plants.

Whiteflies are tiny, sap-sucking insects that are frequently abundant in vegetable and ornamental plantings. They excrete sticky honeydew and may cause yellowing or death of leaves. Whiteflies usually occur in groups on the underside of leaves.

Ants protect and care for honeydew-producing insects such as aphids, soft scales, whiteflies, and mealybugs, increasing damage from these pests. Ants perform many useful functions in the environment, such as feeding on other pests (e.g., fleas, caterpillars, termites), dead insects, and decomposing tissue from dead animals. Ants are annoying when they enter dwellings.

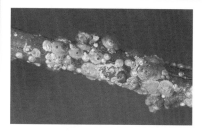

Scales spend most of their lives hidden under a disk-like or waxy covering. They have sucking mouthparts. Adult female scales and many immature forms cannot move or move only when molting. Soft scales produce large amounts of honeydew; armored scales do not.

Snails and slugs are among the most bothersome pests in many garden and landscape situations, especially where conditions are moist. Snails and slugs chew irregular holes in leaves and flowers and can clip succulent plant parts. They leave a silvery trail of mucous.

COMMON INVERTEBRATE PESTS AND TYPICAL DAMAGE CAUSED

Lawn grubs (white grubs) are the C-shaped larvae of various beetles, including the mask chafer. The larvae feed on roots of grass plants. Grub activity can cause the ground to feel spongy; root feeding may be so extensive that the turf can be rolled back like a carpet.

Mealybugs are soft, oval, distinctly segmented insects that are usually covered with a white or gray mealy wax. They suck sap from stems, leaves, and shoots, and like their close relatives, the soft scale insects, mealybugs produce honeydew.

Mites are arachnids, not insects. They have 8 legs during most life stages, no antennae, and no wings. Plant-feeding mites suck fluids from plant cells and live mostly on lower leaf surfaces and on new plant growth. Spider mites may leave webbing on leaves, and other mites may cause distorted plant growth.

SIDEBAR 2.1—WHAT IS HONEYDEW?

Some insects eat plant sap by sucking it in. These insects include aphids, soft scales, whiteflies, and mealybugs. Many of these insects produce a sugary liquid called honeydew. Honeydew does not hurt plants. However, black sooty mold can grow on honeydew, so that less light reaches the leaves. Plant growth may slow down and plants may become less attractive. Honeydew and sooty mold make a sticky mess on trees, sidewalks, cars, and other surfaces under plants.

Honeydew droplet being excreted by an aphid.

Sooty mold on oak leaves infested with aphids.

Ornamental plum coated with honeydew produced by aphids.

Insect Life Cycles

6. Describe the developmental stages of insects with complete and incomplete metamorphosis.

Insects and mites generally hatch from eggs. Immatures increase in size by molting, or shedding, their outer body covering (exoskeleton) and growing a new larger one. The insect changes its shape with each successive molt; the process is called metamorphosis. Insects that undergo major shape changes between the immature and adult stage, such as butterflies and moths, have a pupal stage and are said to have complete metamorphosis (Figure 2-6). Their immature stages are called larvae. Insects that gradually transform from immature to winged adult, such as stink bugs, go through incomplete (or gradual) metamorphosis. Their young are called nymphs.

Figure 2-6. Developmental stages of insects with incomplete and complete metamorphosis.

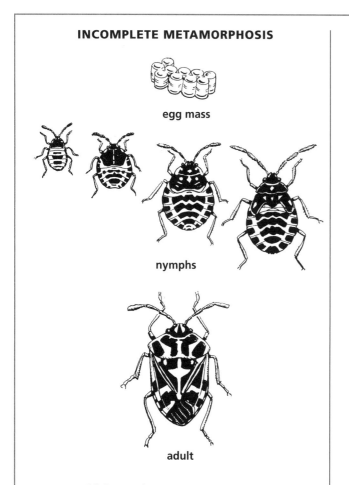

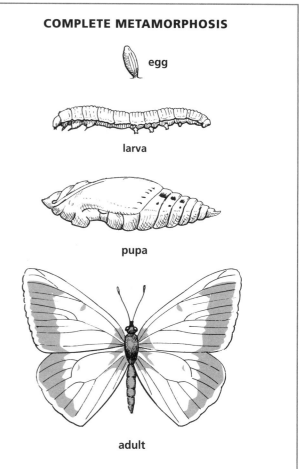

INCOMPLETE METAMORPHOSIS	COMPLETE METAMORPHOSIS

INCOMPLETE METAMORPHOSIS

egg mass

nymphs

adult

COMPLETE METAMORPHOSIS

egg

larva

pupa

adult

Insects with incomplete metamorphosis change gradually. There are three stages of growth: egg, nymph, and adult. Nymphs grow by molting, with each molt looking more like an adult.

Examples: Aphids, true bugs (such as stinkbugs, shown here), grasshoppers, and scales.

Insects with complete metamorphosis go through four stages of growth: egg, larva, pupa, and adult. They pass through a larval stage and a pupal (resting) stage before becoming adults. Larvae look very different from adults.

Examples: Moths, butterflies, beetles, flies, and wasps.

Knowing a pest's life cycle is important to successful pest management. Sometimes the stage you see when you are out in the landscape is not the stage that you can effectively control. For instance soft scales are most noticeable when they are almost mature because they produce a lot of honeydew and are large. The easiest stage to control, however, is the very youngest nymph or crawler stage, which occurs later in the year, after the female has laid her eggs.

WEEDS

Weeds compete with desirable plants for water, nutrients, and light, and reduce the visual beauty of the landscape. Three general categories of weeds may be found in landscapes: broadleaves, grasses, and sedges (Figure 2-7). Identifying weeds and knowing their life cycles are essential for management. Figures 2-8 and 2-9 show four common landscape weeds, including annual bluegrass, bermudagrass, spotted spurge, and dandelion.

7. Know the difference between broadleaf, grass, and sedge weeds.

Figure 2-7. General descriptions of the three categories of weeds.

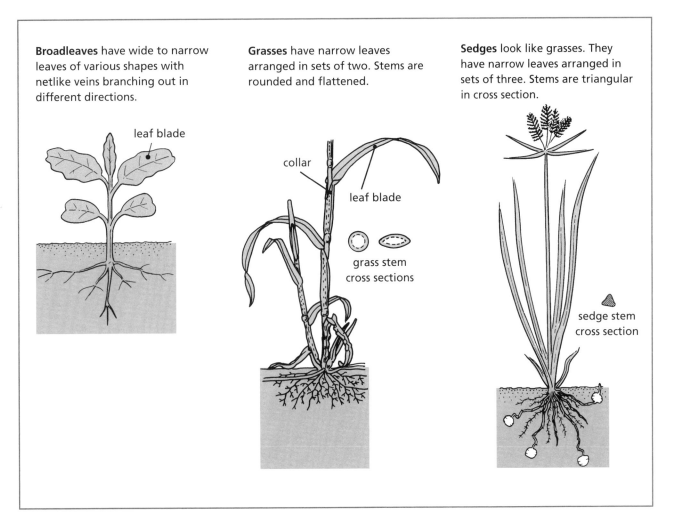

Broadleaves have wide to narrow leaves of various shapes with netlike veins branching out in different directions.

leaf blade

Grasses have narrow leaves arranged in sets of two. Stems are rounded and flattened.

collar

leaf blade

grass stem cross sections

Sedges look like grasses. They have narrow leaves arranged in sets of three. Stems are triangular in cross section.

sedge stem cross section

Figure 2-8. Two common grass weeds—annual bluegrass and bermudagrass, which is a perennial.

Annual bluegrass
Poa annua

Annual bluegrass is an **annual grass** that germinates in late summer or fall and is a problem in the winter and spring. Leaves are often folded at the tip resembling the bow of a boat.

Bermudagrass
Cynodon dactylon

Bermudagrass is a tough **perennial grass** that spreads rapidly using stolons and rhizomes. It thrives in sun and hot weather and is difficult to manage.

Figure 2-9. Two common broad-leaf weeds—spotted spurge, an annual, and dandelion, which is a perennial.

Spotted spurge
Chamaesyce maculata

Spotted spurge is a low-growing mat-forming summer **annual broadleaf** that spreads rapidly on bare soil. Leaves have a darkish spot in the center.

Dandelion
Taraxacum officinale

Dandelion is a **perennial broadleaf** that grows best in full sun. It spreads through seeds produced on its fluffy seed head. It can also grow from its strong taproot, which can be more than a foot deep.

Weed Life Cycles

Most weeds begin their life as a seed that germinates when the right combination of light, temperature, and moisture occurs. The primary root emerges first, and then the shoot and the first leaves. Weed seedlings are usually the easiest stage to manage. Growth of stems and leaves or vegetative growth continues until the plant develops flowers. This begins the reproductive stage.

Annual plants live one year or less (Figure 2-10). They sprout from seeds, mature, and produce seeds for the next generation during this period. Annual weeds are either summer annuals or winter annuals, depending on when they normally mature.

8. Describe the life cycles of annual and perennial weeds.

Figure 2-10. Life cycles of winter annual, summer annual, and perennial weeds.

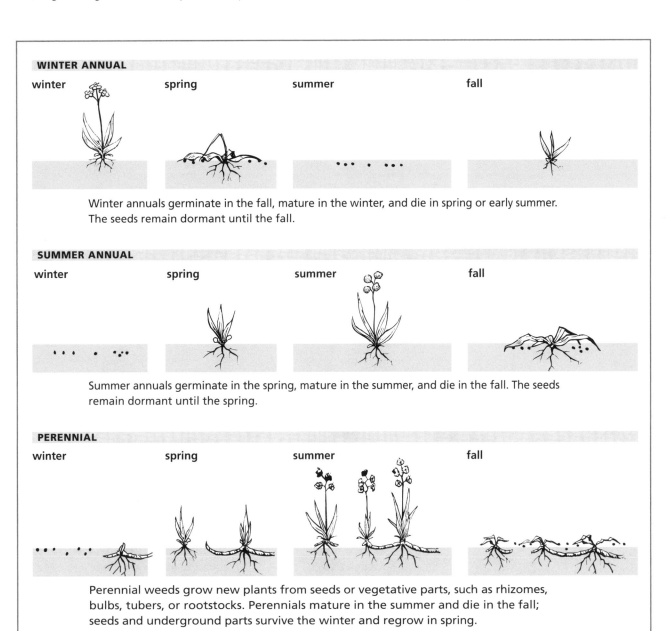

WINTER ANNUAL

winter   spring   summer   fall

Winter annuals germinate in the fall, mature in the winter, and die in spring or early summer. The seeds remain dormant until the fall.

SUMMER ANNUAL

winter   spring   summer   fall

Summer annuals germinate in the spring, mature in the summer, and die in the fall. The seeds remain dormant until the spring.

PERENNIAL

winter   spring   summer   fall

Perennial weeds grow new plants from seeds or vegetative parts, such as rhizomes, bulbs, tubers, or rootstocks. Perennials mature in the summer and die in the fall; seeds and underground parts survive the winter and regrow in spring.

Perennial plants live for more than a year (Figure 2-10). Many perennials, such as certain species of trees, become dormant and lose their leaves each winter. Herbaceous perennials die back entirely during the winter and regrow each spring from roots or plant parts such as tubers, bulbs, or rhizomes. Most perennials also reproduce by seed.

Why Are Perennial Weeds Difficult to Control?

Many perennial weeds are capable of reproducing through vegetative structures, such as rootstocks, rhizomes, stolons, bulbs, and tubers (Figure 2-11). Cutting or chopping the tops off plants does not control them because they can regrow from underground structures. Also, hoeing or rototilling can break up and disperse these structures, leading to new weed plants. These underground structures make many perennial weeds persistent, aggressive invaders in the landscape and difficult to control.

9. Describe how vegetative reproductive structures of perennial weeds, such as rhizomes, bulbs, and stolons, make them difficult to control.

Figure 2-11. Vegetative reproductive structures of perennial weeds.

RHIZOMES
Elongated underground stems that grow horizontally from the plant.

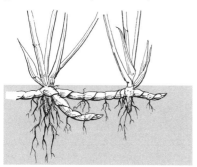

johnsongrass rhizomes

STOLON
A stem that grows horizontally above the ground surface and forms new plants at nodes.

bermudagrass stolons

stolons of kikuygrass

BULB
Underground storage organ consisting of highly compressed leaves.

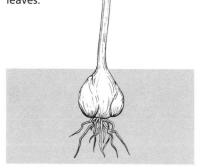

wild garlic bulb

TUBERS
Enlarged fleshy growth arising from stems or roots.

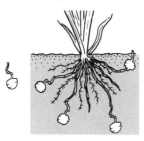

nutsedge tubers

tubers of yellow nutsedge

PLANT DISEASES

Microorganisms that cause plant disease are called pathogens. Fungi, bacteria, and viruses are the more common pathogen groups that cause plant disease. Plant pathogens alter or interfere with the chemical processes that take place within plant cells, producing disease symptoms such as leaf discoloration, wilting, or root rot.

Identifying diseases can be difficult. Symptoms of different diseases can be similar, and symptoms may be similar to those caused by nonliving (abiotic) factors. Often the viruses, fungi, or bacteria causing the disease are not visible to the naked eye, and laboratory analysis by a skilled plant pathologist is required for positive identification.

10. Know that many diseases caused by plant pathogens must be diagnosed by an expert.

The Disease Triangle

Three essential components are required for the development of a plant disease: a pathogen in contact with a host, a susceptible host plant, and an environment favorable to the development of disease. This concept is best displayed in a diagram called the disease triangle, discussed in Sidebar 2.2. When conditions are not right, disease will not develop on a plant even if the pathogen is present.

11. Be able to recognize powdery mildew and the conditions that favor it.

SIDEBAR 2.2—APPLY THE IDEA OF THE DISEASE TRIANGLE

POWDERY MILDEW IN ROSES

All sides of the disease triangle must be present for disease to occur. As conditions on any side become more favorable, the disease will become more severe. For example, for powdery mildew in roses, the following conditions must be present.

1. **Susceptible host.** As a group, roses are easily infected by the pathogen and readily develop disease symptoms. However, some rose varieties are less likely than others to be seriously affected.

2. **Pathogen.** Powdery mildew on rose is caused by the fungus *Sphaerotheca pannosa* f. sp. *rosae*. The fungus produces white growth (mycelium) on leaves, shoots, sepals, and buds. It moves into the plant cells and interferes with normal growth.

3. **Favorable environment.** Powdery mildew is encouraged by shady conditions and mild temperatures (not too hot or too cool). Water on leaf surfaces is not required.

Apply the disease triangle. Proper plant care can break the disease triangle. Roses in uncrowded, sunny locations are likely to have fewer problems with powdery mildew. Roses in the shade are likely to have more problems with powdery mildew. Plant less susceptible cultivars such as *Rosa rugosa* varieties. If favorable environmental conditions continue, a fungicide such as horticultural oil or neem oil may be used to kill the fungus.

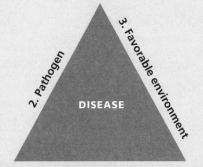

1. Susceptible host

White growth in leaves and buds indicates powdery mildew.

Plant pathogens can spread through the landscape in many different ways (Table 2-2). Gardeners must consider whether the disease triangle elements are present and avoid procedures that encourage plant diseases.

Root and Crown Diseases

12. Describe symptoms and conditions associated with root and crown diseases.

Several root and crown diseases are common in landscapes, especially where overwatering or mechanical injury has been an issue. *Phytophthora* pathogens are among the most common agents associated with root and crown diseases. Affected plants wilt and leaves discolor, stunt, and grow slowly. Twigs and branches die back and entire trees can be killed. Roots may be streaked with brown and rotted tips (Figure 2-12). Trunks may show gumming and cankers.

Root and crown rot pathogens are present in many landscapes. Chemical controls are not available for management in most situations. The most effective way to prevent root and crown disease is to prevent the environmental conditions that favor disease development through proper irrigation and improvement of drainage. For more information, see *Phytophthora Root and Crown Rot in the Garden* (UC IPM Pest Note 74133), available on the UC IPM Web site (**www.ipm.ucdavis.edu**).

Table 2-2. Ways Plant Pathogens Spread. Pathogens commonly spread through the landscape in one or more of these ways.

WAYS PLANT PATHOGENS SPREAD
• Water splashing
• Wind and wind-blown rain
• Insects
• Irrigation runoff
• Contaminated seeds
• Infected transplants
• Soil and debris on boots and shoes
• Contaminated tools and equipment

Figure 2-12. Plants affected by Phytophthora root and crown rot may have both above ground and below ground symptoms. Roots may be rotted and streaked (at left). Above ground, plants look water stressed, and branches and foliage may die (Irish yew tree at right).

VERTEBRATE PESTS

Vertebrates are animals with internal skeletons and backbones. They include fish, frogs, lizards, snakes, birds, and mammals. They become pests if they spread disease, damage plants, make burrows or mounds that become safety hazards, or interfere with the activities or needs of people.

Identify vertebrate pests by comparing their damage symptoms, nests, or droppings to photographs and drawings. For help in identifying and managing vertebrates, see *Wildlife Pest Control Around Gardens and Homes* (UC ANR Publication 21385) and the UC IPM Web site's Pest Notes. The most common vertebrates causing problems in residential landscapes include pocket gophers, ground squirrels, and moles (Figure 2-13).

Figure 2-13. Vertebrate pests that often cause problems in residential landscapes include pocket gophers, ground squirrels, and moles.

	ANIMAL	BURROW
Pocket gopher Gophers can remove or kill plants and can damage sprinkler systems.	 An adult pocket gopher just out of the burrow entrance. Gophers have thick bodies and short legs. They are 6 to 12 inches long. Gophers stay in their burrows and are rarely seen.	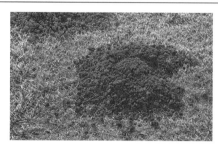 As gophers dig in underground tunnels and push loose dirt to the surface, they form crescent- or horseshoe-shaped mounds. The plugged burrow opening may be off to the side. Mounds of fresh soil are the best signs of gophers.
Ground squirrel Ground squirrels eat plants and damage tree trunks. Their burrows create tripping hazards.	 An adult ground squirrel has mottled, brownish-gray fur and a bushy tail. Their bodies are 9 to 11 inches long. Tails add several inches.	 The burrow entrances of a California ground squirrel are not plugged. They sleep, rest, rear young, store food, and avoid danger by staying within the burrow system.
Mole Moles can eat roots and insects, but most damage is due to their burrows and mound building, especially in lawns.	 Moles are small (5–6 inches long) insect-eating animals with weak eyes. They live almost entirely underground and are rarely seen.	 Moles form volcano-shaped mounds that are pushed up from a tunnel in the center of the mound.

PROBLEM DIAGNOSIS: INFORMATION ABOUT PEST IDENTIFICATION

Know the plant species growing in landscapes you manage, and examine them regularly. Some plants tend to have more serious pest problems than others, so check these regularly for signs of problems. Plants especially prone to pest problems include

- Ash trees
- Azaleas and rhododendrons
- Crape myrtles
- Flowering plum trees
- Fruit trees
- Fuschias
- Monterey pines
- Roses
- Sycamore trees

Likewise, some plants are more susceptible to stress from lack of water or nutrients and other injury. Keeping on top of plant conditions allows you to address pest problems and solve them sooner, when they are less severe, saving you time and money.

Remember that a plant may have more than one problem at the same time. For instance, a plant suffering from lack of water (an abiotic problem) may also be attacked by bark beetles (a biotic problem). In this case, the primary problem—water stress—leads to the secondary problem—bark beetles—and must be corrected to protect surrounding plants from additional bark beetle invasions.

Focus your monitoring activities on areas (Figure 2-14) where problems are most likely to show up. Become familiar with abiotic and pest control resources (see Sidebar 3-3 at the end of the next chapter) including books, Web sites, pamphlets, University of California Cooperative Extension (UCCE) offices, agricultural commissioner offices, and nurseries. Most counties in California have a UCCE office, and many also have UC Master Gardener programs. Consult with them; bring plant or damage samples to discuss. Agricultural commissioner offices in each county can also help with pest identification and pesticide information. See Sidebar 2.3 for a checklist to use for diagnosing plant problems in the landscape.

13. Know where to go to seek information about pest identification.

Figure 2-14. Examples of good locations for monitoring to detect and diagnose problems.

A. Wet area under drippy faucet or sprinkler head favors nutsedge and other weeds.

B. Standing water provides environment favorable for root pathogens. Look for signs of disease.

C. Check rose bushes for pests.

D. Check mulches to see that they are thick enough.

E. Yellow or brown patches of grass from dog urine or fertilizer spill.

F. Thick growth of ground cover favors rats, snails, and earwigs.

G. Poor grass growth in very shady areas. Consider alternate ground covers.

H. Ants may be tending honeydew-producing insects such as aphids or scales. Look for sticky honeydew and sooty mold.

I. Spring growth in trees: Look on new growth for symptoms of disease or insect damage.

SIDEBAR 2.3—CHECKLIST FOR DIAGNOSING PLANT PROBLEMS

CONSIDERATION	NOTES
☐ **What is the affected plant species?** Is the problem occurring on one plant or many plants?	
☐ **When did you first notice the problem?** Has it been there for just a few days or for weeks or months?	
☐ **What parts of the plants are affected?** New or old growth? Do the symptoms seem to be moving in the plant?	
☐ **Have you recently applied fertilizer, herbicide, or other garden chemicals that could have injured the plant?**	
☐ **Check the irrigation system; is it working properly?** Are parts of the landscape waterlogged or underwatered?	
☐ **Has there been an unusual weather event such as frost, hail, a heat spell, or high winds that could cause problems?**	
☐ **Look for patterns in the symptoms.** This may give clues to the cause. Damage that occurs suddenly, especially after fertilizing, spraying, or mechanical injury, may be abiotic damage, especially when more than one plant species is injured. Symptoms that gradually expand may point to a disease or insect problem, especially when present only on one plant species.	
☐ **If the problem is on just one plant species, find common pests and symptoms on that plant.** Go to the UC IPM Web site **(www.ipm.ucdavis.edu)** or use the tables in the back of the book *Pests of Landscape Trees and Shrubs* (UC ANR Publication 3359). Use the *UC Guide to Healthy Lawns* **(www.ipm.ucdavis.edu/ TOOLS/TURF)** to help identify turf problems.	
☐ **Make a tentative diagnosis.** If you don't have enough information, seek help. Sometimes an experienced professional is the only one who can identify a pest problem. Take samples to a county UC Cooperative Extension office or to the county agricultural commissioner's office. They may help identify the problem or send your sample to a diagnostic laboratory.	

◾ Chapter 2 Review Questions

1. Which of the following is not an abiotic disorder that damages plants?
   - ☐ a. mechanical injury
   - ☐ b. chewing damage from caterpillars
   - ☐ c. overwatering
   - ☐ d. pesticide injury

2. Proper identification of pests is important for pest management because
   - ☐ a. misidentification or lack of information about a pest could cause you to make poor management decisions and not solve the problem
   - ☐ b. you must be certain that the damage you see is actually due to a pest and not some other cause
   - ☐ c. damage symptoms caused by pests and abiotic disorders often look similar
   - ☐ d. all of the above

3. If several different species of plants in one area of a landscape suddenly develop brown areas on their leaves, what would you suspect might be the cause?
   - ☐ a. an insect
   - ☐ b. a disease
   - ☐ c. an abiotic factor
   - ☐ d. a fungus

4. All of the following are true of gophers, ground squirrels and moles, EXCEPT
   - ☐ a. They are vertebrate pests.
   - ☐ b. Their borrows damage landscapes.
   - ☐ c. They eat landscape plants.
   - ☐ d. They are natural enemies of pests.

5. If leaves are covered with a sticky sugary substance and black mold, what might you suspect is the cause?
   - ☐ a. an abiotic disorder
   - ☐ b. a bacterial disease
   - ☐ c. overwatering
   - ☐ d. a sucking insect pest

6. Insects that undergo major shape changes between the immature and adult stage are said to have
   - ☐ a. many nymphs
   - ☐ b. gradual metamorphosis
   - ☐ c. mature metamorphosis
   - ☐ d. complete metamorphosis

7. _____ weeds live one year or less. They sprout from seeds, mature, and produce seeds for the next generation during this period.
   - ☐ a. annual
   - ☐ b. woody
   - ☐ c. broadleaf
   - ☐ d. perennial

8. Why are many perennial weeds difficult to kill?
   - ☐ a. they grow very fast
   - ☐ b. they produce a lot of seed
   - ☐ c. they produce underground reproductive structures, such rhizomes, that allow them to regrow
   - ☐ d. they produce poisonous tubers

9. What are the three components of the disease triangle?
   - ☐ a. pathogen, susceptible host, and favorable environment
   - ☐ b. bacteria, wet leaves, and wind
   - ☐ c. pathogen, susceptible host, and many trees
   - ☐ d. none of the above

10. For most efficient use of your time when checking a landscape for pests, focus your efforts
   - ☐ a. on the highest value plants
   - ☐ b. on plant species and areas known to have problems
   - ☐ c. on planting beds rather than lawns
   - ☐ d. on lawns rather than planting beds

11. Write in the correct name of the pest in the photos at right. Choices are: lawn grub, ant, scale, mealybug, snail, mite, aphid, whitefly

(Answer sheet is on pages 206–207.)

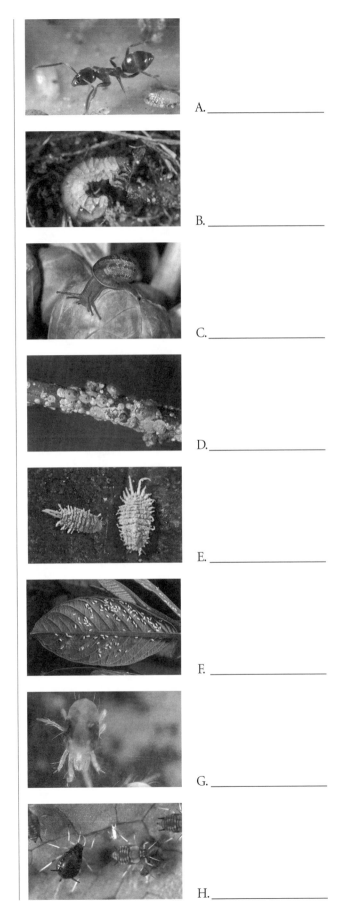

A._____

B._____

C._____

D._____

E._____

F._____

G._____

H._____

3 Integrated Pest Management

The best pest management programs combine several complimentary control methods using a strategy called integrated pest management (IPM). Pesticides are one tool, but many problems can be solved with nonchemical tools.

1. List the components of an IPM program.

2. Know how to routinely check a landscape to keep on top of pest problems.

3. Describe the main pest management tools used in an IPM program, including cultural, biological, mechanical and physical, and chemical.

4. Understand how plants that are less susceptible to pest damage, such as resistant varieties, can be used in an IPM program.

5. Explain how cultural practices such as proper fertilization, irrigation, pruning, and mowing height are important in preventing lawn weed, insect, and pathogen problems.

6. Explain how the following tools can be used to manage weeds in some situations: mulches, landscape fabrics, hand weeding, and weed trimmers.

7. Define natural enemies, explain how they control pests, and know how to protect them.

8. Be able to recognize adults and immatures of the following natural enemies: lady beetles, lacewings, and syrphid flies. Know that aphid mummies indicate parasitic wasp activity.

9. Understand that pesticides kill natural enemies and cause problems.

10. Know the benefits of keeping track of pest problems and management practices on each property.

11. Know how to recognize when pest control efforts have not been successful and what to do next.

12. Know where to find reliable pest management information.

Integrated pest management (IPM) is an ecosystem-based strategy for managing pests that focuses on long-term prevention of pests or their damage through a combination of methods such as

- biological control

- habitat manipulation

- modification of cultural practices

- use of resistant varieties

Pesticides are used only after monitoring or surveying indicates that they are needed according to established guidelines, and pesticide treatments are made with the goal of removing only the target pests. Pest control materials are selected and applied in a manner that minimizes risks to human health, to beneficial and nontarget organisms, and to the environment.

1. List the components of an IPM program.

Managing Pests with Integrated Pest Management

Maintenance gardeners have many tools available for managing pests. Pesticides are one tool, but many pest problems can also be solved with nonchemical tools such as pest-resistant plants, cultivation, mulches, traps, barriers, changes in irrigation practices, or biological control. These other approaches may provide safer, long-term pest control. The best pest management programs combine several complimentary control methods using a strategy called integrated pest management (IPM).

The Components of an IPM Program

There are five components to a successful IPM program (Figure 3-1):

1. Prevention through good cultural practices.

2. Regular monitoring for pests and problems.

3. Pest and symptom identification.

4. Action thresholds: Treat only when necessary.

5. Integration of appropriate management methods.

1. PREVENTION THROUGH GOOD CULTURAL PRACTICES

Many pest problems can be avoided by implementing careful landscape design, thoughtful plant selection, good site preparation, proper planting, and appropriate cultural practices (Sidebar 3.1) such as irrigating and mulching. Planting pest-resistant varieties or tolerant plant species is the best way to avoid problems with many landscape insect pests and diseases. Proper landscape site preparation and plant installation reduces weed establishment and encourages good drainage to prevent disease. Do not accidentally introduce new pests into a landscape! Pests such as weed seeds or nematodes are brought in with infested soil; other pests arrive on new plants that have been infested in the nursery. After plants are established, improper irrigation, fertilization, pruning, and other plant care practices can be directly linked to a wide range of pest problems.

Figure 3-1. The five components of an IPM program.

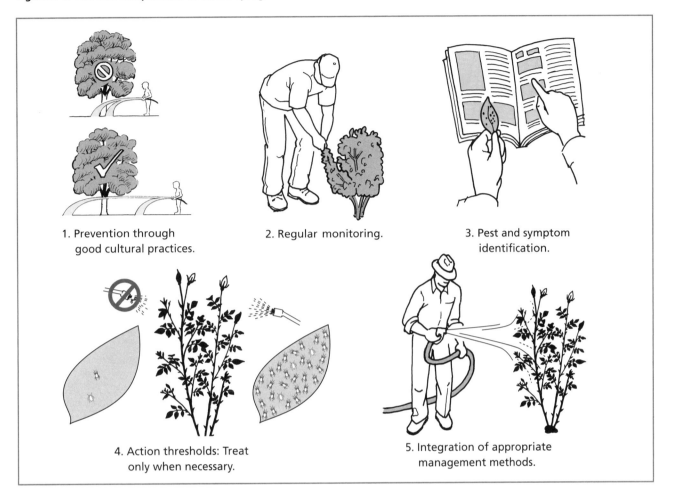

1. Prevention through good cultural practices.

2. Regular monitoring.

3. Pest and symptom identification.

4. Action thresholds: Treat only when necessary.

5. Integration of appropriate management methods.

SIDEBAR 3.1—PROTECT PLANTS AND AVOID DISEASE

PROTECT PLANTS AND AVOID DISEASE BY USING THESE PREVENTIVE MEASURES

- Plant at a time of year that does not favor the pathogen.

- Plant in areas with adequate sunlight and good drainage. Powdery mildew and molds are more serious problems in shady areas. Root diseases are more of a problem in soils with poor drainage.

- Choose plants that do well in your area and are resistant to pests. Use pest-resistant varieties.

- Space the plants apart properly. Crowding can favor disease.

- Do not overwater. Too much water favors root pathogens. Water early in the day so foliage can dry out quickly. Maintain an even water supply during the growing season.

- Do not overfertilize.

- Group plants according to their water and sunlight needs. Do not locate a plant that needs frequent light watering next to one that needs infrequent deep watering.

- Handle plants and plant parts carefully when you transport them. Protect from wind and heat.

- Avoid injuring plants when handling and caring for them.

2. Know how to routinely check a landscape to keep on top of pest problems.

Figure 3-2. Regularly monitor for pests and problems. Keep written records of what you find.

2. REGULAR MONITORING FOR PESTS AND PROBLEMS

Check your landscape regularly for pests, damage symptoms, conditions and practices that can damage plants (Figure 3-2). Learn the problems that commonly occur in your area on each species of plant that you manage. This will help you know what to monitor for and where to look for the pest on and around the plant. Keep written notes (Figure 3-3) of your findings, recording date, time of day, stage of plant development, location, and any unusual weather conditions or association with cultural practices such as irrigation or pesticide application. If you do something to try to correct the problem or kill the pests, keep a record of what you did and the results. Following these procedures will help you to develop a pest management program that works best for you.

3. PEST AND SYMPTOM IDENTIFICATION

Correct pest identification is essential for choosing the right management method. If the weed, insect, pathogen, or other pest causing the problem is misidentified, the selected management practice is unlikely to work. In some cases, an improper control treatment can cause a new problem. See Sidebar 2.3 for a checklist for diagnosing problems. Use the resources listed at the end of this chapter to help identify pests.

4. ACTION THRESHOLDS: TREAT ONLY WHEN NECESSARY

Action or treatment thresholds can help decide whether management actions, including pesticide treatments, are needed to avoid unacceptable plant damage. A low to moderate number of pests on a plant and some amount of damage usually can be tolerated. The difficulty is determining the point at which action must be taken to prevent unacceptable damage. The pest population or damage level when action must be taken to stop undesirable damage often depends on people's attitudes about the aesthetics of a landscape. In a few cases, University of California publications on specific landscape pests give guidelines on when management is required. For instance, for the California oakworm, the UC IPM publication *Pest Notes: California Oakworm* (UC ANR Publication 7422) suggests that if you find more than 25 oakworm caterpillars after inspecting 100 twigs, treatment may be advisable to avoid unsightly defoliation on your oak trees. For most landscape pests, however, there are no specific numerical thresholds and you will need to rely on your experience and the client's tolerance for the pest to determine when treatment is required.

Figure 3-3. Use a form like this to keep records of monitoring and management activities.

RESIDENTIAL PEST MONITORING REPORT

Address: _____

Name of person doing monitoring: _____

Date: _____ Time: _____

RECENT WEATHER CONDITIONS

_____

MAP
(note any problem plants or infested areas)

↑
N

LAWN AREAS

Turf species: _____

Weeds present

    Annuals: _____

    Perennials: _____

Other problems

_____

_____

Date last fertilized: _____

    Quantity applied: _____

Drainage problems: _____

TREES AND SHRUBS
(plant name, pest problem, and degree of infestation)

_____

_____

LANDSCAPE BEDS

    Weeds present

        Annuals: _____

        Perennials: _____

    Mite or insect pests (on which plants?):_____

_____

    Natural enemies present: _____

    Signs of disease (on which plants?): _____

_____

    Other problems: _____

WATERING SCHEDULE
Length of time and frequency

    Lawn: _____

    Beds: _____

MANAGEMENT
Suggested control activities

                    Date done

_____

_____

PESTICIDE APPLICATIONS IN LAST 6 MONTHS
(product, date, and where applied)

_____

_____

_____

FOLLOW UP (was control effective?)

_____

_____

5. INTEGRATION OF APPROPRIATE MANAGEMENT METHODS

Landscape managers have a variety of pest control tools at their disposal. Many tools can be used to prevent problems and control pest populations. Most pest control tools do not eliminate all pest individuals, they only reduce the population. Using two or more complimentary tools usually provides more effective and long-term control than reliance on one tool alone. IPM programs try to integrate the use of several tools against each pest. For instance, in the case of an herbicide application in a lawn, targeted weeds may appear to be eliminated at first, but a new infestation is likely to occur if the lawn has not become vigorous enough to outcompete new invasions through implementation of appropriate maintenance such as regular fertilization. Management methods available to manage landscapes may fall into one of four major categories: cultural (good management practices), biological, mechanical and physical, and pesticides. These categories are described in greater detail in the next section.

■ Pest Management Tools Used in an IPM Program

CULTURAL CONTROLS (GOOD MANAGEMENT PRACTICES)

3. Describe the main pest management tools used in an IPM program, including cultural, biological, mechanical and physical, and chemical.

Cultural controls are modifications of normal plant care activities, such as pruning and irrigation, that reduce pest problems. Some people might call these activities simply "good management practices." Providing plants with proper cultural care is the single most important component of pest management. Good care can prevent many pests from harming plants. Cultural practices such as proper fertilization, irrigation, and mowing height are important in preventing weed, insect, and pathogen problems in lawns and landscapes. Examples of successful cultural control practices are discussed below.

Resistant Plant Varieties

4. Understand how plants that are less susceptible to pest damage, such as resistant varieties, can be used in an IPM program.

Choosing plant species or varieties that are resistant to or tolerant of pest activity (host plant resistance) can reduce pest problems, especially plant diseases. Host plant resistance refers to plant varieties that suffer less damage than do other varieties usually because the pest is not able to survive or reproduce as effectively. Pest tolerance refers to a plant that can withstand the damage caused by normal pest populations.

Some varieties may possess physical or chemical properties that discourage pest feeding, reproduction, or survival. Others may be able to support large pest populations without suffering considerable damage. For instance, some crape myrtle varieties are resistant to powdery mildew, and some fuchsia species are resistant to the fuchsia gall mite. Get more information on resistant varieties from your UC Cooperative Extension office or specialists at a plant nursery.

Water Management

Proper management of water can reduce pest problems. Too little water can result in small plants, poor root systems, and slower growth. As a result, these weak plants cannot compete with weeds or resist damage. Too much water can lead to environmental conditions that favor the development of some diseases (Figure 3-4) and weed growth. Too much water may also weaken a plant, lowering its resistance to insects and diseases.

To prevent problems, design your irrigation system and prepare soil to promote even water distribution and good drainage. Early morning or just before dawn is the best time to irrigate (Figure 3-5). Irrigating at this time reduces water loss from evaporation while minimizing the length of time when foliage is wet, discouraging the development of certain leaf diseases. Schedule irrigation by observing plants, monitoring soil moisture, or following recommendations such as the lawn irrigation guidelines in the *Lawn Watering Guide for California* (UC ANR Publication 8044). Drip irrigation systems (Figure 3-6) deliver water only to desirable plants and thus reduce weed problems and improve water efficiency.

Fertilizing

Fertilize only as needed. Avoid overfertilization, especially with high-nitrogen fertilizers. Too much fertilizer promotes excessive succulent foliage, which can increase populations of certain pests, such as mites, aphids, and psyllids that prefer new growth. Many woody ornamentals require no fertilizer for healthy growth in most soils. Lawns must be fertilized to remain vigorous and outcompete weeds, but follow

Figure 3-4. Don't let the area around the base of trees or shrubs stay wet for a long time. Moisture at the base of the trunk promotes diseases such as Phytophthora root rots. Plant on a central mound surrounded by a basin, as shown on the right. Do not plant in a hole, as shown on the left.

Figure 3-5. Early-morning irrigation prevents plant disease by allowing leaves to dry by midday. Many diseases need several hours of wet leaf surfaces to infect plants.

Figure 3-6. This drip irrigation system will help save water. After installation, it will be covered with organic mulch. Drip irrigation reduces soil compaction, salinity, and weed growth problems that come with sprinklers.

fertilizing guidelines carefully (Figure 3-7). Begin a regular lawn fertilization program approximately 6 weeks after planting. In general, lawns must be fertilized about four times a year with no more than one pound of actual nitrogen per 1,000 square feet per application. Follow University of California guidelines for fertilizing lawns and landscape trees listed in references such as *Practical Lawn Fertilization* (UC ANR Publication 8065) and *Fertilizing Landscape Trees* (UC ANR Publication 8045).

Mowing

5. *Explain how cultural practices such as proper fertilization, irrigation, pruning, and mowing height are important in preventing lawn weed, insect, and pathogen problems.*

Be sure you know the dominant species of grass in each lawn you take care of. Each turfgrass species has specific mowing height requirements (Table 3-1). Mowing some grasses too short can weaken the turfgrass and increase weed invasions. Mowing too high can hurt the appearance or usefulness of the turf.

Figure 3-7. Fertilizing lawns properly will keep them healthy. Healthy lawns can compete with invading weeds and other pests.

Table 3-1. Recommendations for Mowing Grasses. Mowing turf too short or too long reduces its resistance to pests.

RECOMMENDATIONS FOR MOWING GRASSES		
TURF SPECIES[1]	**SET MOWER TO (inches)**	**MOW WHEN TURF REACHES (inches)**
Annual ryegrass	1.5–2	2.25–3
Perennial ryegrass	1.5–2.5	2.25–3.75
Tall fescue	1.5–3	2.25–4.5
Colonial bentgrass	0.5–1	0.75–1.5
Rough bluegrass	1–2.5	1.5–3.75
Bermudagrass	1–1.5 0.5–1 (for hybrids)	1.5–2.25 0.75–1.5 (for hybrids)
Zoysiagrass	0.5–1	0.75–1.5

1. For help in identifying your turf grass species, see the *UC Guide to Healthy Lawns* at the UC IPM Web site, **www.ipm.ucdavis.edu/TOOLS/TURF.**

Mow grasses more frequently when they are actively growing. A standard guide is to remove no more than one-third of the leaf blade at each mowing. If too much is removed at one time, it can take some time for the grass to recover, giving weeds a chance to invade. Lawns with weed invasions often appear uneven. Mow weedy lawns frequently enough to reduce their patchy appearance and prevent weeds from flowering and producing seeds. Be sure that mower blades are sharp enough so that the turfgrass leaves are not ripped or shredded. If mowers are moved from weedy lawns to other lawns, be sure to wash off the blades to avoid transport of weed seeds, rhizomes, stolons, and other plant parts that can spread weeds. Avoid mowing lawns when the soil is wet, such as after rain or irrigation; moving a mower over wet soil can compact the soil.

Pruning

Woody plants are commonly pruned to direct plant growth and improve performance. However, improper pruning damages plants and provides entryways for pests such as borers and wood decay organisms (Figure 3-8). Follow pruning guidelines illustrated in Figure 3-9 to prevent injury to trees. Only qualified arborists should prune large trees or those near power lines.

Proper pruning can control or prevent certain pests (such as borers and fire blight disease). Correctly prune plants when they are young to minimize the need to remove large limbs later, avoiding large pruning wounds. Remove damaged or diseased limbs. Where disease is a concern, disinfect pruning tools to minimize spread. When pruning, carry a spray bottle with a 10% solution of bleach to disinfect blades when moving to a new branch or tree. Consider pruning out pests such as insects or diseased plant parts if they are confined to a small portion of the plant. Where appropriate, prune to increase air circulation within the canopy, which reduces humidity and the incidence of certain diseases such as brown rot or blossom and twig blight on stone fruits.

Learn more about pruning by referring to *Fruit Trees: Training and Pruning Deciduous Trees* (UC ANR Publication 8057) or *Fruit Trees: Pruning Overgrown Deciduous Trees* (UC ANR Publication 8058).

Figure 3-8. Incorrect pruning can lead to pest problems. The tree on the left was topped. The large wounds left by topping often do not close. Open wounds may be attacked by internal decay and wood-boring insects such as the flatheaded borer (right). Drop crotch pruning (Figure 3-9) avoids these problems.

Figure 3-9. Proper techniques for pruning a branch and removing an upper limb (drop-crotch pruning).

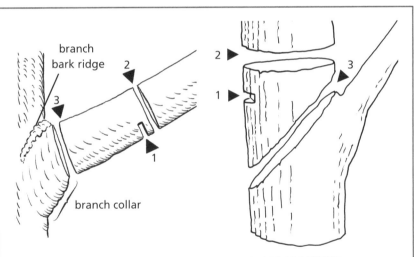

REMOVING A BRANCH

Remove a branch by making the pruning cut just outside the branch bark ridge and branch collar as indicated by the number 3 in the drawing. When removing a limb larger than about 2 inches in diameter, make three cuts in this order: (1) Cut from below, about one-fourth of the way through the limb and 1 or 2 feet from the trunk. (2) Cut about 2 inches past the first cut, cutting from above until the limb drops. (3) Make a final cut at number 3.

DROP-CROTCH PRUNING

Drop-crotch pruning removes an upper limb back to a lower lateral. This technique should be used instead of topping. Topping is poor pruning and leaves stubs. To avoid tearing bark when cutting large limbs, use the 3-cut method shown above and at left.

MECHANICAL AND PHYSICAL CONTROLS

Mechanical and physical control methods include various practices that mechanically destroy pests or present a physical barrier to pest infestation. Examples include traps, mulches, destruction of weeds by handweeding or weed trimming, flaming, solarization, and pest barriers. Examples of successful mechanical and physical control practices include the following.

Traps

A variety of traps can be employed to manage animal pests. Sticky traps or surfaces are used to catch whiteflies and certain insects such as black vine weevils or ants that crawl up trunks. Cone-shaped bait traps capture flies and yellowjackets. Traps are a major control method for managing rodents such as rats, moles, ground squirrels, and pocket gophers (Sidebar 3.2).

Mulches

6. *Explain how the following tools can be used to manage weeds in some situations: mulches, landscape fabrics, hand weeding, and weed trimmers.*

Mulching (Figure 3-10) is one of the easiest and most effective ways to manage weeds in many landscapes. Mulches control weeds by limiting light, which is required for weed establishment. Not only do mulches provide good weed control, they also help conserve water, prevent soil loss, and can be used to improve water penetration into soil or regulate soil temperature. One drawback with mulches is their tendency to provide hiding places for snails, slugs, earwigs, sowbugs, and certain other invertebrate pests. Fresh mulch may also support mushrooms and slime molds; however, these do not harm plants and die off as the mulch dries.

Before any mulch is applied, be sure the soil is weed free. Although very effective against newly germinating weeds, mulch often fails to control established perennial weeds such as johnsongrass, bermudagrass, nutsedge, and field bindweed. Remove these weeds and any vegetative reproductive structures (tubers, rhizomes, stolons) manually as soon as they appear. Keep mulches away from plant crowns (or the base of plants). Mulches may hold moisture, providing conditions that can lead to crown diseases. Two types of mulches may be used: plant-based mulches or non-plant-based mulches.

Plant-based (or organic) mulches include wood chips, yard waste (leaves, clippings, and wood products), compost, and hardwood or softwood bark chips or ground bark. The thickness or depth of mulch necessary to adequately control weed growth depends on the mulch type and the weed population in the area. The larger the particle size of the mulch,

SIDEBAR 3.2—POCKET GOPHER TRAPS

Trapping is a safe and effective method to control pocket gophers. Several types and brands of gopher traps are available. The most common are shown below. On the right, a two-pronged pincher trap, such as the Macabee trap, is triggered when the gopher pushes against the vertical pan. On the left, the choker-style box trap is shown.

To set traps, locate the main tunnel with a probe. Use a shovel or garden trowel to open the tunnel wide enough. Set traps in pairs facing opposite directions. By placing traps with their openings facing in opposite directions, a gopher coming from either end of the burrow can be caught. The box trap is easier to use if you've never set gopher traps before. However, setting it requires more excavation than if you are using a Macabee trap. Box traps are especially useful when the diameter of the gopher's main burrow is small (less than 3 inches) because they fit better into a small tunnel.

Wire your traps to stakes so you can remove them from the burrow easily. Keep light out of the burrow by covering the opening with dirt clods, sod, cardboard, or other material. Fine soil can be sifted around the edges to make a light-tight seal.

Check traps often and reset them when needed. If a gopher is not caught within 3 days, reset the traps in a different location. For more information, see *Pocket Gophers,* UC IPM Pest Note 7433, available on the UC IPM Web site at **www.ipm.ucdavis.edu/PMG/ PESTNOTES/pn7433.html**.

If you normally visit a landscape site only weekly, you may need to visit more often to check traps. Another method is to set traps when you first arrive at a site and pull them when you leave.

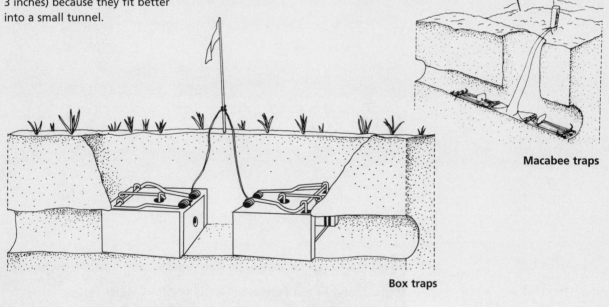

Macabee traps

Box traps

Figure 3-10. Plant-based mulches can give a pleasant, natural appearance. They can improve plant growth and help control weeds.

the greater the depth required to exclude all light from the soil surface. Coarse-textured mulches can be applied up to 4 inches deep and provide long-term weed control. Fine-textured mulches pack more tightly and should be applied only to a depth of about two inches. Plan to periodically replenish landscape mulches, regardless of particle size, because of decomposition (Figure 3-11), movement, or settling. If seedlings germinate in mulches, a light raking, hoeing, or handweeding will remove young weeds. Placing a permeable landscape fabric under mulch results in greater weed control than organic mulch used alone.

Non-plant-based mulches include rocks and various manufactured materials. The most important manufactured materials are geotextiles, or landscape fabrics. Landscape fabrics are porous and allow water and air to pass through them, unlike plastics that are sometimes used. Although these materials are relatively expensive and time-consuming to install, they become more cost-effective than plastic if the planting is to remain in place for 4 or more years. Landscape fabrics are used mainly for long-term weed control in woody ornamental trees and shrubs. Normally a plant-based mulch such as wood chips or bark is placed over the fabric to make it more attractive and improve its durability. There are differences in the weed-controlling ability among the landscape fabrics: fabrics that are thin, lightweight, or have an open mesh make it easier for weeds to grow through than more closely woven or nonwoven fabrics. Most landscape fabrics and plastic mulches are not biodegradable. See Table 3-2 for information on common mulch materials.

Figure 3-11. The organic mulch beneath these shrubs has decomposed, allowing aggressive weeds to invade. Remove the perennial weeds completely (this may require herbicides) and add additional mulch.

COMMON MATERIALS USED AS MULCHES	
PLANT-BASED (ORGANIC) MULCHES	
Compost	May harbor weed seeds if not properly composted. Holds water, so if placed too close to tree trunks may promote crown disease. Weeds grow easily in it. Apply 2 inches deep. Best in annual beds or vegetable gardens for short-term mulching.
Grass clippings	May contain weed seeds. Mats and reduces water penetration, especially if applied too thick and not dried out before applied. Not generally recommended.
Ground bark	Attractive but decomposes rapidly unless used with landscape fabric. Weed seeds grow easily in it and must be pulled out. Can tie up nitrogen as it decomposes when mixed in soil. Don't apply more than 2 inches deep. Often free and is a good source of organic matter. Best for short-term mulching in annual beds or for use on top of landscape fabric.
Medium-sized bark chips	Longer lasting than smaller particles like ground bark. Needs to be replenished as it decomposes. Excellent as a topping for landscape fabric. Best overall choice for a plant-based mulch to be used without fabric. Apply 3 to 4 inches deep and keep replenishing.
Peat moss	Not a good mulch. Resists wetting. May blow away. Expensive. Better as a soil amendment for alkaline soils when worked into the soil.
Wood chips	A good topping for landscape fabric. Where there is a lot of runoff, it may float away. May decompose faster than bark chips.
NON-PLANT-BASED MULCHES	
Landscape fabric	Excellent mulch for permanent plantings of woody landscape plants. Allows for air and water penetration. Many different products are available. May last up to 5 years when properly maintained with plant-based mulch on top.
Newspaper	Two to three sheets of newspaper can be placed under organic mulches in landscape beds on top of drip irrigation; remains effective for the whole season.
Plastic	Inexpensive but breaks down rapidly. Not permeable to air and water. Requires drip irrigation. Weeds can grow through torn places. Use black plastic, since clear plastic encourages weed growth. Unattractive unless covered with plant-based mulch. Landscape fabric or plant-based mulches are generally a better choice.
Rock	Attractive as a top mulch for landscape fabrics. Tends to become weed infested if used alone. May get too hot and injure roots. Hard to clean. Time-consuming to remove.

Table 3-2. Common Materials Used as Mulches. Use a mulch that is right for the landscape project.

Destruction of Weeds

Physical removal by hand or with tools is an important management technique for weeds in landscapes.

Frequent removal of weeds by hand (handweeding) when they are small and have not yet set seed, rapidly reduces the number of annual weeds (Figure 3-12). If weeds are scattered at a site, hand-weeding may be the preferred management method.

Many tools are available to make cultivation and mechanical weeding easier. Garden and supply stores display a variety of hoes of various sizes and shapes. Both broadleaf and grassy annual weeds can be controlled using a hoe, but grass species must be cut off below the soil surface to prevent new sprouts from growing out of the crown. Trowels and other

Figure 3-12. Weeds can be pulled by hand, or you can use hand tools.

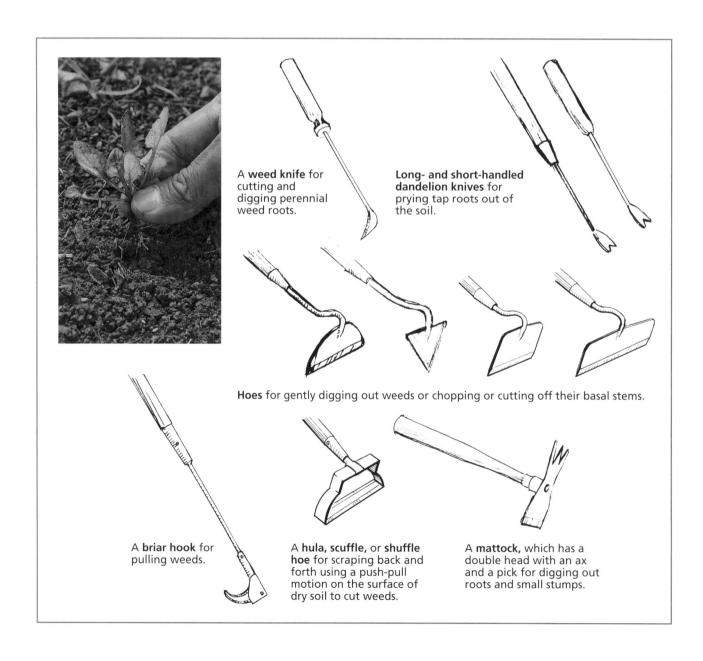

A **weed knife** for cutting and digging perennial weed roots.

Long- and short-handled dandelion knives for prying tap roots out of the soil.

Hoes for gently digging out weeds or chopping or cutting off their basal stems.

A **briar hook** for pulling weeds.

A **hula, scuffle,** or **shuffle hoe** for scraping back and forth using a push-pull motion on the surface of dry soil to cut weeds.

A **mattock,** which has a double head with an ax and a pick for digging out roots and small stumps.

digging tools are useful for removing underground parts of plants. Rototillers can be used in larger areas. It is easier to remove weeds when they are in the seedling stage before they have developed a substantial root system, so weed regularly—once a week or so—especially when landscape plants are young. Once perennial weeds have developed a sturdy root system, the entire plant must be removed to kill them.

Weed trimmers can be used to mow grasses or other tall non-woody vegetation around trees and shrubs before the weeds bloom and form seeds. Be aware that repeated mowing without other control methods can lead to weed shifts to low-growing broadleaf species and grasses that produce seed on plant parts below mowing levels.

Avoid damaging desirable plants with weed trimmers, especially young or thin-barked plants. Trunk damage can girdle and kill young trees or promote attack by wood-boring insects. Before using a weed trimmer, place flexible metal or plastic shields around trunks (Figure 3-13). Customers are sure to be upset if they lose specimen trees to you or your workers damaging the bark.

Flaming

Flaming is a weed management technique that is used in landscapes, row crops, orchards, roadsides, and industrial sites to control young weeds in open areas. In flaming, commercially available propane burners are rapidly passed over young weeds to kill them. Flaming produces temperatures over 1,000°C, heating the plant sap, disrupting cell membranes, and causing cell walls to burst; the weed wilts and dies within seconds. A quick pass over the plant is all that is necessary; do not burn the weed to the ground.

Figure 3-13. Place plant guards around tree trunks for protection before you use a weed trimmer.

Flaming is more effective on broadleaf weeds than on grasses. Young perennial weeds are also susceptible but require more than one treatment. Be careful not to flame over dry vegetation and dry wood chips or near buildings and other flammable materials, and do not get the flame near desired plants. Flaming is most appropriate against weeds in sidewalks and other areas where there is little risk of fire. Don't use flamers on windy days. Permits may be required to use flamers in some areas.

Solarization

Solarization before planting can effectively control most annual and shallow-rooted perennial weeds for 6 months to 1 year. By retaining the sun's heat, solarization can reduce pathogen numbers near the soil surface. Soil solarization is effective only in warmer areas of the state that have warm, sunny summers. To solarize the soil, cover moist, bare, smooth soil with 2-mm-thick clear plastic for about 4 to 6 weeks during the sunny, dry part of the year. Plant soon after the plastic is removed and avoid deep cultivation, which may bring some buried weed seeds to the surface to germinate. See *Soil Solarization: A Nonpesticidal Method for Controlling Diseases, Nematodes, and Weeds* (UC ANR Publication 21377) or *Pest Notes: Solarization* on the UC IPM Web page for more information.

Pest Barriers

Barriers include headers (Figure 3-14) to keep lawns out of planting beds, sticky bands on trees for ants, and copper barriers to keep snails and crawling insects out of trees. Consider using mowing strips, planter beds, and borders to reduce weed encroachment and delineate planting types.

Figure 3-14. Pest barriers, such as headers, can keep grass and weeds out of planted beds. Separate shrub areas from lawns or ground covers by using headers. Headers are barriers made of concrete, metal, plastic, or wood. They extend 8 inches or more below ground and 2 to 3 inches above ground.

BIOLOGICAL CONTROLS

Biological control is any activity by one organism that reduces the harmful effects of another. Living natural enemies are the agents of biological control. Virtually every pest has natural enemies that reduce its population under certain circumstances. Populations of many potential pests are kept below damaging levels most of the time by biological control agents that naturally occur in and around landscapes. These naturally occurring biological control agents often go unnoticed by pest managers until their activities are disrupted (often by a pesticide application), and a new organism becomes a pest. Biological control in landscapes is limited primarily to the management of insect and mite pests, although natural enemies such as hawks or owls may reduce rodent populations.

What Are Natural Enemies?

Natural enemies are organisms that kill, decrease the reproductive potential, or otherwise reduce the numbers of a pest, usually an insect or mite. They are constantly at work in landscapes. Natural enemies used for the biological control of insects can be grouped according to their habits as predators, parasites, or pathogens.

Predators

A predator is an organism that attacks, kills, and feeds on several or many other individuals (its prey) in its lifetime. Some predators are specialized and feed only on one kind of insect, but most are generalists that feed on many kinds of insects. Well-known predators include spiders (Figure 3-15), lady beetles (Figure 3-16), green (Figure 3-17) and brown lacewings, syrphid flies (Figure 3-18), praying mantids, assassin bugs, and predatory mites. Hawks and owls are predators of rodents.

7. Define natural enemies, explain how they control pests, and know how to protect them.

8. Be able to recognize adults and immatures of the following natural enemies: lady beetles, lacewings, and syrphid flies. Know that aphid mummies indicate parasitic wasp activity.

Figure 3-15. All spiders are predaceous and mainly eat insects. Spiders usually avoid people, and most are harmless.

Figure 3-16. Lady beetles are easily recognized by their shiny, rounded shape and short, clubbed antennae. Both larvae and adults of lady beetles eat other insects. The convergent lady beetle, shown here, mostly feeds on aphids and occasionally on whiteflies, other soft-bodied insects, and insect eggs.

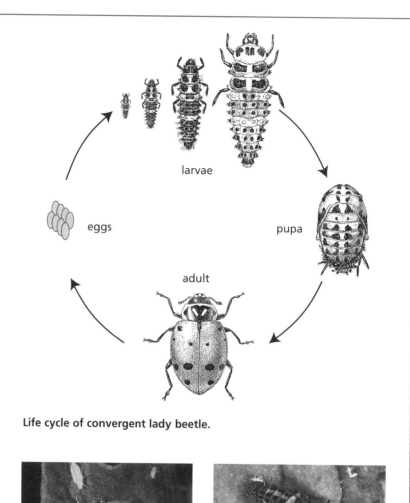

Life cycle of convergent lady beetle.

An adult lady beetle feeding on an aphid.

Lady beetle larva.

Lady beetle pupa.

Lady beetle eggs.

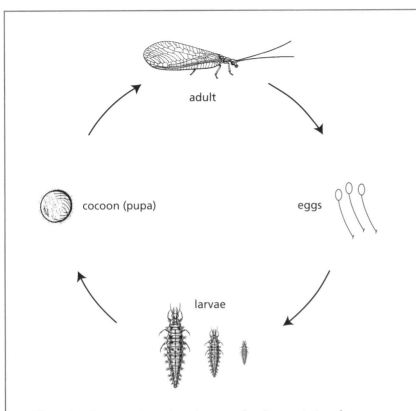

adult

cocoon (pupa)

eggs

larvae

Life cycle of a green lacewing. Average development time from egg to adult is about 1 month.

Adult green lacewing.

Lacewing larva feeding on an aphid.

Figure 3-17. Green lacewings are common predators found in landscapes. All lacewing larvae eat other insects, but adults of many species are not predaceous. Lacewing larvae often feed on aphids. Caterpillars, leafhoppers, mealybugs, psyllids, whiteflies, mites, and insect eggs are also eaten by lacewings.

Figure 3-18. Syrphid flies are found where aphids are present in landscapes and gardens. Adults hover around flowers and feed on pollen. They are often confused with honey bees and wasps. The larvae are important predators. They eat aphids and other soft-bodied insects. Although syrphid larvae resemble caterpillars, unlike caterpillars, they do not have true legs.

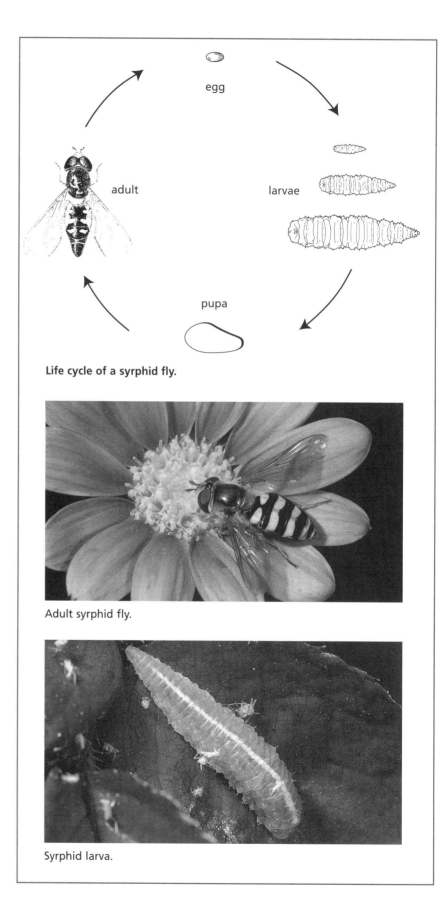

Life cycle of a syrphid fly.

Adult syrphid fly.

Syrphid larva.

Parasites

A parasite is an organism that lives and feeds in or on a larger animal (host). Insects that parasitize other invertebrates (sometimes called parasitoids) are parasitic only in their immature stages and kill their host just as they reach maturity (Figure 3-19). Most insect parasites are tiny wasps or flies. An adult parasite may lay eggs in hundreds of pest individuals, with a resulting quick reduction in the pest population.

Figure 3-19. Life cycle of an insect parasite that attacks aphids.

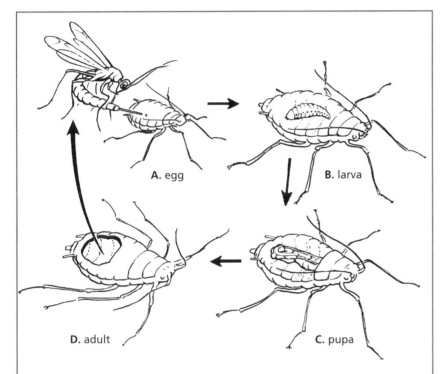

A. egg   B. larva

D. adult   C. pupa

A. An adult parasitic wasp lays an egg inside the live aphid.

B. The egg hatches into a parasite larva that grows as it feeds inside the aphid.

C. After killing the aphid, the parasite pupates.

D. An adult wasp emerges from the dead aphid, then flies off to find and parasitize other aphids.

Figure 3-20. These aphids have been killed by a parasitic wasp. The wasp larva feeds inside, kills the aphid, and turns its skin into a crusty mummy. Once they become adults, the wasps cut round holes in the mummies and emerge to mate and reproduce.

Parasitism is often overlooked. At first glance, parasitized hosts can look like healthy insects. For some hosts, such as aphids, you can tell that they have been parasitized from a change in color. Once killed, parasitized pests such as aphids may be mummified so that their outer surfaces harden and remain unusually well preserved even after the host dies and the parasite departs. Emergence holes left by adult parasites are often visible in the surface of dead hosts (Figure 3-20).

Pathogens

Pathogens, infectious microorganisms that injure or kill their hosts, can cause disease in plants or animals. Pathogens that attack pest insects or mites are beneficial and can be important in biological control. Bacteria, fungi, nematodes, protozoans, and viruses are the most common groups of pathogens affecting insects. A few pathogens or products derived from pathogens are available as insecticides and are classified as microbial insecticides. The most common ones are *Bacillus thuringensis* (Bt) and spinosad.

The only type of commercially available insect pathogens that are not registered as pesticides are entomopathogenic (insect-attacking) nematodes (Figure 3-21). These nematodes are sometimes applied to control lawn grubs or larvae of clearwinged moths or carpenter worms that bore into trees.

Figure 3-21. Insect-killing nematodes emerge from an infected beetle larva. Nematodes can control insect pests such as grubs and caterpillars in lawns.

Protecting Natural Enemies

The beneficial activities of naturally occurring natural enemies in a landscape is one reason that many plant-feeding insects do not ordinarily become damaging pests. You can do several things to encourage biological control agents already present in the landscape you manage. The most important thing is to avoid the use of broad-spectrum insecticides such as pyrethroids, organophosphates, or carbamates whenever possible. Sometimes you can provide habitat that is more favorable for biological control agents. Certain plants in a landscape may enhance the activities of natural enemies of insect pests and indirectly reduce some pest problems. Nectar-producing flowering plants within or near a landscape can attract, support, and increase the activities of natural enemies. Another way to encourage natural enemies is to keep ants out of trees where they protect honeydew-producing pests such as aphids and soft scale from natural enemies (Figure 3-22).

9. Understand that pesticides kill natural enemies and cause problems.

PESTICIDES

Pesticides are substances applied to control, prevent, or repel pests, or to reduce the problems they cause. Pesticides are an important component of many IPM programs. You can quickly obtain temporary control of certain pests if you choose the correct pesticide and apply it at the right time in the appropriate manner. However, if you use an incorrect pesticide, wrong rate, or improper application method, you can do more harm than good. Chapter 4 discusses pesticides in more detail.

Figure 3-22. Ants protect honeydew-producing insects (like soft scales and aphids) from their natural enemies. With no natural enemies to keep them under control, these pests can become serious problems.

Careful Use of Pesticides

Along with the target pest, some pesticides—usually insecticides—often kill predators and parasites. In addition to immediately killing natural enemies that are present at the time of spraying, many pesticides leave toxic residues on foliage that kill predators or parasites that migrate in after spraying. When natural enemies are killed, new pests may become problems, creating a secondary pest outbreak (Figure 3-23). A secondary outbreak occurs when pesticides, usually insecticides, applied against a target pest kill natural enemies of other species, causing another species to become a pest.

Eliminate or reduce the use of broad-spectrum, persistent insecticides whenever possible. Carbamates, organophosphates, and pyrethroids (three major classes of pesticides) are especially toxic to natural enemies (Table 3-3). When pesticides are used, apply them in a selective manner (such as spot applications), time applications to minimize impacts on natural enemies (such as dormant season applications), and choose insecticides that are more specific in the types of invertebrates they kill. Wherever possible, rely on low-persistence insecticides (such as insecticidal soap, narrow-range oil, and the microbial spinosad) or use selective materials, such as the microbial insecticide *Bacillius thuringiensis* (Bt).

Figure 3-23. Applying insecticides that kill natural enemies often results in secondary outbreaks of insects and mites. Sometimes spraying causes big mite outbreaks within a few days.

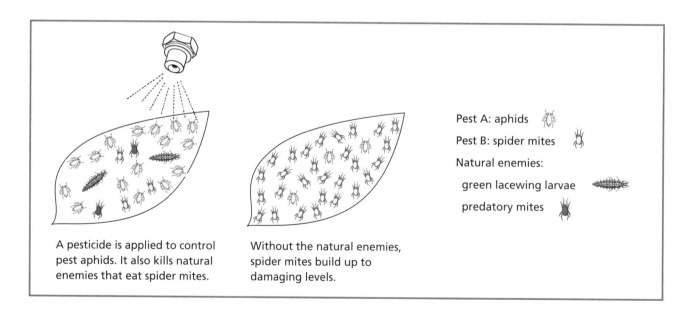

Pest A: aphids

Pest B: spider mites

Natural enemies:

green lacewing larvae

predatory mites

A pesticide is applied to control pest aphids. It also kills natural enemies that eat spider mites.

Without the natural enemies, spider mites build up to damaging levels.

Table 3-3. Toxicity of Common Types of Insecticides to Natural Enemies. Avoid insecticides that may harm beneficial organisms.

TOXICITY OF COMMON TYPES OF INSECTICIDES TO NATURAL ENEMIES		
INSECTICIDE	**TOXICITY TO NATURAL ENEMIES**	
	Contact (immediate killing)	**Residual (long-term killing)**
Microbials *Bacillus thuringiensis* spinosad	none low to high	none short
Oil, soap	moderate	none
Botanicals (insecticides derived from plants)	moderate	short
Pyrethroids (permethrin, bifenthrin, etc.)	high	long
Carbamates and organophosphates	high	moderate to long
Neonicotinoids (imidacloprid)	moderate to high	long

■ Record Keeping and Evaluation

Keep notes on each visit to a landscape site (Figure 3-24). See Figure 3-3 for a sample form for recording useful information. A map or drawing of each landscape site you visit is also helpful. These written records help you determine whether pests or natural enemy populations are increasing or decreasing. They also aid in forecasting possible pest outbreaks. Keeping good landscape records helps you determine which treatments are effective. Refer to them in subsequent years to find out what pests were problems in the past and how they were managed. Records can also help you comply with pesticide regulations, including pesticide use reports. You can also provide these reports to clients to document your work.

10. Know the benefits of keeping track of pest problems and management practices on each property.

Figure 3-24. Take notes about pest problems in landscapes you manage.

Whenever you employ a control method, follow up later to see whether you are getting the results you expect. The correct time to do a follow-up survey depends on the pest and treatment. For instance, for insecticides or postemergent herbicides, follow-up should occur a few days after application. For preemergent herbicides, you must wait a month or more after application to determine whether they have been effective. In any case, if pests are not controlled and continue to be a problem, one of the following factors may be the reason.

11. Know how to recognize when pest control efforts have not been successful and what to do next.

- The method you chose was not effective.

- You misidentified the pest and as a result used an ineffective method.

- The method was not properly applied (for example, wrong time, wrong pesticide application rate, wrong place, or wrong pesticide application equipment).

- Some methods, such as baits for ant control or an application of the herbicide glyphosate, may take days or weeks for the effect to be noticeable.

- Some methods, such as insecticidal soaps, require repeated applications.

Be sure you know the reason for the pest control failure before taking further action. For instance, do not reapply a pesticide without being certain about why it did not work the first time. If you cannot resolve the problem yourself, seek expert help. Keep written records on the effectiveness of management practices to help you make more informed decisions in the future.

■ Information Resources

The best choice of management methods varies by pest and situation. Some insecticides are effective on aphids but do not control caterpillars. Resistant varieties of plants may be available for some plant diseases but not others. Hoeing does a good job on young annual weeds but is not effective against established perennials like bermudagrass.

12. Know where to find reliable pest management information.

This book does not provide you with all the information you need to identify the best management strategy for most pests. Once you have identified your pest, seek information on how to manage it. Become familiar with the UC IPM Web site (**www.ipm.ucdavis.edu**) as it has many useful tools for many pests. There are *Pest Notes* and other pages covering hundreds of weeds and landscape pests. The "Healthy Lawns" section is an interactive tool to help you diagnose lawn problems and solve them. Become familiar with other UC resources, (Sidebar 3.3) including books, Web sites, and pamphlets.

Every county has a University of California Cooperative Extension (UCCE) office and an agricultural commissioner's office, and many also have UC Master Gardener programs. Consult with them; bring pests or plant damage samples to identify and ask about pest management information.

SIDEBAR 3.3—RESOURCES

RESOURCES ON PLANT PROBLEMS, ABIOTIC CONDITIONS, PLANT PESTS, AND THEIR IDENTIFICATION

BOOKS

University of California Agriculture and Natural Resources Publications (UC ANR)

To order a publication visit the online catalog at **www.anrcatalog.ucdavis.edu** or call **800-994-8849**

Weeds of the West
PUBLICATION 3350

Pests of Landscape Trees and Shrubs: An Integrated Pest Management Guide
Second Edition
PUBLICATION 3359

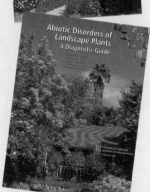

Abiotic Disorders of Landscape Plants: A Diagnostic Guide
PUBLICATION 3420

Weeds of California
PUBLICATION 3488

Pests of the Garden and Small Farm
Second Edition
PUBLICATION 3332

Natural Enemies Handbook: The Illustrated Guide to Biological Pest Control
PUBLICATION 3386

Landscape Pest Identification Cards
PUBLICATION 3513

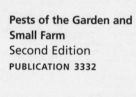

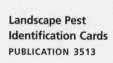

SIDEBAR 3.3—RESOURCES

Wildlife Pest Control around Gardens and Homes
Second Edition
PUBLICATION 21385

IPM in Practice: Principles and Methods of Integrated Pest Management
PUBLICATION 3418

WEB SITES

UC IPM Program Web site
www.ipm.ucdavis.edu

Go to the UC IPM Web site for *Pest Notes* on over 140 specific landscape pests and weeds as well as photos and information on many other pests, natural enemies, pesticides and other pest management methods.

University of California
ANR publications Web site
www.anrcatalog.ucdavis.edu

Go to this Web site to find any UC ANR publication mentioned in this book plus many more of interest to landscape managers.

www.ipm.ucdavis.edu/PMG/menu.homegarden.html

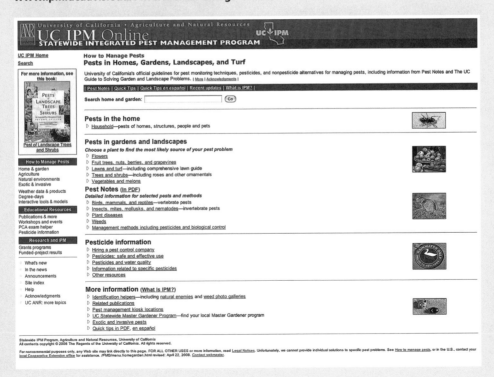

■ Chapter 3 Review Questions

1. To manage pests, integrated pest management programs primarily rely on
   - ☐ a. pesticides
   - ☐ b. biological control
   - ☐ c. a combination of methods
   - ☐ d. action thresholds

2. There are five components to a successful IPM program. They include the following: prevention through good cultural practices; regular monitoring for pests and problems; action thresholds: treat only when necessary; and integration of appropriate management methods. One component is missing. It is
   - ☐ a. pest and symptom identification
   - ☐ b. organically acceptable pesticides
   - ☐ c. removing target organisms
   - ☐ d. cultural practices

3. Which of the following is an example of a cultural control practice?
   - ☐ a. traps
   - ☐ b. applying an herbicide
   - ☐ c. releasing natural enemies
   - ☐ d. setting irrigation timers to water lawns in early morning

4. What is one reason why you should avoid over-watering plants?
   - ☐ a. it may promote root diseases
   - ☐ b. it will result in small plants
   - ☐ c. it attracts insects
   - ☐ d. it will make pests harder to find

5. Why is it important to choose resistant or tolerant plant varieties?
   - ☐ a. reduce pest problems, especially plant diseases
   - ☐ b. reduce reliance on pesticides
   - ☐ c. improve long-term pest management through prevention
   - ☐ d. all of the above

6. Mowing turfgrass too short can
   - ☐ a. prevent disease problems
   - ☐ b. increase weed problems
   - ☐ c. increase fertilizer requirements
   - ☐ d. prevent absorption of pesticides

7. Mulches suppress weeds by
   - ☐ a. encouraging weed-feeding insects
   - ☐ b. limiting light required for weed establishment
   - ☐ c. discouraging people from walking near landscape plants
   - ☐ d. acting as a natural herbicide

8. Write the name of the aphid predator next to its photograph.
   lady beetle
   syrphid fly
   green lacewing

   A._____

   B._____

   C._____

9. Insecticides can cause pest outbreaks by
    ☐ a. killing natural enemies of pests
    ☐ b. reducing photosynthesis
    ☐ c. causing phytotoxicity
    ☐ d. insecticides never cause pest outbreaks

10. Why is it a good idea to keep good records of
    pest management actions for each landscape
    you manage?
    ☐ a. you will be able to predict the weather
    ☐ b. you will not have to comply with pesticide
          regulations
    ☐ c. it will help you determine which treatments
          are effective against pests
    ☐ d. all of the above

11. What are some good sources of information for
    finding out how to control a specific pest?
    ☐ a. UC Cooperative Extension office
    ☐ b. books from the University of California
    ☐ c. UC IPM Web site **www.ipm.ucdavis.edu**
    ☐ d. all of the above

(Answer sheet is on pages 206–207.)

4

Pesticides and Their Hazards

Pesticides are important tools for managing pests, but if you use them improperly, you risk harming yourself, others, the plants you are protecting, and the environment.

1. Know that all pesticides are toxic to some organisms and can cause problems.

2. Recognize what factors affect pesticide effectiveness and potential to harm.

3. Know how pesticides are classified according to target pest.

4. Define pesticide selectivity and explain why it is important.

5. Be familiar with different pesticide formulations.

6. Describe the best timing for applying preemergent and postemergent herbicides.

7. Explain the difference between contact and systemic herbicides.

8. Explain the difference between systemic insecticides and other insecticides.

9. Explain how pesticides move in the environment in air, water, and sediment and injure non-target organisms.

10. Recognize the causes and effects of phytotoxicity (injury to plants) from landscape and turfgrass pesticide applications.

11. Explain how people get exposed to pesticides in landscape and turf settings.

12. Know how pesticides enter the body.

13. Know the health effects of pesticide exposure.

PESTICIDES ARE important tools for managing pests, but pesticides pose hazards as well. If you use them improperly, you risk harming yourself, others, the plants you are protecting, and the environment. Choosing and using pesticides requires special knowledge, experience, and appropriate training. Knowing how and why a specific pesticide controls the target pest allows you to use it more effectively. This chapter will help you choose the right pesticide and know its potential hazards.

■ Pesticide Basics

TOXICITY

1. Know that all pesticides are toxic to some organisms and can cause problems.

Toxicity is the ability of a pesticide or other material to injure a person, animal, plant, or other organism. The level of toxicity is a permanent characteristic of a pesticide chemical and does not change. However, the likelihood of injury due to application of any pesticide chemical may be reduced or increased depending on pesticide formulation, dilution, application method, exposure, and other factors.

All pesticides are toxic to some organisms at some level. "The dose makes the poison" is another way to describe how pesticides that have little effect in tiny amounts can cause serious harm to people and other living organisms when present in larger quantities. The risk of harm is related to the amount of exposure (the dose) and the toxicity of the pesticide product. Pesticides that cause injury at lower doses are more toxic than those that require higher doses to cause similar injury.

Pesticide toxicity is commonly measured as the lethal dose that will kill half the population of a test organism. This measure is called the LD_{50} (Figure 4-1). Oral (through the mouth) and dermal (through the skin) LD_{50}s are shown on the pesticide product's Material Safety Data Sheet (MSDS).

You can compare the LD_{50}s of different pesticides to learn how toxic they are to test animals. The lower the LD_{50}, the more toxic the pesticide. (Figure 4-2).

Figure 4-1. The amount of a pesticide that will kill half of the group of test animals is the pesticide's LD_{50}. In this illustration, the test animals are rats. The LD_{50} for this pesticide is 10 milligrams of pesticide for each kilogram of a rat's body weight. Half of the rats die when fed 10 milligrams per kilogram of the pesticide. This can be written LD_{50} = 10 mg/kg.

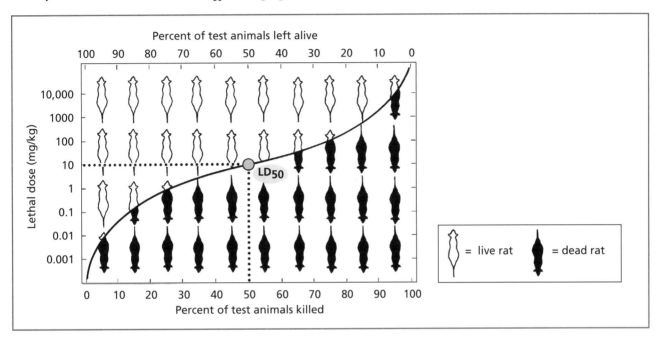

Figure 4-2. Relative toxicities of some pesticides used in landscapes. When the LD_{50} is lower, smaller amounts are needed to kill test animals.

CHEMICAL NAME	DISULFOTON	METALDEHYDE	CARBARYL	GLYPHOSATE
Trade name	2 in 1 Systemic Rose & Flower Care	Slug & Snail Death (3.25)	Sevin Ready-To-Spray Bug Killer	Remuda Full Strength
(EPA Registration #)	(72155-49)	(8119-11)	(264-334-71004)	(228-366-54705)
	insecticide	molluscicide	insecticide	herbicide
Relative amount required to kill half of the population of test animals				
Oral LD_{50} (mg/kg)	347 mg/kg	630 mg/kg	1,947 mg/kg	over 5,000 mg/kg
Weight equivalent for a person (who weighs 60 kg or 132 pounds)	less than 1 ounce	slightly over 1 ounce	approximately 4 ounces	more than 10 ounces
Signal word	WARNING	CAUTION	CAUTION	CAUTION

Pesticide Toxicity Classifications

Federal regulations group pesticides into categories according to their acute toxicity and potential to injure people or the environment. Pesticide labels indicate these categories by using signal words (Figure 4-3):

- DANGER and POISON: Category I
- DANGER: Category I
- WARNING: Category II
- CAUTION: Category III and IV

A highly toxic pesticide will include the signal word DANGER as well as the word POISON and a skull and crossbones. These are the most dangerous and should be handled very cautiously. DANGER (and DANGER–POISON) pesticides are the most toxic. CAUTION pesticides are the least toxic to people and generally pose less risk. However, there is a lot of variability in toxicity among pesticides with the CAUTION signal word. Different label and regulatory requirements apply to each category.

In California you need a permit from the county agricultural commissioner's office to buy, possess, and use most Category I pesticides, and you also must be a certified applicator. See Chapter 1 for information on becoming a certified applicator.

Acute versus Chronic Toxicity. Signal word toxicity classifications and LD_{50} measurements are based on a single exposure to the pesticide

Figure 4-3. Signal words on labels tell you the relative hazard of pesticides. Pesticides with a skull and crossbones and the words DANGER–POISON are the most toxic pesticides. Use them with extreme care.

DANGER–POISON	DANGER	WARNING	CAUTION
Highly toxic	Highly toxic	Moderately toxic	Slightly toxic

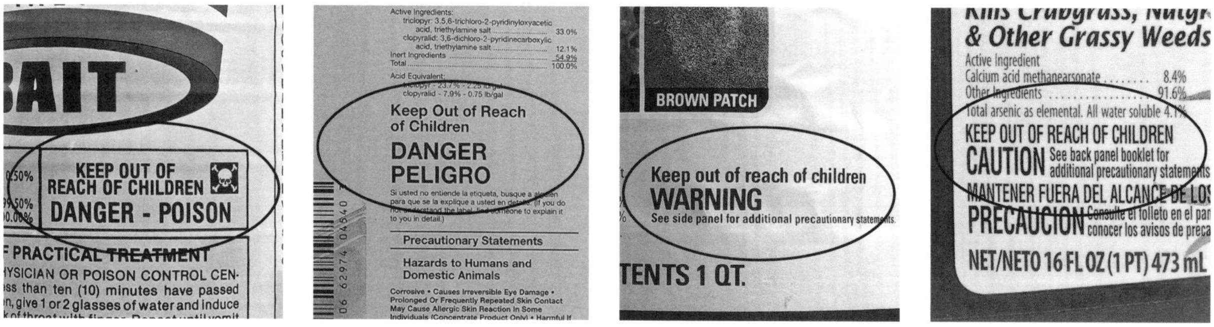

and do not provide information about possible long-term health effects of repeated exposures to lower doses of a pesticide over a long time. The LD_{50} rating measures only acute toxicity, or the ability of a pesticide to quickly kill an organism with a single dose. Some pesticides that do not have a high acute toxicity as measured by LD_{50} can pose serious health problems when people are exposed over time. This type of toxicity is called chronic toxicity. Typical effects of chronic toxicity are cancer, birth defects, and nervous system problems, which develop over a long time. The likelihood that a pesticide application will cause injury is affected by the toxicity of the pesticide and also the application rate or dose, the way it is formulated, the environment, and how it is applied and handled.

FACTORS THAT INFLUENCE A PESTICIDE'S EFFECTIVENESS AND POTENTIAL TO CAUSE HARM

The toxicity of a pesticide to the pest you are trying to control is only one factor that determines whether a pesticide will control the target pest or cause harm to the environment or human health (Figure 4-4). Other factors include

2. Recognize what factors affect pesticide effectiveness and potential to harm.

- application procedures

- weather and water

- condition of the treated plant

- special site considerations such as the soil type, surrounding areas, sensitive organisms, and people

How fast a pesticide breaks down into less toxic compounds has a big impact on its effectiveness and its potential to cause harm. Pesticides that remain toxic in the environment for a long time, known as persistent pesticides, are more likely to have negative impacts on the environment. The time it takes for half of a pesticide to break down in the environment into other compounds is called its half-life. You can find out what a pesticide's half-life is by checking the MSDS. See the following chapter for more information about the MSDS.

Soil microbes, soil pH, the quality of the water used in mixing, and impurities combined with the pesticide can also lengthen or shorten the time it takes a pesticide to break down. Sometimes impurities are introduced into pesticide products during manufacture, formulation, storage, or while you are mixing them. Mixing one pesticide product with another may also increase or decrease toxicity and change the half-life of the tank mix.

Figure 4-4. Chemistry, application procedures, and site conditions affect a pesticide application's potential to control a pest or cause harm.

FIVE FACTORS THAT INFLUENCE PESTICIDE SAFETY OR EFFECTIVENESS

1. **Chemical properties of the pesticide product**
   - toxicity
   - formulation
   - volatility

2. **Application procedures**
   - equipment type
   - rate
   - handling procedures
   - protective equipment and clothing

3. **Weather and water**
   - sunlight
   - temperature
   - wind
   - rain, humidity, dew, irrigation

4. **Condition of treated plant**
   - drought stress
   - other pest problems
   - growth stage
   - nutritional deficiency

5. **Special considerations of the site**
   - near to people, schools, pets
   - nontarget sensitive organisms
   - proximity of creeks, rivers, drains
   - slope
   - soil type
   - surrounding natural areas or sensitive plants

Water pH

One important environmental factor that influences effectiveness of a pesticide is the acidity or pH of the water you are using to mix it. Some pesticides lose effectiveness when water is alkaline (over pH 8). The effect of pH depends on the specific pesticide.

Weather and Irrigation

The time it takes for a pesticide to break down is also affected by temperature, humidity, and exposure to sunlight, wind, and rain. Certain ingredients of the pesticide may volatilize, or evaporate and turn into a gas. Many pesticides break down or volatilize rapidly when it is windy or temperatures are high. Temperature can make a big difference in the success or failure of your pesticide application by affecting the way a pesticide interacts with pests, the plant, and other organisms. Many pesticide labels warn against making an application when temperatures are very high or low to prevent plant injury or to improve effectiveness. Pesticides may also break down rapidly by exposure to ultraviolet light, which is most intense during clear, sunny weather. Rainfall, fog, and even heavy dew may dilute or degrade pesticides or wash them off the treated surfaces. High moisture can also cause granular pesticides to stick to leaves, causing plant injury.

Weather and the way pesticides are applied can also affect the likelihood that pesticides will move off-site to cause problems. Rainwater can wash pesticides into or over the soil, possibly causing groundwater or surface water contamination, especially if water washes onto hard or impermeable surfaces such as pavement or roads. Pesticides can also be carried away from the application site through water movement from irrigation.

Strong winds may cause uneven pesticide coverage or blow the pesticide off target and reduce effectiveness. Wind can blow pesticides away from the target site, causing drift; however, some air movement helps improve coverage of treated surfaces.

The effects of rain or irrigation on the condition of treated plants may be important. For instance, some herbicides are less effective on water-stressed weeds. Other pesticides, such as insecticidal oils, may damage trees or shrubs that are water stressed. Some herbicides need water to activate in the soil.

In summary, checking weather and other environmental conditions (Figure 4-5) before applying a pesticide is important because these conditions may affect a pesticide's

- ability to control the pest

- potential for injury to plants

- persistence, or how fast it will break down

- likelihood of moving in the environment

Site Considerations

The site location, slope, soil type, proximity to children, recreational areas, and water bodies, as well as many other factors that could be affected by the pesticide application, must be considered before applying pesticides. Nontarget organisms, endangered species, and the environment must be protected from pesticides moving off-site.

TYPES OF PESTICIDES (PESTICIDE CLASSIFICATION)

3. Know how pesticides are classified according to target pest.

Pesticides are classified in several ways. One common classification is by the target pests they are intended to control. For example, insecticides control insects, and herbicides control plants. Table 4-1 lists common pesticide types used in landscape pest management.

Pesticides can also be classified according to chemical group. Pesticides in the same chemical group often have common characteristics. The mechanism by which they control pests, toxicity to certain pest groups, environmental or health hazards, and persistence in the environment are other ways that pesticides may be classified. Pesticide selectivity or formulation can also be used to classify pesticides.

Figure 4-5. Before you apply pesticides, know what weather conditions to expect.

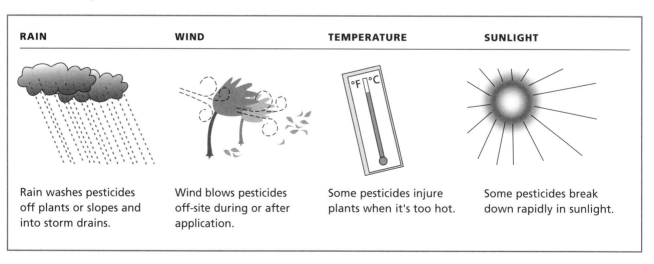

RAIN	WIND	TEMPERATURE	SUNLIGHT
Rain washes pesticides off plants or slopes and into storm drains.	Wind blows pesticides off-site during or after application.	Some pesticides injure plants when it's too hot.	Some pesticides break down rapidly in sunlight.

Table 4-1. Examples of Pesticides Commonly Used in Landscapes.

EXAMPLES OF PESTICIDES COMMONLY USED IN LANDSCAPES		
PESTICIDE TYPE **PESTS CONTROLLED**	**EXAMPLE OF PEST**	**EXAMPLES OF** **ACTIVE INGREDIENTS**
Acaricides **or miticides** control mites	spider mite	jojoba oil neem oil petroleum oil
Fungicides control fungi	powdery mildew on rose	chlorothalonil copper sulfur
Herbicides control weeds	dandelion	2,4-D dicamba fluazifop glyphosate trifluralin
Insecticides control insects	aphid	carbaryl disulfoton imidacloprid malathion permethrin insecticidal soap horticultural oils
Molluscicides control snails and slugs	brown garden snail	iron phosphate metaldehyde

4. *Define pesticide selectivity and explain why it is important.*

Pesticide Selectivity

Pesticide selectivity indicates the range of organisms and life stages affected by the pesticide. A broad-spectrum insecticide kills a wide variety of pests and nontarget organisms. A selective pesticide controls a smaller group of closely related organisms. Selective insecticides are generally desirable in IPM programs because they often have fewer harmful impacts on beneficial organisms and lower health risks for humans and wildlife. Selective pesticides target chemical processes unique to one pest or pest group. Selective herbicides often target one group of plants, for instance, broadleaves or grasses. 2,4-D is an example of an herbicide that kills many broadleaf weeds but is safe to use on most grasses, making it useful for managing many weeds in lawns. Selectivity can also be achieved through the use of application techniques that aim a pesticide right at the target pest so it does not contact nontarget organisms or by timing applications carefully.

Pesticide Formulations

5. *Be familiar with different pesticide formulations.*

A pesticide product is a mixture of the active ingredient(s) and other materials (sometimes referred to as "inert" ingredients) combined into a pesticide formulation. The type of formulation determines how the product will be applied and how it should be mixed before application. Specialized equipment, such as bait stations or spreaders (Figure 4-6) for some granules, may be required for application of certain formulations. For maintenance gardeners, most liquids are applied either right from the original container (ready-to-use products) or with backpack or compressed air applicators. Some labels include formulation information in the product name. The more common pesticide formulations used by maintenance gardeners and their properties are described in Table 4-2. Some must be diluted with liquid and require constant mixing (agitation), while others are applied dry.

Figure 4-6. Some pesticide formulations may require special application equipment. Spreaders like this are used to apply granular pesticides.

Table 4-2. Pesticide Formulations Used in Landscapes.

PESTICIDE FORMULATIONS USED IN LANDSCAPES				
FORMULATION TYPE	SAMPLE PRODUCT	COMMENTS	MIX WITH WATER?	SPECIAL EQUIPMENT NEEDED?
Ready to use; ready to spray; also includes aerosols		Ready to use. Common for home use and spot applications.	no	no
Wettable powder		Do not inhale. Keep agitating (shaking) after mixing.	yes	yes
Emulsifiable concentrate		Keep agitating after mixing. May contain solvents that are irritating and contribute to air pollution. Penetrates soil and wood. May cause more plant injury than wettable powders.	yes	yes
Flowable; flowable concentrate		Keep agitating after mixing. May contain solvents that are irritating and contribute to air pollution.	yes	yes
Granules		Be sure it lands where desired. Do not allow it to stick to wet leaves. Small chance of drift because of larger particle size.	no	yes
Dust		Fine particles can irritate lungs and skin. Small particle size can lead to drift. Do not breathe dust.	no	yes
Bait or pellet		Be sure pets and children are not attracted. Use bait stations to keep nontarget animals away from rodenticide baits.	no	Sometimes placed in bait stations. For gophers, use special applicators to place in burrows.
Pesticide and fertilizer combination (sometimes called "weed and feed")		Combination of fertilizer and pesticide. Often used on lawns or turf. Generally not recommended because best timing for fertilizing and applying pesticide may not be the same. Do not apply combination products when only fertilizers are needed.	no	yes

Choosing Pesticides

The first step in choosing a pesticide is to accurately identify the pest (e.g., the insect, weed, plant pathogen) that is causing the problem. If the pest is misidentified, you will not be able to choose an effective pesticide. Seek out help from your UC Cooperative Extension office or other resources if you can't identify the pest.

If a pesticide is needed, select one that will control your pest and also pose the fewest risks to human health and the environment. You often have a number of choices. A good source of information for least toxic pesticides for use against specific pests is the UC IPM Pest Note series available at your UCCE office or at the UC IPM Web site (**www.ipm.ucdavis.edu**). Always be sure that the pest and plant (or site) that you are treating are listed on the pesticide product label.

Herbicides. Herbicides are classified in several ways including according to

- the product formulation
- when they are applied relative to plant growth stage
- how they control weeds

Herbicide formulations vary according to their usefulness in different situations and required application equipment. Common herbicide formulations are granules (typically applied dry), wettable powders, flowables, and emulsifiable concentrates. Maintenance gardeners often apply herbicides using a backpack or compressed air applicator.

Preemergent herbicides. Preemergent herbicides are applied before weeds germinate and will kill germinating weeds for several weeks or months after application (Figure 4-7). Preemergent herbicides generally do not kill established weeds or plants. They are relatively safe for application around existing landscapes.

6. *Describe the best timing for applying preemergent and postemergent herbicides.*

The timing of a preemergent herbicide application is determined by when the target weed germinates or by when the weed is in the stage that is most sensitive to the herbicide. In general, late summer or early fall applications of preemergent herbicides are used to control winter annuals. Late winter or early spring applications are used to control summer annuals and seeds of perennial weeds. Some preemergent herbicides applied when soil temperatures are cool may not be effective because the weeds do not take them up fast enough.

7. *Explain the difference between contact and systemic herbicides.*

Postemergent herbicides. Postemergent herbicides are applied to weeds that have green growth above the soil (see Figure 4-7). They may be classified as contact or systemic (translocated) herbicides (see Figure 4-8). Contact postemergent herbicides usually kill only

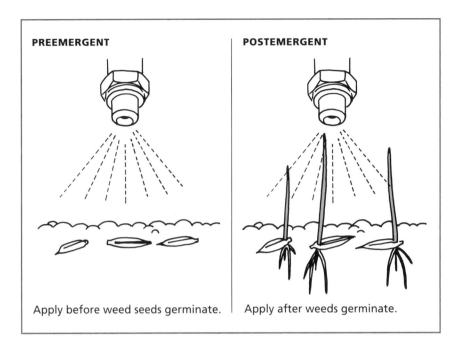

Figure 4-7. Herbicides may be classified as preemergent or postemergent.

Figure 4-8. Contact and systemic herbicides kill plants differently.

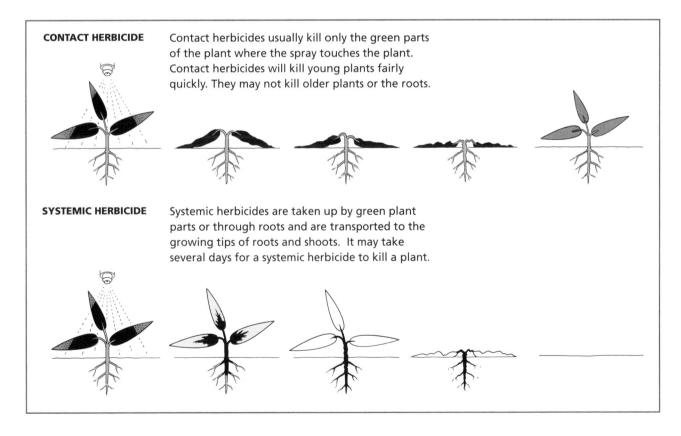

those green plant parts on which spray is deposited (usually leaves and stems), so thorough coverage is important for good control. It is best to control the plants when they are small to minimize the amount of herbicide needed.

Translocated (systemic) herbicides may be taken up by green parts of the plant and translocated (transported) to the growing tips of roots and shoots, so it may not be necessary to spray the entire plant to kill it; or they are applied to soil and taken up through the roots to the leaves and need not be sprayed on the leaves. Some herbicides are translocated (moved) both ways. For example, dicamba can be taken up by leaves and shoots or through the roots. The principal advantage of systemic herbicides is that they can control many perennial weeds. For best control, perennial weeds should be growing vigorously and have many mature leaves when they are sprayed. Depending on the season and stage of plant growth, the effect of some translocated (systemic) herbicides may not be visible until some time after they are applied. For example, the effect of glyphosate (Round-up) may not be seen until 4 to 7 days after application.

Selectivity. Herbicides may be selective or nonselective (broadspectrum). Selective herbicides kill only certain groups of plants. They can be used around certain desirable plants as directed on the label. For example, phenoxy herbicides such as MCPA and 2,4-D are used in lawns because they kill most broadleaf weeds but not grasses when properly used. Nonselective (broad-spectrum) herbicides kill both grass and broadleaf weeds, as well as desirable plants with which they come in contact. Nonselective herbicides, such as glyphosate, should be used where there are no desirable plants nearby or under circumstances where they can be applied so that the material contacts only weeds and not the green bark or foliage of desirable landscape plants. Landscape plants may be damaged by direct spraying or from herbicides that reach plants through drift, volatilization, or by contacting roots in treated soils. Selectivity can be achieved with a broadspectrum herbicide (Figure 4-9). For example, glyphosate can be used selectively when applied around the base (dead bark) of trees, vines, or shrubs, as long as it does not come in contact with leaves. Roses or citrus with green bark will be injured.

Figure 4-9. The rose at left has been injured by contact with a nonselective herbicide, glyphosate. Shoots are puckered, and leaves are feathered and discolored.

Insecticides. A variety of insecticides are available for landscape use. Effective use of insecticides within an IPM program requires choosing the most selective material that controls the pest. Insect and mite management in the landscape relies to a great extent on naturally occurring biological control. Every effort should be made to choose insecticides that do not kill predators or parasites that attack insect pests. See Table 3-3 for some common landscape insecticide groups and their impacts on natural enemies.

Some insecticides are referred to as contact poisons or as stomach poisons. A contact insecticide provides control when target pests come in physical contact with it. Stomach poisons must be eaten to affect the pest. For instance, *Bacillus thuringiensis* (Bt) acts as a stomach poison. If a Bt spray is applied when or where the target pests (caterpillars) are not feeding, it will have no impact. Many insecticides have both contact and stomach action.

Some insecticides are systemic (Figure 4-10). After application, they are taken up by the plant through the roots, stems, or leaves and are moved around through the plant. Commonly used systemic insecticides include imidacloprid and acephate. For good control with nonsystemic insecticides, complete coverage of the plant or areas where the insects are present is required. Good coverage is not a requirement with systemics, since the chemical will be moved in the plant to places where the insects feed.

8. Explain the difference between systemic insecticides and other insecticides.

Figure 4-10. Nonsystemic insecticides must be applied to all infested parts of the plant. Systemic insecticides are taken up by the plant and translocated to leaves or other parts.

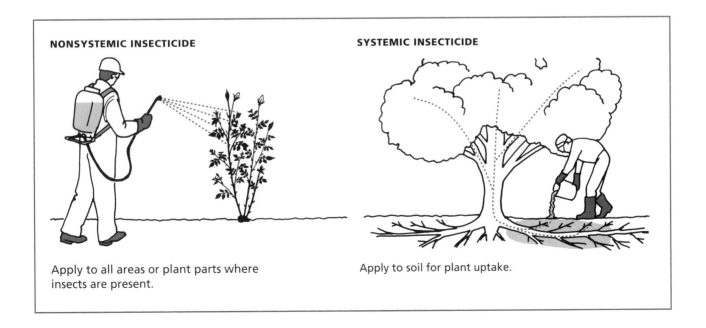

NONSYSTEMIC INSECTICIDE

SYSTEMIC INSECTICIDE

Apply to all areas or plant parts where insects are present.

Apply to soil for plant uptake.

Fungicides. Pesticides used to control fungal diseases are called fungicides. Many fungicides are available for managing a variety of fungal diseases, and new products are added every year. Most fungicides are surface protectants that must be applied before the fungal spores germinate and enter the plant (Table 4-3). Their presence usually prevents the spores from germinating or kills the spores once they germinate. If infection occurs, protectant fungicides cannot prevent disease. Eradicant fungicides, such as petroleum or plant-based oils, may reduce existing infections.

When selecting a fungicide it is important to choose the most effective material for the situation (Figure 4-11). Protectants (preventive fungicides) have limited usefulness once an infection has started. Precise timing of fungicide applications is very important for the control of plant pathogens. Keep track of weather, especially temperature and moisture, because disease outbreaks can build rapidly after changes in the weather, especially rain.

Table 4-3. Eradicant and Preventive Fungicides for Powdery Mildew.

ERADICANT AND PREVENTIVE FUNGICIDES FOR POWDERY MILDEW			
CHEMICAL OR CLASS	CONTROLS EXISTING INFECTIONS? (ERADICANT)	PREVENTIVE FOR DISEASE? (PROTECTANT)	TRADE NAME OR EXAMPLES
Horticultural oils	yes	somewhat	neem oil, jojoba oil, narrow range petroleum oil
Sulfur	no	yes	wettable sulfur
Potassium bicarbonate	somewhat	yes	Kaligreen
Biological fungicide	no	yes	Serenade
Myclobutanil	yes	yes	Immunox

Figure 4-11. When you can see fungus growth on the leaf, as shown on this crape myrtle, it is too late to use protectant fungicides.

■ Pesticide Hazards

Several types of potential hazards are associated with pesticide use. If you are exposed to pesticides, you could suffer short-term or long-term health problems. If you are careless and allow pesticides to drift or otherwise get into the environment, nearby landscape maintenance workers, residents, or pets may be injured. Exposure to residues may also cause harm. Environmental contamination by pesticides may lead to loss of water quality or injury to nontarget organisms. It is important to recognize the hazards associated with pesticide applications in turf and landscape situations and learn how to prevent them.

HOW DO PESTICIDES MOVE THROUGH THE ENVIRONMENT?

Environmental contamination results when pesticides are carried away from the target area through wind, water, or soil (Figure 4-12). As much as 55% of an applied pesticide may leave the treatment area due to spray drift, volatilization, leaching, runoff, and soil erosion. Pesticides that drift or move onto adjacent areas may damage desired plants and can contaminate lakes, rivers, streams, and oceans. Some pesticides can run off or leach (move down through the soil) from a treated area to groundwater and into wells.

Sometimes, environmental damage can occur even when the pesticides you have applied remain in the treated area. If humans, pets,

9. Explain how pesticides move in the environment in air, water, and sediment and injure non-target organisms.

Figure 4-12. Pesticides may move off the application site by drifting in air or being washed off with water and soil.

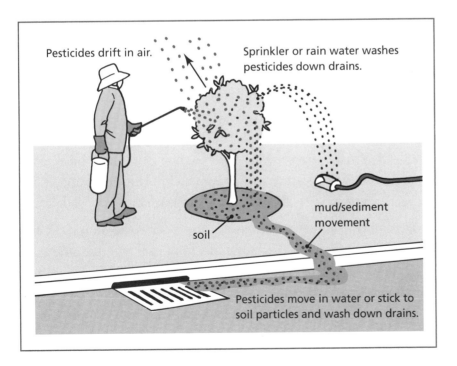

Pesticides drift in air.

Sprinkler or rain water washes pesticides down drains.

mud/sediment movement

soil

Pesticides move in water or stick to soil particles and wash down drains.

or wildlife are in a treated landscape area or enter the area soon after an application, they may be poisoned. Some pesticides (persistent pesticides) remain toxic in the environment for many weeks, months, or even years after they have been applied. In other cases, pesticide breakdown products may be as toxic or more toxic than the applied chemical. The type of formulation, the quantity of pesticide applied, and the application location also influence how long a pesticide remains potentially damaging.

Pesticide Movement through the Air

Pesticides can become airborne in many ways. Pesticide droplets or particles may be blown into the air. Liquid pesticides may also vaporize or become a gas. Or, they may cling to dust or soil particles that are blown into the air. Drift is the movement of pesticides in the air away from the treatment site through any of these means during application. Drift can damage susceptible plants or cause environmental contamination away from the application site. Drift into residential areas, school grounds, or anywhere that people may be exposed can pose health risks. Drift also reduces the effectiveness of a pesticide application because the material does not land on the target pest to control it.

Many factors influence drift, including application equipment, nozzle size, and weather. Drift is most likely when making applications in windy conditions. Low relative humidity and high temperatures also increase the potential for drift by causing spray droplets to evaporate faster.

Pesticide Movement in the Soil

Pesticides get into soil through several routes. They may be applied directly to the soil surface or incorporated (worked) into the top few inches of soil. When pesticides are applied to plants, some always lands on the soil. Pesticides can also enter the soil through spills, drift, and runoff. Once in the soil, pesticides can be taken up into the bodies of invertebrates (such as earthworms), taken up by plants, volatilize into the air, mobilize in water through erosion or leaching, or break down.

The soil type influences how long the pesticide will remain. The tendency for pesticides to remain in the soil varies with the amount of clay and organic matter in the soil. The higher the percentage of clay and organic matter in the soil, the greater the number of sites where pesticide molecules can attach themselves; however, pesticides may break down more rapidly in soils with more organic matter due to the presence of microorganisms. Pesticides tend to be retained longer in soils with high clay content than in sandy soils (Figure 4-13). The more water-soluble a pesticide is, the more rapidly it can move through the soil (leach), especially in sandy soils, which can result in groundwater contamination.

Pesticide Movement in Water

Many pesticides readily move in water. In urban areas, pesticides may reach creeks and rivers through storm drains and household drains. Runoff from rain and landscape or turf irrigation washes pesticide residues down the streets through gutters into storm drains. The runoff flows through pipes that often lead directly into creeks, lakes, and rivers (Figure 4-14). Dumping unused pesticides from spray tanks or containers into gutters has the same effect and is illegal.

Disposing of pesticides or wash water from cleaning personal protective equipment or application equipment into

Figure 4-13. Soil type affects the movement of pesticides.

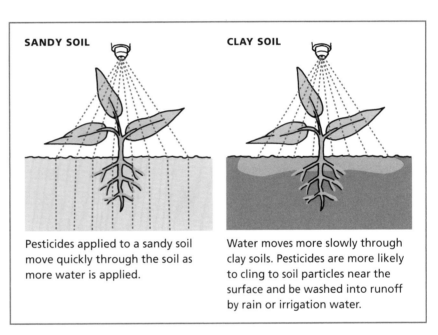

SANDY SOIL

CLAY SOIL

Pesticides applied to a sandy soil move quickly through the soil as more water is applied.

Water moves more slowly through clay soils. Pesticides are more likely to cling to soil particles near the surface and be washed into runoff by rain or irrigation water.

Figure 4-14. Pesticides can move through storm drains or household drains into creeks and rivers.

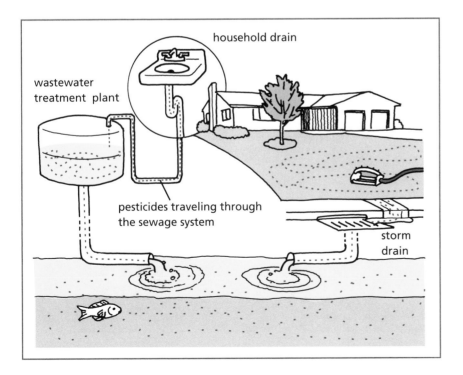

household drain

wastewater treatment plant

pesticides traveling through the sewage system

storm drain

sewers may also contaminate surface water. Sewers carry wastewater from toilets, sinks, showers, and other plumbing drains to treatment plants. While wastewater treatment plants send incoming wastewater through a thorough treatment and disinfecting process before releasing water into a river, the treatment process does not detoxify pesticide chemicals.

For more information on how to avoid contaminating surface water with pesticides see "Pesticides and Water Quality" on the UC IPM Web site, **www.ipm.ucdavis.edu/WATER/U/index.html**.

THE IMPACT OF PESTICIDES ON NONTARGET ORGANISMS

Some pesticides may be harmful to nontarget organisms at the application site and in the surrounding environment. Nontarget organisms include all plants and animals other than the pest being controlled by a pesticide application (Figure 4-15).

Impact of Pesticides on Natural Enemies of Pests

When you apply a pesticide, natural enemies such as predators or parasites of pests can be destroyed along with the target pest. Disrupting the natural control of pests by destroying their natural enemies often leads to an increased dependency on pesticides. To learn more about how pesticides kill natural enemies, see Chapter 3.

Figure 4-15. There can be many nontarget organisms in landscape settings.

Impact of Pesticides on Wildlife

Wildlife may also be harmed by pesticide applications either as a result of accidental poisoning or through destroying wildlife food sources and habitats. Examples of wildlife in urban areas include birds, butterflies, bees, rabbits, squirrels, gophers, snakes, raccoons, turtles, toads, and deer. Even if a pesticide exposure does not directly cause illness or death, it may weaken a nontarget animal and indirectly cause death by leaving the animal unable to get food and water or protect itself from predators.

Impact of Pesticides on Aquatic Organisms

Fish and other aquatic organisms may be injured by pesticides that get into waterways or bodies of water such as ponds that are part of the landscape, even at low concentrations. Pesticides enter waterways through drift, by direct application, by leaching, or through runoff.

Impact of Pesticide Use on Desirable Plants

If you improperly apply herbicides you may unintentionally kill nontarget plants, including those in nearby landscapes or in natural and undeveloped areas. Phytotoxicity (Sidebar 4.1), or injury to plants, may be a problem with a specific pesticide on certain

10. Recognize the causes and effects of phytotoxicity (injury to plants) from landscape and turfgrass pesticide applications.

SIDEBAR 4.1—FACTS ABOUT PHYTOTOXICITY

Phytoxicity is plant injury from pesticides or other chemicals. Herbicides often cause phytotoxic symptoms when they drift onto plants. Some insecticides, fungicides, and plant growth regulators can also cause phytotoxicity when label directions are not followed.

Phytotoxicity is more likely to occur on water- or heat-stressed plants or on plants that have low vigor. Phytotoxicity symptoms are often difficult to diagnose without knowing the affected plant's cultural and chemical treatment history.

Chemical phytotoxicity symptoms vary according to chemical but may include

- yellow to brown leaf spots

- chlorosis (yellowing) or necrosis (death) of leaf tips, leaf margins, and areas between leaf veins (interveinal)

- leaf curling, cupping, twisting, yellowing, or scorching

- leaf stunting

- premature leaf drop

Injury symptoms of phytotoxicity differ from symptoms of diseases caused by pathogens. Injury symptoms of phytotoxicity do not spread as time passes. The symptoms do not move to undamaged foliage or plants. Oil solvents or carriers in a pesticide (not the pesticide's active ingredient) may also produce injury symptoms or may make the symptoms more severe than normal.

Glyphosate (a broad-spectrum herbicide) damage to citrus shoot: stunted, narrow leaves; fewer leaves than normal; and buds that open only partially after exposure to the herbicide.

Figure 4-16. Phytotoxicity (plant injury) can be caused by pesticides.

Sycamore leaves on branch at right are curled and distorted. The herbicides dicamba or triclopyr were taken up by tree roots to cause this damage.

Marginal leaf burn on rose was probably caused by oil spray applied when temperatures were too hot.

Grass killed by glyphosate herbicide.

Drift from 2,4-D broadleaf herbicide used to manage weeds in lawns caused twisting and curling of this hibiscus stem and leaves.

landscape plants (Figure 4-16). The pesticide active ingredient is not always what causes phytotoxicity. Solvents in the formulation or impurities (such as salts) in the water mixed with the pesticide may also cause plant injury. Environmental conditions such as temperature and humidity at the time of application can also increase risk of plant injury.

HOW ARE PEOPLE EXPOSED TO PESTICIDES IN LANDSCAPE AND TURF SETTINGS?

11. Explain how people get exposed to pesticides in landscape and turf settings.

People can be exposed to pesticides in several ways (Figure 4-17). You are at greatest risk for exposure when mixing and applying pesticides and when entering or working in treated areas soon after application. People who live or work near where you are applying pesticides may also be exposed. When you treat a lawn, children or others may be exposed if they play on the lawn before the pesticide has dried or the

Figure 4-17. People can be exposed to pesticides during mixing or application. People can be exposed after application, too.

WHILE MIXING PESTICIDES

splashing

spills

breakage

WHILE APPLYING PESTICIDES

drift on nearby people

when PPE not worn

AFTER APPLICATION

residues on plants or treated surfaces

residues on protective gear or clothing

labeled reentry period has elapsed. Additionally, exposure can happen as a result of excessive use or improper storage of pesticides in and around residences. One of the most tragic types of pesticide injury occurs when pesticides are stored in food or drink containers and are unintentionally consumed (Figure 4-18). Many cases have been reported of children drinking pesticides from soft drink containers. Accidental ingestion of pesticide products by children accounts for a major portion of pesticide poisonings that do not occur on the job. Never store concentrated or diluted pesticides in containers commonly used for food or drink: it is illegal. Containers that hold products that humans consume should NEVER be used for pesticides.

Following the pesticide label instructions, wearing proper personal protective equipment, practicing good hygiene, storing pesticides properly, and using other protective measures reduce hazards to people. Good hygiene also includes washing pesticide application clothing separately from family laundry (Figure 4-19).

Poisoning or injury sometimes results from a single exposure to a large quantity of pesticide. In other cases, injury does not occur until you have been exposed repeatedly over a period of time. It is quite common for individuals to vary in their sensitivity to the level of pesticide exposure. Some people may show no reaction to a dose that causes severe illness in others.

Figure 4-18. Children are often pesticide poisoning victims. Improper storage of pesticides at home is the main way children find and eat, drink, or touch pesticides. Never store pesticides in food or drink containers.

CHANGING OUT OF PESTICIDE APPLICATION CLOTHING AND REMOVING PPE

Use care not to contaminate your body.

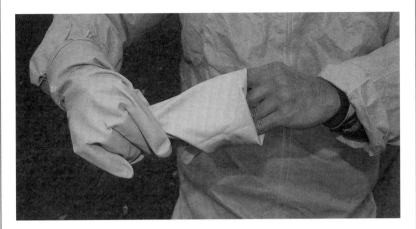

WASHING PESTICIDE APPLICATION CLOTHING

Set it aside and wash separately from family laundry. Wear gloves when handling pesticide clothing. Use hot water wash with detergent. Clean the washing machine before using it again for regular laundry by running an empty cycle with detergent and hot water. Hang clothing to dry.

Figure 4-19. Handle pesticide application clothing and PPE carefully when removing and cleaning it. Keep this clothing separate from regular family laundry.

How Do Pesticides Enter the Body?

The most common ways for pesticide exposure to occur are through the skin, eyes, lungs, and mouth (Figure 4-20).

12. Know how pesticides enter the body.

Skin Exposure. Skin, or dermal, contact is the most frequent route of pesticide exposure. Some pesticides may cause a skin rash or irritation when they contact the skin (Figure 4-21). Oil-soluble pesticides are more likely to pass through skin and affect internal organs

Figure 4-20. Pesticides can enter your body through these four paths of exposure.

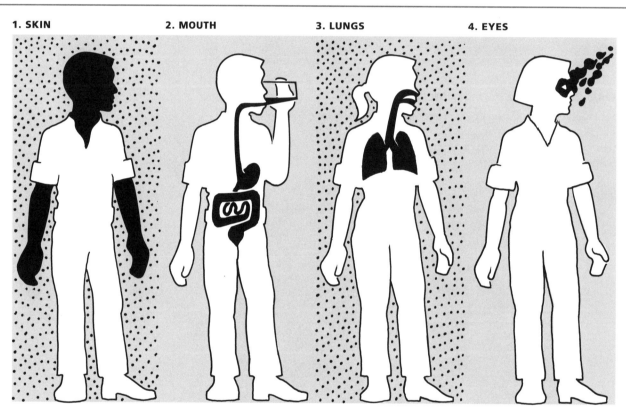

1. SKIN

Skin contact is the most common type of pesticide exposure. If some pesticides contact the skin they may cause a skin rash or mild skin irritation. Other pesticides may cause more severe skin injury, such as burns. Pesticide absorbed through the skin can cause internal poisoning: the blood carries the pesticide to other organs in the body.

2. MOUTH

It is rare for someone to accidentally drink a pesticide. More often, pesticides are taken in when spray materials or pesticide dusts splash or blow into your mouth during mixing or application. Sometimes pesticides are taken in when someone consumes contaminated food or drink. Smoking while handling pesticides increases your risk of taking in pesticides.

3. LUNGS

The lungs quickly absorb certain pesticides. The blood transports these pesticides to other parts of the body. Some pesticides cause serious lung injury. Use the correct respiratory protective measures to avoid breathing dusts and vapors during mixing or application.

4. EYES

The eyes provide another way for pesticides to get into your body. The active or inert ingredients of some pesticide formulations are caustic to the eyes.

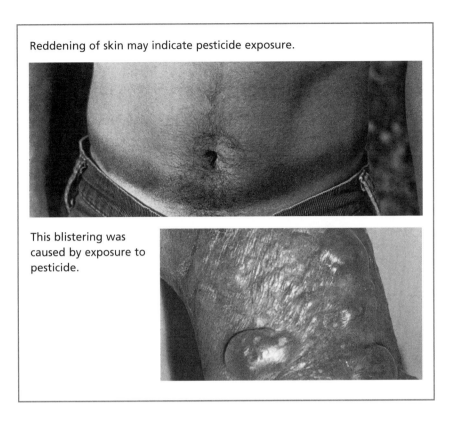

Reddening of skin may indicate pesticide exposure.

This blistering was caused by exposure to pesticide.

Figure 4-21. A skin rash is a common symptom of pesticide exposure.

than those that are soluble in water. Skin around the head, armpits, and groin absorbs pesticides many times faster than the skin of the hands or forearms (Figure 4-22). Always wear chemical-resistant gloves when handling pesticides or their containers.

Eye Exposure. The active or other ingredients of some pesticide formulations may be abrasive and can scratch the eyes. Also, solvents used to formulate some liquid pesticides can harm eyes. Besides their vulnerability to injury, the eyes provide a route for entry of certain pesticides into your body, especially when mixing the concentrate. Always protect your eyes by wearing a face shield, goggles, or safety glasses with side (temple), front, and brow protection.

Lung Exposure. Some pesticides cause serious lung injury. Avoid breathing dusts or vapors during mixing or application. Always wear label-recommended respirators during mixing and application or choose a different pesticide that does not require a respirator. If you do use a respirator, make sure it is properly fit-tested, is in good condition, and is the right type for the pesticide you are using.

Figure 4-22. Some parts of the body absorb pesticides faster than other parts. The skin on the head area, armpits, and groin can absorb pesticides much faster than skin on the forearms or hands.

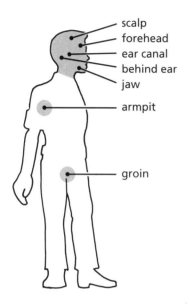

scalp
forehead
ear canal
behind ear
jaw

armpit

groin

13. Know the health effects of pesticide exposure.

Mouth Exposure. Exposure through the mouth (oral) occurs when spray materials or pesticide dusts splash or blow into your mouth during mixing or application. Linings of your mouth, stomach, and intestines readily absorb some pesticides. Sometimes even small amounts may make you sick. To protect yourself and others:

- Never put pesticides into food or drink containers.

- Keep all pesticides in their original packages.

- Do not mix or measure pesticides with utensils that someone could use later for food preparation or serving.

- Always wash your hands thoroughly before eating or drinking.

- Keep food and drink away from areas where pesticides are being applied or stored.

- Always wash hands after handling pesticides and before smoking or using the restroom.

The Health Effects of Pesticide Exposure

The type and severity of injury or poisoning depends on the toxicity and mode of action of the pesticide you are using, the amount absorbed into your body, how fast it is absorbed, and how fast your body is able to break it down and excrete it.

You can lessen the severity of pesticide-related injury through prompt first aid and medical treatment (described in the next chapter). Very small doses often produce no poisoning symptoms. Depending on the toxicity of the pesticide, larger doses may cause severe illness or death. Effects of exposure may be localized—such as irritation of your eyes, skin or throat—or generalized—such as when pesticides are absorbed through your skin or into the digestive system and carried to your internal organs. Certain pesticides may affect several internal systems at the same time. The extent of damage is related to the characteristics of the pesticide and its dose.

Age and body size often influence the response to exposure. Infants and young children are usually more affected by smaller doses than adults. Also, adult females more often are affected by lower doses than adult males. Smaller doses may be more harmful to the elderly or sick than to younger adults.

Symptoms of Pesticide Exposure. Symptoms are any abnormal changes in your body that you see or feel. At times, pesticide exposures cause symptoms that can be detected by medical examination or laboratory tests. Different symptoms may occur depending on the pesticide exposure and the type of pesticide and how your body reacts. Sometimes pesticide exposure is confused with symptoms resulting from other causes, such as allergies, plants that cause skin irritation, anxiety, or the flu. For example, excessive alcohol consumption can give you a headache or make you nauseous, but this can be a symptom of pesticide poisoning as well. Also, many of the symptoms of heat illness (see below) resemble pesticide poisoning. It is very important to pay attention to symptoms when handling or being around pesticides, and to always seek medical attention if you might be experiencing a pesticide-related illness. For more details, refer to the section "Types of Injuries from Pesticides."

Symptoms of Heat Illness. Heat illness is a serious medical condition that occurs when the body builds up more heat than it can cope with. Heat illness, even in mild forms, makes people feel sick and impairs their ability to do a good job. The early signs of heat illness include headaches, dizziness, lightheadedness, muscle cramps, and feeling unusually tired and weak. Left untreated, this leads to more serious heat illness including heat exhaustion and heat stroke. Heat stroke is a serious illness, and unless victims are cooled quickly, they can die. Symptoms of more serious heat illness include unusual behavior, irritability, mental confusion, nausea or vomiting, rapid pulse, excessive sweating or hot dry skin, seizures or fits, fainting, and loss of consciousness.

Heat illness is not caused by exposure to pesticides, but it may affect pesticide handlers and others who work in hot conditions. Wearing personal protective equipment—clothing that protects the body from contact with pesticides—can increase the risk of heat illness by limiting the body's ability to cool down. On hot days start work early, wear light-colored protective clothing (Sidebar 4.2), take frequent breaks, drink water often, and stop work before you begin to experience heat illness. High temperature, high humidity, and direct exposure to sunlight increase the likelihood of heat illness. Air movement from wind or fans may provide cooling. Because hard work causes the body to produce heat, a person is more likely to develop heat illness when working on foot than when driving a vehicle.

Seek immediate medical attention if you experience heat illness symptoms that are not resolved by immediate corrective actions.

SIDEBAR 4.2—HEAT ILLNESS

People applying pesticides can suffer from heat illness when working under hot conditions. Heat illness is especially dangerous when you wear protective equipment. To avoid heat illness, apply pesticides in the morning before temperatures rise.

HOW TO AVOID HEAT ILLNESS

Before you begin a pesticide handling task, think about making adjustments in the task itself or in the workplace conditions:

- Reduce your workload—the amount of effort a task takes.
- Wear loose, light-colored PPE and a wide-brimmed hat to protect yourself from sunlight.
- Increase your drinking water intake (drink 3–4 glasses per hour).
- Take more frequent rest breaks in a cooler, shaded area.
- Avoid working during the hottest part of the day.
- Gradually adjust to working in the heat (acclimation).

IF EXPERIENCING HEAT ILLNESS

- Move to a cool, shaded area.
- Loosen or remove heavy clothing.
- Drink water or an electrolyte beverage (such as Gatorade).
- Fan and mist the person with water.

Get emergency medical services immediately when you suspect even the first symptoms of heat illness. Get help even if the person protests. A person who shows symptoms of serious heat illness should not be left alone.

Types of Injuries from Pesticides. When you have been exposed to a large enough dose of pesticide to produce injury or poisoning, you may experience either immediate or delayed symptoms. Sometimes symptoms from pesticide exposure may not show up for weeks, months, or even years. These delayed symptoms may either come on gradually or appear suddenly; they may be difficult to associate with their cause because of the lapse of time between when you were exposed to the pesticide and when you start to get sick.

Injury, illness, and poisoning symptoms vary among different pesticides. The level of sickness you experience is related to the amount and type of pesticide and how it entered your body. Exposure to some insecticides can cause tiredness, headache, dizziness, blurred vision, a rash, itchy eyes, nausea and vomiting, or cramps and diarrhea. These symptoms may go away within a short period of time and sometimes are difficult to distinguish from allergy symptoms, a cold, or the flu. Although these symptoms can indicate pesticide poisoning, they also may be signs of other physical disorders or diseases. Diagnosing pesticide poisoning requires a medical examination. It is very important to get immediate medical care for anyone affected by pesticide exposure.

You or your employees and others can be injured either by a single massive dose being absorbed during one pesticide exposure or from smaller doses absorbed during repeated exposures over an extended period of time. You may experience an illness that is acute (having a sudden onset) and lasts either for a while or a short duration, or your illness may become chronic (persisting over a long time). Injuries caused by pesticides are usually reversible; that is, they can either be repaired by the body's natural processes or through some form of medical treatment. Exposure to large doses of some pesticides, however, may cause irreversible or permanent damage that results in a chronic illness, disability, or death. Make every effort to determine the source of exposure so you can prevent it from happening again.

■ Chapter 4 Review Questions

1. Which signal word means the *least* amount of hazard?
   - ☐ a. WARNING
   - ☐ b. CAUTION
   - ☐ c. DANGER
   - ☐ d. POISON

2. The acute toxicity of a pesticide is usually measured by its
   - ☐ a. no observable effect level (NOEL)
   - ☐ b. long-term health effects
   - ☐ c. LD_{50}
   - ☐ d. half-life

3. What pest do molluscicides control?
   - ☐ a. rodents
   - ☐ b. natural enemies
   - ☐ c. fungi and bacteria
   - ☐ d. snails and slugs

4. A _____ pesticide kills a wide range of pests and nontarget organisms, whereas a _____ pesticide controls a smaller group of closely related organisms.
   - ☐ a. persistent, selective
   - ☐ b. selective, broad-spectrum
   - ☐ c. broad-spectrum, selective
   - ☐ d. strong, weak

5. _____ formulations are pre-mixed pesticides in containers such as aerosol cans or hand pump squirt containers.
   - ☐ a. flowables
   - ☐ b. baits
   - ☐ c. granules
   - ☐ d. ready-to-use

6. A contact postemergent herbicide
   - ☐ a. is applied before weeds germinate
   - ☐ b. must be translocated in the plant to be effective
   - ☐ c. usually causes injury to any green part of the plant it comes in contact with
   - ☐ d. provides systemic weed protection

7. Insecticides or herbicides that are taken up by the crop, plant, or animal and move, after application, to other plant tissues are called
   - ☐ a. systemic insecticides
   - ☐ b. contact insecticides
   - ☐ c. internal insecticides
   - ☐ d. stomach insecticides

8. Most fungicides are surface _____ that must be applied before the fungal spores germinate and enter the plant.
   - ☐ a. oils
   - ☐ b. protectants
   - ☐ c. eradicants
   - ☐ d. pathogens

9. Pesticides move through the air in three ways:
   - ☐ a. leaching, runoff, and drainage
   - ☐ b. volatilization, spray drift, and dust-borne particles
   - ☐ c. spray drift, leaching, and fog
   - ☐ d. rain, runoff, and spills

10. In urban areas, pesticides may reach creeks and rivers through
    - ☐ a. storm drains
    - ☐ b. grass clippings
    - ☐ c. pesticide containers
    - ☐ d. birds and other wildlife

11. Which of the following could contribute to phyto-toxicity problems when spraying a pesticide onto plants?

☐ a. drift of a broadleaf herbicide applied to a lawn

☐ b. application to the soil of an herbicide that is taken up by plant roots

☐ c. oil spray to control mites

☐ d. all of the above

12. The **main** reason food containers should not be used for storing pesticides is

☐ a. pesticides soften plastic and corrode metal

☐ b. people may mistake the contents for something to eat or drink

☐ c. these containers cannot be properly sealed

☐ d. these containers are not accurate enough for measuring pesticides

13. Which of the following is the most frequent route of pesticide exposure among pesticide workers?

☐ a. oral (through the mouth)

☐ b. dermal (through the skin)

☐ c. inhalation

☐ d. eye

14. The seriousness of a pesticide injury from an exposure usually is related to the

☐ a. time of day an exposure occurs

☐ b. toxicity and dose of the pesticide

☐ c. type of application equipment used

☐ d. frequency of application of that pesticide

(Answer sheet is on pages 206–207.)

5

Protecting People and the Environment and Handling Emergencies

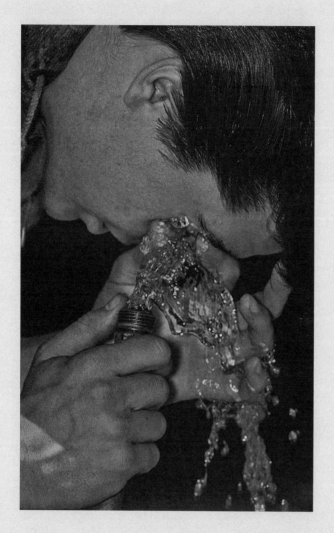

When using pesticides, you must take a number of precautions to protect people and the environment. In the previous chapter you learned how pesticides harm the environment and injure people. This chapter outlines steps that will help you use pesticides safely. It also outlines procedures to follow if an accident or emergency occurs.

KNOWLEDGE EXPECTATIONS
Protecting People and the Environment and Handling Emergencies

1. Describe where to find information about pesticide hazards and safety, for example, pesticide labels, Material Safety Data Sheets (MSDSs), and the Pesticide Safety Information Series (PSIS) leaflets.

2. Know how to select pesticides that are less hazardous to people, water quality, and wildlife by comparing label information.

3. Be aware of the hazards of vertebrate control materials and snail baits for pets and nontarget organisms.

4. Know how to select, fit, care for, and use personal protective equipment when handling pesticides.

5. Know that you can be contaminated by touching pesticide application equipment, which exposes you to harmful pesticide residues.

6. List precautions that can be taken to protect people and pets that might enter a treated area.

7. Know how to prevent pesticide drift and other off-site movement.

8. Know how to keep pesticides out of the environment through proper application and disposal practices.

9. Know proper personal hygiene after handling pesticides, including laundering.

10. Know how to recognize pesticide exposure symptoms and respond to emergencies.

11. Know how to respond to spills, leaks, or other releases of pesticides.

12. Know how to respond to pesticide fires.

13. Know what to do when pesticides are misapplied.

14. Know that you will be liable if you apply a pesticide that injures plants, people, animals, or property.

W**HEN USING** pesticides, you must take a number of necessary precautions to protect people and the environment. In the previous section you learned how pesticides harm the environment and injure people. This section outlines steps that will help you use pesticides safely.

■ Information Sources about Pesticide Hazards and Safety

All pesticides are potentially toxic and can cause problems. Be sure to learn about pesticide hazards BEFORE you use a product (Figure 5-1). You can learn about pesticide hazards and safety by studying the pesticide label, Material Safety Data Sheets (MSDSs), and the Pesticide Information Series (PSIS) (Figure 5-2). These documents provide important information about the dangers to you, to people and animals, and to the environment and how you can prevent problems.

1. Describe where to find information about pesticide hazards and safety, for example, pesticide labels, Material Safety Data Sheets (MSDSs), and the Pesticide Safety Information Series (PSIS) leaflets.

Figure 5-1. Read the label and use good work practices to prevent personal injury.

Read the label.

Wear PPE.

Use good work practices.

Clean up after handling pesticides.

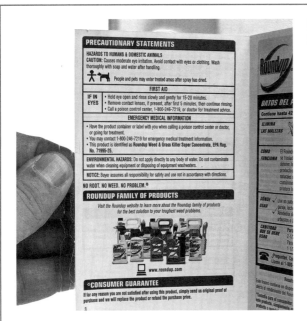

Pesticide label

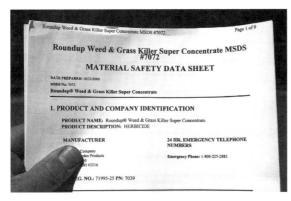

Material Safety Data Sheet (MSDS)

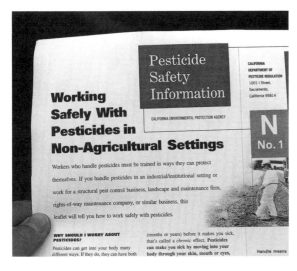

Pesticide Safety Information Series (PSIS) leaflet from the agricultural commissioner and Department of Pesticide Regulation

Figure 5-2. Find information about pesticide hazards and safety on the pesticide label, on the MSDS, and in PSIS leaflets.

THE PESTICIDE LABEL

The pesticide label is the most important source of information when you use a pesticide. The information on pesticide labels is put there for your protection. If you read, understand, and follow this information, you will reduce the chance of an accident or exposure that could cause an injury or illness.

Look for signal words (DANGER, WARNING, CAUTION) and a skull and crossbones. Signal words identify the acute toxicity of the pesticide formulation. However, acute toxicity is not the only kind of hazard associated with pesticides. Some chemicals that do not have high acute toxicity can cause cancer or birth defects in unborn babies or other long-term problems.

Check the label for required personal protective equipment (PPE) (Figure 5-3). Make sure that you have and use this PPE and that it is in good condition. Review the label for any special environmental precautions. Always be sure that the label lists the application site or plant type you will treat. Consult the label and the agricultural commissioner's office for information on how to dispose of unwanted pesticide and empty containers.

If you don't understand the label, do not use the product. First, ask your supervisor or the chemical supplier to tell you what the label says

Figure 5-3. Personal protective equipment (PPE) includes devices and clothes that protect you from pesticide exposure.

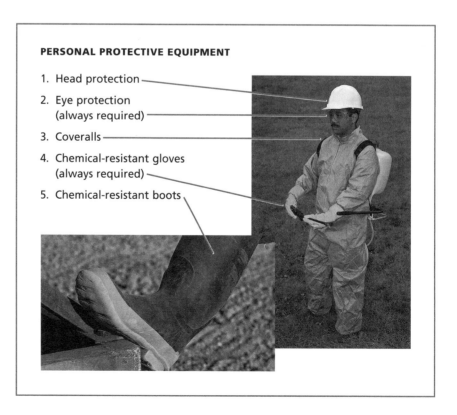

PERSONAL PROTECTIVE EQUIPMENT

1. Head protection
2. Eye protection (always required)
3. Coveralls
4. Chemical-resistant gloves (always required)
5. Chemical-resistant boots

and how to follow all of the directions. Call the manufacturer's phone number that may be provided on the label. Make sure you understand the entire label before you apply any pesticide. Chapter 1 provides information about how to understand a pesticide label. If you need the label in another language, ask the supplier if it can be obtained.

MATERIAL SAFETY DATA SHEET

The Material Safety Data Sheet (MSDS) provides valuable facts about the pesticide's hazards (Figure 5-4), including information on acute and long-term health effects that could result from exposure to the pesticide formulation. These sheets are prepared by manufacturers for each pesticide product and are made available upon request to every person selling, storing, or handling pesticides.

When you buy a pesticide, be sure to ask for an MSDS. If the store where you purchase your pesticides can't supply you with one, call the manufacturer (manufacturers' phone numbers are often provided on the label) and ask them to send you one. You may need to note the bar code and EPA registration number from the product container to get the correct MSDS from the manufacturer. You may be able to get an MSDS online, but be sure it's for precisely the same product formulation that you have.

MSDS sheets are helpful because they describe the chemical characteristics and hazards of the pesticide ingredients. The MSDS also lists fire and explosion hazards, health hazards, incompatibility characteristics, and the types of PPE needed for safe handling and emergency

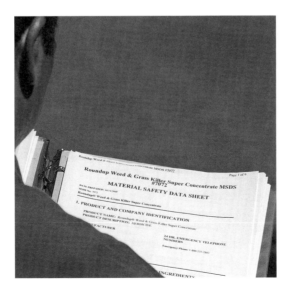

Figure 5-4. Be sure to have the MSDS for every pesticide you use.

response. Storage information and emergency spill or leak cleanup procedures are also described. LD_{50} and LC_{50} ratings (lethal doses and lethal concentrations, based on laboratory animal test data) are given for various test animals. If the MSDS seems to conflict with the information on the pesticide label, you must always follow the label directions.

Keep MSDSs in a safe place at a central location at the workplace, away from your pesticide storage area. Maintain a notebook with an MSDS for every pesticide used on the landscapes you maintain.

PESTICIDE SAFETY INFORMATION SERIES

The Pesticide Safety Information Series (PSIS) leaflets describe how to properly and safely use pesticides. These leaflets were developed by the California Department of Pesticide Regulation. The leaflets are available in English, Spanish, and Punjabi on the Internet at **www.cdpr.ca.gov/docs/whs/psisenglish.htm** or from your county agricultural commissioner's office. Maintenance gardeners should use the N series PSIS. The A series are for agricultural crops.

▪ Using Pesticides Safely

Pesticide safety requires thoughtful selection and careful application of pesticide products. Following label directions, using protective equipment, preventing environmental contamination, and maintaining personal hygiene are all important for protecting people and the environment.

SELECTING A PESTICIDE

2. Know how to select pesticides that are less hazardous to people, water quality, and wildlife by comparing label information.

Remember that a pesticide may not be necessary to solve a pest problem in a landscape. It is important to first correctly identify the cause of a problem and evaluate options to correct it. Before you choose to use a pesticide, review the pest management tools listed in Chapter 3. To correctly select a pesticide that is less hazardous to waterways, people, and wildlife, consider the following guidelines:

- Look at signal words on the pesticide label. First choose pesticides with the signal word CAUTION and next those that are labeled WARNING. Pesticides with signal words DANGER or DANGER–POISON are the most toxic.

- Compare precautionary statements on pesticide labels. Precautionary statements describe the human and environmental hazards associated with a pesticide. Avoid pesticides that are extremely toxic to fish and wildlife.

- Avoid using persistent, broad-spectrum pesticides, which injure many nontarget organisms as well as pests. Apply safer materials such as the microbial insecticide *Bacillius thuringiensis*, less-persistent insecticides, or insecticidal soaps and narrow-range oils that break down rapidly in the environment.

- Determine how much pesticide you need and buy only the amount you can use in a reasonable period of time. Avoid storing or transporting excessive amounts.

- Make sure the pesticide you choose kills the target pest.

- Be aware of the hazards for pets and nontarget organisms, especially with rodenticides (Sidebar 5.1), insecticides, and snail baits (Sidebar 5.2).

3. Be aware of the hazards of vertebrate control materials and snail baits for pets and nontarget organisms.

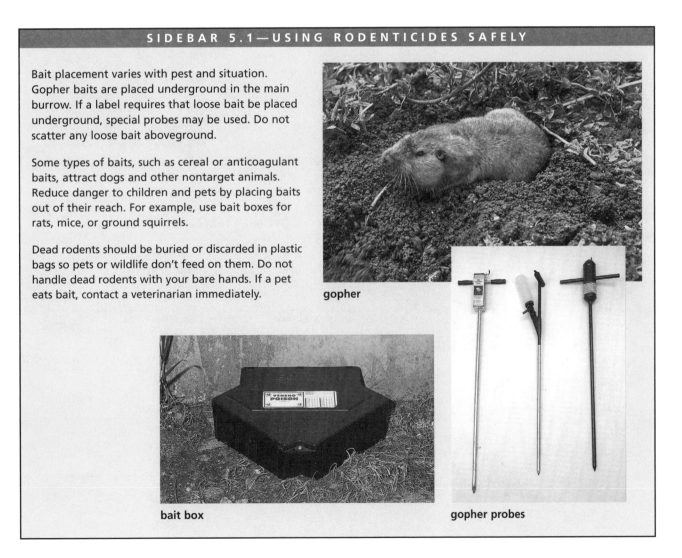

SIDEBAR 5.1—USING RODENTICIDES SAFELY

Bait placement varies with pest and situation. Gopher baits are placed underground in the main burrow. If a label requires that loose bait be placed underground, special probes may be used. Do not scatter any loose bait aboveground.

Some types of baits, such as cereal or anticoagulant baits, attract dogs and other nontarget animals. Reduce danger to children and pets by placing baits out of their reach. For example, use bait boxes for rats, mice, or ground squirrels.

Dead rodents should be buried or discarded in plastic bags so pets or wildlife don't feed on them. Do not handle dead rodents with your bare hands. If a pet eats bait, contact a veterinarian immediately.

gopher

bait box

gopher probes

SIDEBAR 5.2—HAZARDS OF SNAIL BAITS

Baits can be effective at controlling snails and slugs when used properly. However, some snail baits pose hazards in landscape environments.

Metaldehyde baits are poisonous to dogs and cats. The pelleted form is especially attractive to dogs. Do not use metaldehyde baits where children or pets cannot be kept away. The higher the concentration of metaldehyde, the more toxic it is to dogs and wildlife. Never pile bait in mounds or clumps because this attracts pets and children.

Better choices are snail and slug baits containing iron phosphate. Iron phosphate is safe for use around domestic animals, children, birds, fish, and other wildlife.

READING AND FOLLOWING PESTICIDE LABELS

After selecting a pesticide to use, learn how to carry out all safety and precautionary requirements on the label for that product. Before you apply the pesticide

- look for the signal word. (Choose pesticides with the word CAUTION where possible, although even these may have negative impacts.) Note precautions for use such as PPE, work clothing, and other ways to mix and apply safely.

- know what active ingredients are in the pesticide. Know the rate of pesticide to be applied. Know how to mix the pesticide with water for the desired rate of application.

- review the label for any special environmental precautions. Survey the application site for any environmental concerns.

- be certain the label lists the intended landscape application site (or plant type) and pest. It is legal to use a pesticide in California on a pest not listed on the label; however, the method and site of the pesticide application must be listed on the label.

- consult the label for information about how to dispose of unwanted pesticide and compare this information with your county or regional disposal requirements.

- be prepared for emergencies by having emergency phone numbers and instructions for getting medical help on site.

PESTICIDE APPLICATOR SAFETY: PERSONAL PROTECTIVE EQUIPMENT

Before you mix and apply pesticides you must learn how to select, fit, care for, use, and remove personal protective equipment (PPE). Included in PPE are special clothing (such as coveralls) and devices (chemical-resistant gloves, boots, and head protection and eye protection) worn to minimize human body contact with pesticides or pesticide residues.

PPE helps protect your body and clothing from pesticide exposure. Some PPE also protects your eyes or feet. However, PPE is effective only if it fits correctly and you use it properly. Always keep it clean and well maintained. Clean it at the end of each work period before using it again by washing it in soapy water. Allow it to air dry out of the sun. Wear chemical-resistant gloves when removing personal protective equipment after a pesticide application to avoid transferring residues onto your body.

You also wear work clothing when you mix and apply pesticides. Some labels specify work clothing requirements. Work clothing includes garments such as long-sleeved shirts, long pants, short-sleeved shirts, and short pants (if the pesticide label allows), shoes, and socks. Work clothing is not considered PPE. Do not wear a cloth baseball cap (Figure 5-5). Cloth baseball caps do not provide protection and in fact are a potential source of head contamination when pesticides come into contact with caps. Even when coveralls are not required, you may choose to wear them over your work clothing for increased safety.

Follow the pesticide label for the protective clothing and equipment you must use (Figure 5-6). You will find directions about PPE

4. Know how to select, fit, care for, and use personal protective equipment when handling pesticides.

Figure 5-5. Don't wear a baseball cap while applying pesticides if any will get on the hat. The cap will keep the pesticide on your skin, and you could get sick from this exposure.

Figure 5-6. Choose your personal protective equipment carefully.

Disposable coveralls. Lightweight disposable coveralls are strong and resistant to tearing or puncturing. After use, throw them away when soiled unless they are contaminated with undiluted pesticide. Dispose of clothing contaminated with undiluted pesticide at a hazardous materials disposal site.

Reusable coveralls. Most reusable coveralls are made of fabric. After use, wash them separately from other laundry in hot water to remove dirt and any pesticide residues.

Gloves. Use chemical-resistant unlined gloves made from nitrile, natural rubber, latex, butyl, or neoprene. Do not use leather or fabric gloves unless the label requires them. Clean gloves with soap and water after use.

Eye protection. Always wear eye protection during all pesticide handling activities. Eye protection is safety glasses with brow and side (temple) protection, goggles, or face shields. Clean eye protection with soap and water after use.

Protective footwear (boots). Chemical-resistant protective footwear is made from rubber or a synthetic material such as PVC, nitrile, neoprene, or butyl. Wear these over your shoes or in the place of shoes. Protective boots must have good footing. Do not wear sandals when handling pesticides or walking in treated areas.

Head protection. If the label requires head protection, wear a water-resistant wide-brimmed hat or a hooded waterproof jacket. Don't wear a baseball cap!

in the PRECAUTIONARY STATEMENTS section of the pesticide label. You may find that different types of PPE are required for mixing than what you must use during application.

You can be contaminated by handling pesticide equipment (Figure 5-7). Wear PPE for activities after application such as cleaning nozzles, taking pesticide application equipment in and out of a truck, and handling pesticide measuring equipment. Wear your PPE to protect you from all possible exposure to pesticides or their residues.

Before removing PPE and pesticide application clothing, stop and think about how you will protect yourself from exposure to pesticide residues on your PPE. When removing safety clothing and gear after pesticide-related activities, take care to prevent skin exposure.

PUBLIC AND ENVIRONMENTAL SAFETY

Protect the public from exposure to pesticides during and after application (Figure 5-8). It is your responsibility to keep people away from treated areas during and after you make the application until the spray dries or other entry restrictions have passed. As a courtesy, inform all people who may go into an area that pesticides have been applied and explain how they can avoid exposure. To protect people

- notify residents before the pesticide application

- apply pesticides when people and pets are not going to be around

- prevent drift or other off-site movement of pesticide materials outside the treatment area

- prevent water used for irrigation or other purposes from running off pesticide-treated areas

- after each pesticide application, warn the residents to stay away from treated areas until dry (or longer if the label requires this) and to keep children and pets away

5. Know that you can be contaminated by touching pesticide application equipment, which exposes you to harmful pesticide residues.

Figure 5-7. Prevent personal exposure by using the right protective equipment when you handle pesticides or application equipment. For instance, wear gloves when cleaning nozzles.

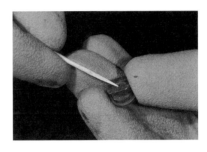

6. List precautions that can be taken to protect people and pets that might enter a treated area.

Figure 5-8. Prevent residents from becoming exposed to pesticides.

COMMUNICATE	APPLY SAFELY

• Tell residents before and after you apply pesticides. • Keep people and pets away from treated areas during and after application until the pesticides have dried out or as long as indicated on the label directions.	• Apply pesticides carefully, just to the target site. • Make sure that water runoff does not carry the pesticide you are applying.

PRECAUTIONS FOR PREVENTING ENVIRONMENTAL CONTAMINATION AND PROTECTING HUMAN HEALTH

Take steps to protect environmental and human health every time you handle pesticides. Precautions to take when you transport, store, mix, apply, and dispose of pesticides are described below (Figure 5-9).

Transporting. There is always a risk of an accident when using a vehicle to transport pesticides. Spilled materials may cause serious human exposure as well as environmental damage. Chemicals that spill onto roads may wash into ditches, streams, and rivers during rainstorms and create the potential for serious environmental damage, including surface water and groundwater contamination. Pesticide spills may also contaminate the vehicle, its occupants, or other cargo, so a good practice is to place pesticide containers into a secondary containment in the cargo area of the vehicle. Secondary containment could be as simple as a plastic pan that will hold the pesticide container and catch any leaks. To avoid contamination, pesticides should not be carried with seeds or fertilizers. Pesticides must not be carried in the driver or passenger section of a vehicle.

Mixing. Mix only the amount of pesticide needed for the job. Before mixing any pesticides, check your application equipment to be

Always keep pesticides in a locked cabinet. Never leave them out in the open.

Watch for damaged containers. They are not safe.

Always transport pesticides safely. Secure them in the nonpassenger part of vehicles. Use secondary containment during transport so that if a container leaks, the spillage is easy to clean without contaminating the truck or your body.

Figure 5-9. Know how to store and transport all pesticides and pesticide service containers.

sure there are no cracked hoses or other leaks and that the filters, screens, and nozzles are clean. Have an emergency supply of soap, clean water, and single-use towels nearby for washing in case of an accident, as well as materials to absorb a pesticide spill (e.g., cat litter). Do not overfill your spray tank. Use a backflow prevention device or air gap (see Chapter 6) on filling pipes to prevent backflow of contaminated water into water supplies. Never place water delivery hoses directly into spray tanks. Never leave your sprayer unattended while it is being filled with water. If a spill occurs, clean up and dispose of the waste quickly and safely in accordance with regulations. Follow cleanup guidelines on the MSDS.

Applying. Safe application techniques require that you work with the weather, control droplet size and spray pattern, and be familiar with the application site and have an awareness of its hazards. Develop application approaches for the site to address hazards and environmental conditions, and leave a buffer zone of untreated landscape between treated and sensitive areas.

Before beginning a pesticide application, check the landscape characteristics and note all potential hazards. Be especially careful around waterways, playgrounds, or occupied areas. Check for plants, animals, or structures that might be damaged by pesticides or by the movement of the equipment through the area. Note any water features that might have fish or other aquatic life that require protection.

Reduce the potential for drift from pesticide applications. Do not spray during windy conditions (Figure 5-10). A little bit of air movement can be helpful, and winds less than 5 miles per hour help provide good pesticide distribution within trees and leafy plants, especially if your sprayer is not equipped with a blower. However, stronger winds, especially those over 10 miles per hour, increase drift potential. Spraying is illegal if the wind speed is high enough to cause substantial drift. Check the pesticide label and local regulations for wind speed restrictions or requirements. Reduce drift of pesticides off the target site by using nozzles that produce large droplets.

Whenever possible, make applications during optimal weather conditions. Rainfall, fog, and even heavy dew can affect pesticide applications because the moisture may dilute and degrade pesticides and may wash the material off treated surfaces. Although light rainfall (¼ to 1 inch) can help activate certain preemergent herbicides, high rainfall amounts can wash pesticides off the application site and cause water contamination.

Pesticides can also be carried away from the application site through water movement as a result of irrigation. Time the watering and pesticide applications so this does not happen.

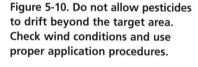

7. Know how to prevent pesticide drift and other off-site movement.

Figure 5-10. Do not allow pesticides to drift beyond the target area. Check wind conditions and use proper application procedures.

Disposing of Pesticides. Even when your equipment is properly adjusted or calibrated, pesticides may remain in your spray tank after completing an application. The best way to dispose of this material is to apply it to an untreated application site on the label. Many diluted pesticide mixtures do not store well, so you must use them quickly. Store any mixtures in a cool area at an even temperature. If you are unable to use up a mixture, place it into an accurately labeled pesticide service container (see Chapter 1) and safely store it for later disposal at a hazardous waste disposal site.

Don't ever dump leftover pesticides down sinks, drains, sewers, or on the ground. It is both illegal and a potential source of environmental and groundwater contamination. When a pesticide container is empty and rinsed, it must be disposed of properly.

To clean most liquid containers, triple-rinse them immediately as you empty the container so that the rinse solution goes into the spray tank along with the last drops of the concentrated pesticide (See Chapter 1, Sidebar 1.1). Use a secondary container (Figure 5-11) to catch any drips or spills.

Even triple-rinsed containers may still contain traces of pesticide, so never use them for another purpose. Punch a hole in the bottom to assure that the container cannot be used again. Rinsed containers should be stored in a locked area until they can be disposed of properly. Obtain specific disposal information from the county agricultural commissioner's office.

Storing. Store pesticides in their original tightly closed containers. Keep pesticide residues off the outsides of containers. Keep containers off the ground to reduce their exposure to moisture. Some baits may attract rodents, so these should be stored in rodent-proof containers. Protect pesticides from extremes in temperature and containers from moisture.

Ideally, a pesticide storage area will be a separate building, away from people, living areas, food, animal feed, and animals. The area must have good ventilation and

8. Know how to keep pesticides out of the environment through proper application and disposal practices.

Figure 5-11. Use a secondary container (such as a cat litter box or plastic basin) beneath your working area to catch drips or spills.

lighting. If storing on your truck, be sure to keep pesticides in a closed, locked enclosure. If storing category I or II (signal word DANGER or WARNING) pesticides, the storage area must be posted with warning signs. A locked cabinet in a garage or a locked storage shed may be a suitable pesticide storage location (see Chapter 1).

Do not store most pesticides for longer than 2 years. Before pesticides exceed their shelf life, use them in an appropriate application or transport them to an approved hazardous waste disposal site.

Keep a record of all pesticides being stored. Indicate on this record the date of purchase and the date you placed each chemical in your storage area. Check stored pesticides on a regular basis. Inspect the condition of containers and look for leaks and spills. Immediately clean up any spilled pesticide in the storage area and take damaged containers to hazardous waste sites.

PERSONAL HYGIENE

9. Know proper personal hygiene after handling pesticides, including laundering.

Follow these instructions when handling pesticides to protect yourself.

- Always wear all required PPE when working with pesticides.
  - Clean PPE after use and no less than daily when in use.
  - Wear disposable PPE such as coveralls that can be discarded after each day's use. If they become contaminated with pesticides during the workday, change to clean coveralls immediately, after decontaminating your body.
- If you have been handling pesticides or working in treated areas, wash your hands with soap and water before you eat, drink, use any tobacco product, put on makeup, or use the bathroom (Figure 5-12).
- Never eat in areas where pesticides are stored, mixed, or applied.
- Don't let other people handle your dirty work clothes without notifying them that there is possible pesticide contamination. Wash them separately from regular laundry.
- Shower (Figure 5-13) and put on clean clothes right after you finish your work.
- Wash reusable clothing daily, as described in Figure 4-19. Handle with care since pesticide residues can come in contact with your body from contaminated clothing.

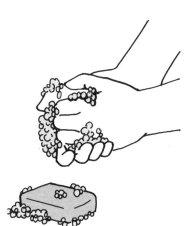

Figure 5-12. Wash hands with soap and water after handling pesticides or pesticide containers.

Pesticide Emergencies

Accidents happen. Even when we take precautions, mistakes happen. It ˌery important to know what to do when problems occur and to plan ahead. Pesticide emergencies can be caused by leaks, spills, fires, thefts, misapplication, or lack of care in storage or handling. Accidents may take place while you are transporting, handling, or opening containers; errors can arise during mixing or applying pesticides. You must be prepared for emergencies even when you use good work habits and follow proper pesticide handling procedures.

BE ON THE ALERT FOR
ACCIDENTAL EXPOSURE TO PESTICIDES

Exposure can occur if pesticides get onto your skin, into your eyes or mouth, are swallowed, or if you inhale vapors, dusts, or fumes (see Figure 4-20). The most common way people are exposed to pesticides is through the skin. Skin on various parts of the head and the groin area is especially able to absorb pesticides. Whatever the route of exposure, pesticides can affect you externally (contact) or internally (systemic). Either type of exposure is dangerous and immediate corrective action is required.

Some people may be especially sensitive to pesticides. These people show signs of allergic reactions when exposed to some types of pesticides. Allergic symptoms often include breathing difficulties, sneezing, watery and itchy eyes, skin rashes, anxiety, and general discomfort. Sensitive people should avoid exposure to pesticides that produce allergic reactions. The allergic reaction could be to the pesticide active ingredient or to other chemicals that are included in the pesticide formulation.

The type of exposure, what the product contains, and your body's reaction determine what first aid and medical treatment is required. Serious pesticide exposure can result in poisoning, which can stop breathing or cause convulsions, paralysis, skin burns, blindness, or death. Serious exposure can occur from small amounts that are not cleaned off your body or from a massive exposure, such as when equipment breaks.

Be especially alert for signs of exposure in high-risk situations. Some of the most serious accidents occur during mixing and transporting of pesticides. Undiluted pesticide concentrates are much

Figure 5-13. Take a shower and wash your hair after handling pesticides.

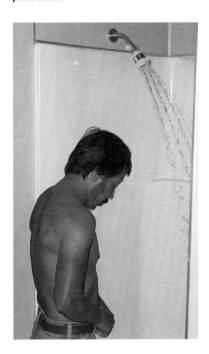

10. Know how to recognize pesticide exposure symptoms and respond to emergencies.

more dangerous than diluted pesticides. All pesticides, however, may be hazardous.

Prepare for Emergencies

Planning ahead helps you respond better to emergencies (Table 5-1). Always have the label for the pesticide you are using at the application site. You should have an extra, clean, dry copy of pesticide labels on the truck in case of an accident or injury, since the label provides key information for medical and emergency responders.

Keep an updated list of nearby medical facilities capable of treating pesticide-related injuries posted in your work vehicle and posted at your work location (Figure 1-17). Have a copy handy not only of the pesticide labels but also the MSDS for all pesticides you use. For more pesticide information, consult the National Pesticide Information Center (NPIC) (1-800-858-7378). Professional medical care must be obtained at once when there has been possible pesticide exposure or when a person shows any signs of pesticide poisoning. This requires safely transporting the injured person to a medical facility for treatment or calling 9-1-1 for an ambulance.

Also be sure you have at the work site all the materials you need to handle emergencies, including first aid supplies, clean water, and materials for cleaning up spills as described later in this section.

Table 5-1. Checklist for Preparing for Pesticide Emergencies.

CHECKLIST FOR PREPARING FOR PESTICIDE EMERGENCIES

- ☐ Be prepared for an accident. When accidents happen, the best response is a quick response.

- ☐ Develop an emergency response plan for pesticide exposures and accidents (spills, leaks, and fires).

- ☐ Train all of your handlers how to handle emergencies.

- ☐ Obtain first aid supplies and keep a set in each truck or workplace. Keep them updated.

- ☐ Obtain a spill cleanup kit (Figure 5-23) and keep a set in each truck or workplace. Keep materials clean and updated.

- ☐ Be sure to have adequate clean water for routine washing during the work period, emergency washing of the entire body, and eye flushing.

- ☐ Obtain information about the pesticides you are using, including copies of the label and MSDS for each pesticide you use and put them in the truck or at the workplace. Contact the National Pesticide Information Center (www.npic.orst.edu) for more pesticide information.

- ☐ Take training on first aid procedures, including rescue breathing and CPR.

- ☐ Locate and make arrangements for emergency medical care for you and your employee handlers before you need emergency care.

- ☐ Post the name, location, emergency telephone number, and address of the emergency care facility in your vehicle and at your workplace.

FIRST AID

First aid is the help given to a person injured or made ill from an accident or natural disaster before professional help can be obtained. First aid reduces the amount of injury or illness and saves lives. First aid is not a substitute for professional medical care.

The PRECAUTIONARY STATEMENTS section of the pesticide label provides specific first aid information for pesticide related injuries or illnesses (Figure 5-14). Read and understand these statements before starting to use a product. The section on HAZARDS TO HUMANS AND DOMESTIC ANIMALS is key to knowing the risks and correct responses to emergencies with the pesticide you are using. Become familiar with the information in this section before using any pesticide. Another good source of first aid information is the MSDS.

If you or any other person may have been exposed to any pesticide, obtain first aid and seek medical care immediately (Figure 5-15). If you are feeling ill or showing symptoms of pesticide exposure, get first aid, even if time has passed since the exposure. If you do not think you were exposed but you are feeling ill and have been handling pesticides, seek help.

Don't transport yourself to a medical facility if you have been exposed to a pesticide. Call 9-1-1 for an ambulance or get someone to

Figure 5-14. Example of a precautionary statement on a pesticide label. Know about the first aid treatments for each pesticide you use.

Figure 5-15. If you have been exposed to pesticides, stop work immediately, remove contaminated clothing, and get professional medical care.

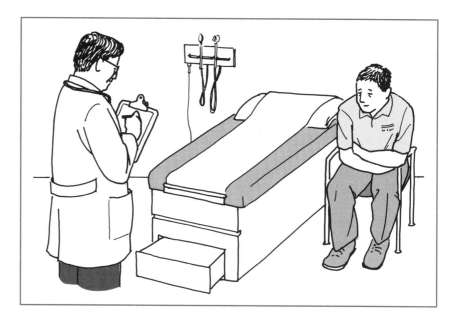

drive you. Be sure to bring the label or MSDS for the pesticide you were exposed to.

Decontaminate (wash) the exposed parts of your body as quickly as possible and prevent further exposure. If you are giving first aid to another person, wear protective clothing so you are not also exposed. First aid responders can easily become victims if they are not careful.

Keep first aid supplies and emergency information in your work vehicle (Figure 5-16). These supplies should include decontamination instructions plus a supply of clean water, soap, and clean disposable towels for whole-body washing; clean coveralls or other change of clothing; and medical treatment facility information. The wash water temperature should be cool (not too hot or cold), and the water should be clean and fresh so it does not cause harm if swallowed or if it comes in contact with the eyes during decontamination or washing. You can use drinking water as wash water as long as you have plenty of water.

Everyone handling pesticides should know where these supplies are located ahead of time. Explaining about first aid supplies and how they are to be used should be part of your pesticide safety training. To prepare yourself for emergencies, enroll in an American Red Cross first aid course and cardiopulmonary resuscitation (CPR) training. Sidebars 5.3, 5.4, 5.5, and 5.6 describe first aid steps to follow when someone comes in contact with pesticides through one of the four types of exposure (skin, eyes, inhalation, or swallowing).

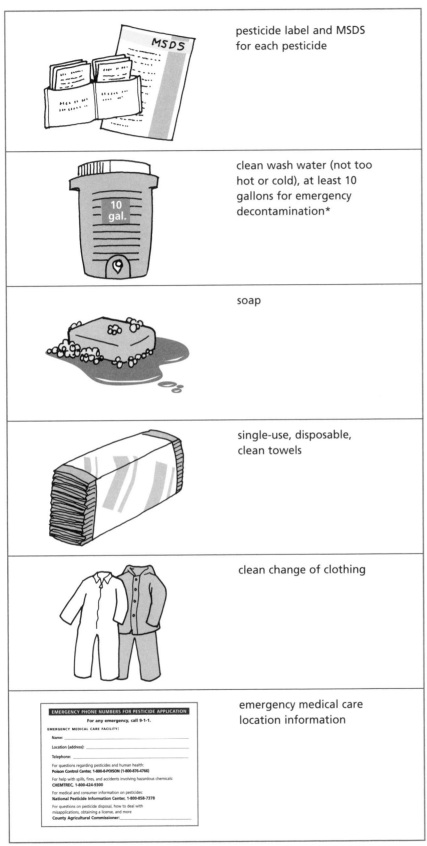

pesticide label and MSDS for each pesticide

clean wash water (not too hot or cold), at least 10 gallons for emergency decontamination*

soap

single-use, disposable, clean towels

clean change of clothing

emergency medical care location information

Figure 5-16. Keep first aid supplies and other emergency response tools in the work vehicle. Include information on how to decontaminate exposed people.

* If the pesticide product labeling requires protective eyewear, each pesticide handler must have at least 1 pint of water immediately available for emergency eye flushing.

SIDEBAR 5.3—HOW TO RESPOND TO SKIN EXPOSURE

Skin contact with concentrated or diluted pesticides can cause serious injury. When pesticides contact skin directly or soak through clothing to the skin, it can cause burns, blisters, or rashes (Figure 5-17). Skin absorption can cause poisoning effects to internal organs. If a pesticide touches your skin or clothing

- immediately remove contaminated clothing
- wash the affected areas with plenty of clean water and soap

If soap is not available, wash with water and as soon as possible, wash again with soap and more water. (Figure 5-18).

Follow these steps if anyone's skin is exposed to pesticides.

1. **Leave the contaminated area.** Immediately move everyone away from the source of contamination. Quickly get away from vapors, fumes, or spilled pesticide. Prevent further contamination and exposure. Assure that no one else enters the contaminated area.

2. **Prevent ongoing exposure.** Remove contaminated clothing and quickly wash affected skin with large amounts of clean water and soap. Prevent further exposure by safely bagging the contaminated clothing.

3. **Restore breathing.** If the victim has stopped breathing, call out for help and begin rescue breathing. Continue rescue breathing until the victim resumes breathing without help or until professional medical help arrives. If the person has stopped breathing and has no pulse, begin CPR and continue until help arrives.

4. **Get medical attention.** Call 9-1-1 for an ambulance or safely provide transportation to the nearest medical facility as quickly as possible, if any poisoning symptoms are exhibited or for any major exposure. Assure that the pesticide does not contaminate the transportation vehicle. If possible, take a pesticide label or MSDS. At least provide the pesticide product name and EPA registration number (see Figure 1-9) to the professional medical staff at the facility. This will help them determine the best treatment.

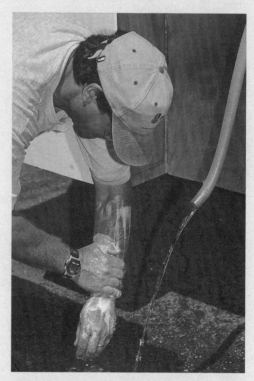

Figure 5-17. Rashes may appear immediately after pesticide exposure or later.

Figure 5-18. If you get pesticides on your skin, wash exposed parts of the body with soap and plenty of water.

SIDEBAR 5.4—HOW TO RESPOND TO EYE EXPOSURE

Many pesticides are corrosive or otherwise damaging to the eyes. Quickly flushing the eyes is important. Prompt first aid, followed by medical care, can help minimize serious injury. Follow these steps in case anyone's eyes are exposed to pesticides.

1. **Leave the contaminated area.** Immediately move everyone away from the source of contamination. Quickly get away from vapors, fumes, or spilled pesticide. Prevent further contamination and exposure. Assure that no one else enters the contaminated area.

2. **Flush the eyes.** Immediately flush the affected eyes with a gentle stream of clean water (Figure 5-19). If available, use an eye flushing station fitted with two fountains that direct gentle streams of water upward to the eyes.

   Get water from a designated container for emergency eye flushing, a water faucet at the work site, or even from a water cooler. Use a hose or a clean cup or glass to pour the water. Tilt the head back while gently pouring water onto the bridge of the nose, so the water runs over the affected eye. Do not contaminate the other eye. Be sure the water temperature is tepid (not too hot or cold). If the eye wash water is too hot or too cold, you could increase damage to the eyes.

Hold the eyelids open (with clean fingers) to assure thorough, gentle flushing. Use a slow stream of water and flush the eyes for at least 15 minutes. Continue to hold the eyelids open to assure that water reaches the affected eye tissues. Do not use any eye wash chemicals, eye drops, or drugs in the water, since this may increase the extent of injury. See the label directions if you wear contact lenses and remove them as directed on the label.

3. **Obtain medical care.** Call 9-1-1 immediately so paramedics can be on the way while the eye is being flushed. After you've flushed the eye, if no ambulance is available, ask someone to drive you to the nearest medical facility right away. Do not delay the eye flushing since it needs to be done immediately. If possible, take a pesticide label and MSDS. At least provide the pesticide product name and EPA registration number (see Figure 1-9) to the professional medical staff so they know what the eye has been exposed to.

Figure 5-19. If you get a pesticide in your eye, wash it with clean, running water for 15 minutes and get professional medical care.

SIDEBAR 5.5—HOW TO RESPOND TO PESTICIDE INHALATION (BREATHING)

Inhaling pesticide mists, dusts, vapors, or fumes can cause serious lung injury (Figure 5-20). It may cause internal poisoning after being absorbed into other parts of the body through the lungs. Immediately take first aid measures to reduce injury or prevent death. Follow these steps if anyone has inhaled pesticide dust or vapors.

1. **Leave the exposure area.** Get to fresh air immediately. If you are the victim, avoid unnecessary physical exertion, because it strains the heart and lungs. If you must enter a contaminated area to help someone, wear PPE, especially respiratory protection equipment, to prevent exposure.

2. **Loosen clothing.** Loosening clothing makes breathing easier. This also releases pesticide vapors or fumes trapped between clothing and the skin. It also reduces the risk of further dermal exposure for you or the victim. Remove any contaminated clothing.

3. **Restore breathing.** If the victim has stopped breathing, call out for help as you begin rescue breathing. Continue rescue breathing until the victim resumes breathing without help or until professional medical help arrives. If the person has stopped breathing and has no pulse, begin CPR and continue until help arrives.

4. **Treat for shock.** Inhalation injury can cause a person to go into shock. When shock occurs, blood does not circulate properly through the body and organs begin to fail. Keep the injured person calm and lying down. Cover the person with a blanket, coat, or similar cover to prevent them slipping further into shock. Do not give any drink when a person is in shock.

5. **Watch for convulsions.** If the person is still upright, protect the victim from falls or injury in case seizures or convulsions occur. If the person is lying down and seems to be experiencing shock symptoms, keep air passages clear by making sure the head is tilted back.

6. **Get immediate professional medical care.** Call 9-1-1 for an ambulance or safely provide transportation to the nearest medical facility as quickly as possible if any poisoning symptoms are exhibited or for any major exposure. Provide medical staff with the pesticide product name and EPA registration number (see Figure 1-9). If a pesticide label or MSDS is available, bring it.

Figure 5-20. Breathing pesticides can be harmful. Get to fresh air quickly. Loosen clothing. Seek medical help.

SIDEBAR 5.6—HOW TO RESPOND TO SWALLOWED PESTICIDES

This is an emergency!

Act quickly when anyone has swallowed a pesticide or when a pesticide comes in contact with the mouth (Figure 5-21). Immediately give first aid by following the instructions on the pesticide label or the MSDS. If the label or MSDS is not available, follow these steps.

1. **Immediately call 9-1-1 for an ambulance and to get medical advice.** This is an emergency. You may request connection with the Poison Control Center or you may call Poison Control at **1-800-222-1222** for first aid information (Figure 5-22).

2. **If directed to do so, dilute the swallowed pesticide.** If the person is conscious and alert, give large amounts of water (1 quart for an adult or a large glass for a child under 7). Do not give any liquids to an unconscious or convulsing person.

3. **Don't induce vomiting unless you are directed by the pesticide label, MSDS, or the Poison Control Center.** If a corrosive or petroleum-based pesticide has been swallowed, vomiting could seriously harm the lungs and digestive system.

   If advised to induce vomiting or if the person is already vomiting, make sure the person is kneeling or lying on their right side.

4. **Obtain professional medical care.** Call 9-1-1 for an ambulance or transport the poisoning victim to the nearest medical facility. Provide as much information as possible about the swallowed pesticide, including the pesticide product name and pesticide registration number (see Figure 1-9). If a pesticide label or MSDS is available, bring it.

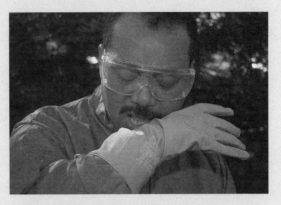

Figure 5-21. Getting pesticides in your mouth is a serious medical emergency. Get medical treatment immediately. For most pesticides that are swallowed, it is not safe to vomit.

Figure 5-22. Call the California Poison Action Line if you think someone has been poisoned. Services are available in over 100 languages.

Figure 5-23. Keep a pesticide spill cleanup kit in your truck.

PERSONAL PROTECTIVE EQUIPMENT

gloves, protective eyewear, disposable coveralls, chemical-resistant boots, and protective head covering

ABSORBENT MATERIAL

sawdust, vermiculite, dry coarse clay, cat litter, commercial absorbent, newspapers or paper towels

AND

broom and scoop or shovel to pick up the contaminated material

WASTE CONTAINER

container with lid (a pail, heavy-duty garbage bag, or sealable plastic bag) for the contaminated waste

MARKER OR PEN

for labeling containers with pesticide name

PHONE NUMBERS

emergency and county agricultural commissioner phone numbers

PESTICIDE LEAKS AND SPILLS

All pesticide leaks or spills should be treated as emergencies. Leaks or spills can occur while transporting, storing, mixing, or using pesticides. You must develop an emergency response plan that describes what you will do in each type of situation and include the equipment, tools, and other materials you will need. Have a pesticide spill cleanup kit (Figure 5-23) in your truck for safely containing leaks and spills. Concentrated pesticide spills are much more dangerous than pesticides diluted with water, but both types must be treated seriously.

Find out in advance where to get assistance with spill cleanup. When spills occur on public roadways, immediately call 9-1-1. The 9-1-1 emergency dispatcher will contact the agencies that need to respond to the emergency. All leaks or spills of pesticides, no matter where they occur, must also be reported immediately to the local county agricultural commissioner. Refer to the MSDS for specific information about spill cleanup procedures.

Cleaning Up Pesticide Leaks and Spills

Follow these steps to clean up pesticide leaks and spills (Figure 5-24).

1. **Clear the area.** Keep people and animals away from the contaminated area. Contain the spilled or leaked pesticide with constructed berms or barriers made with an absorbent material such as cat litter. Do not allow any smoking near a spill. If the spill occurs in an enclosed area, shut off all electrical appliances and motors that could produce sparks and ignite a fire or explosion.

2. **Move injured people from the site.** If someone is injured, exposed to the pesticide, or contaminated, remove them from the site to a place safe from further exposure. If necessary, wear personal protective clothing to remove the victim from the place of exposure. Provide first aid. Send for professional medical help.

3. **Wear protective clothing.** Before beginning any cleanup, review the pesticide label or MSDS for information on the PPE required. If that information is not available, put on chemical-resistant (rubber) boots, gloves, and protective clothing, as well as eye protection and respiratory protection equipment.

11. Know how to respond to spills, leaks, or other releases of pesticides.

Figure 5-24. Learn how to handle a spill or leak in advance.

Read the MSDS for the pesticides you will use. Note the section on ACCIDENTAL RELEASE MEASURES.

Clear the area of people so no one is contaminated.

Wear protective clothing, contain the pesticide, and clean it up with absorbent material.

Properly dispose of spilled material at a hazardous waste site. If you have a large amount of material, call CHEMTREC at **1-800-424-9300**.

4. **Contain the leak.** If the container is leaking, stop the leak by transferring the pesticide to another container or by patching the leaking container (paper bags and cardboard boxes can be patched with strong tape). Prevent the spill from spreading. Starting at the edges of the spill and working inward, cover it with something absorbent, such as sawdust or cat litter. Be sure to keep pesticides out of storm drains and gutters.

5. **Clean up the pesticide.** Sweep the absorbent material and pesticide into sealable plastic bags. If the pesticide is highly toxic or if the spill is large, a professional spill team should be called to do the cleanup, such as **CHEMTREC (1-800-424-9300)**.

6. **Clean nonporous surfaces and safety equipment.** If the spill occurred on a cleanable surface such as concrete or asphalt, use a broom to scrub the contaminated surface with a strong detergent solution. Clean up the detergent solution with absorbent material (such as cat litter) and place all of the waste with the contaminated material in a sealable, labeled container. Equipment such as brooms, shovels, and dustpans must be cleaned or disposed of. When you finish, clean your PPE.

7. **Dispose of the spilled material.** Local regulations on disposal of hazardous materials may vary. Check with the county agricultural commissioner for instructions on how to dispose of the container and its contents.

PESTICIDE FIRES

Fires involving pesticides are very dangerous because they produce toxic smoke. Hazardous materials responders need to know what is burning so they can use the correct and safest methods on the fire. Follow these steps when pesticide fires break out (Figure 5-25).

1. **Call the fire department.** Immediately call 9-1-1 to contact the nearest fire department. Inform them that the fire involves pesticides. Provide them with the names of the pesticides and any other chemicals in the fire, along with the names of other chemicals near the burning area. If possible, provide MSDSs to the arriving fire units.

2. **Clear the area.** Get people out of the immediate area of the fire; there may be considerable risk of toxic fumes and explosions. Do not put out the fire yourself as it could spread the pesticide.

3. **Evacuate people.** Evacuate and isolate the area around and downwind of the fire. If you can do it safely, protect animals and move equipment and vehicles that could be damaged by the fire or fumes, or that would impair fire fighting efforts.

12. Know how to respond to pesticide fires.

Figure 5-25. Pesticide fires are dangerous because they produce toxic smoke. Call 9-1-1. Do not put out the fire yourself.

CALL EMERGENCY 9-1-1
FIRE • POLICE • MEDICAL

MISAPPLICATION OF PESTICIDES

13. Know what to do when pesticides are misapplied.

A pesticide misapplication can be an emergency if it poses a danger to people, property, or the environment. Making a misapplication is a serious problem; do not compound the damage by failing to take responsible corrective action. If the wrong pesticide has been applied to a site, immediately notify the property owner and the county agricultural commissioner. This is especially important if fruits or vegetables grown for consumption have been improperly treated.

Types of Misapplications

A misapplication is defined as the intentional, accidental, or negligent use of a pesticide on a site not allowed by the label or applying pesticides in a manner inconsistent with the label (Figure 5-26). Some examples are

- applying a pesticide to a plant or site not listed on the label

- using more pesticide than allowed on the label

- using improper application or mixing procedures

- disposing of leftover pesticides or containers improperly

Application of pesticide above the rate specified on the label can be a danger to human health as well as an environmental threat. Overapplication may occur as a result of incorrect calibration of application equipment, improper measurement of pesticide or water, or poor mixing of pesticides in your spray tank. Pesticide residues may last longer than expected, presenting greater hazards to people or damaging treated plants or nontarget organisms. Using too little pesticide usually does not pose a hazard but may result in inadequate control of pests.

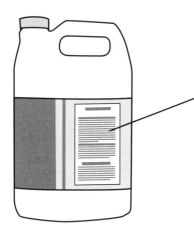

Figure 5-26. Pesticide mistakes can be prevented. Avoid common errors such as incorrect pesticide handling procedures, off-site movement (drift), or lack of proper protective clothing. Read the label, understand it, and follow it.

DIRECTIONS FOR USE

Broadcast Treatment of Ornamental Turf
Apply 1/3 to 3/4 fluid ounce per 1,000 square feet of TURFLON ESTER in enough water to provide uniform coverage of the target area to control actively growing broadleaf weeds growing in perennial bluegrass, perennial ryegrass, or tall fescue. Do not use on other turfgrass species (see General Use Precautions) unless injury can be tolerated. To minimize turf injury, do not treat if turf is under heat or drought stress and make repeat applications at least 4 weeks apart.

Spot Treatment on Ornamental Turf
Mix 3/8 to 3/4 ounce of TURFLON ESTER per 1,000 square feet in enough water to provide uniform coverage of the target area and apply at any time broadleaf weeds are susceptible. Note: Do not apply more than 1.5 fluid ounces per 1,000 square feet of TURFLON ESTER in a single application.

Environmental Hazards
This pesticide is toxic to fish. Do not apply directly to water, or to areas where surface water is present or to intertidal areas below the mean high water mark. Do not contaminate water by cleaning of equipment or disposal of equipment washwaters.

Once an improper application has been discovered, take immediate action. Notify the property owner and the county agricultural commissioner of the problem and seek information and advice on what remedies can be taken. If possible, contact the pesticide manufacturer for help in determining what corrective action measures can be taken. Remember, quick action is of the utmost importance when trying to reduce damage.

PESTICIDE INJURY AND LIABILITY

You are legally responsible for all pesticides that you apply. If the application injures plants, animals, people, or property, you are responsible. You may be required to pay the medical bills of those injured by pesticide applications.

14. Know that you will be liable if you apply a pesticide that injures plants, people, animals, or property.

If the pesticide you are applying moves off-site through drift or other manner and causes human injury or damages nearby plants, animals, property, or the environment, you may be subject to fines, jail sentences, and loss of your applicator certificate or license. In addition, courts may hold you responsible in lawsuits for personal injury or damages. Accurate records of all your pesticide applications may help in your defense, if someone brings a claim of negligence against you.

Commercial pesticide applicators and maintenance gardeners must have liability insurance or adequate financial resources (Figure 5-27) to protect themselves from claims associated with pesticide use. Of primary importance is the protection of people, animals, and the environment. Responsible, quick action is key.

Figure 5-27. Maintenance gardeners must have liability insurance or adequate financial resources in case of accidents. As part of the application process, you will provide proof of liability insurance or sign the financial responsibility statement.

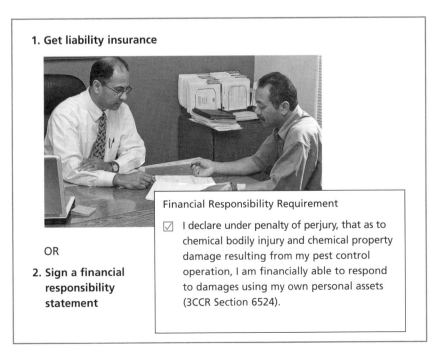

1. Get liability insurance

OR

2. Sign a financial responsibility statement

Financial Responsibility Requirement

☑ I declare under penalty of perjury, that as to chemical bodily injury and chemical property damage resulting from my pest control operation, I am financially able to respond to damages using my own personal assets (3CCR Section 6524).

Chapter 5 Review Questions

1. All pesticides can be toxic and cause problems. You can learn about pesticide hazards and safety by studying
   - ☐ a. pesticide labels
   - ☐ b. Material Safety Data Sheets (MSDSs)
   - ☐ c. Pesticide Safety Information Series (PSIS) leaflets
   - ☐ d. all of the above

2. How do you select the personal protective equipment for applying a pesticide?
   - ☐ a. use whatever personal protective equipment is available
   - ☐ b. follow the pesticide label requirements
   - ☐ c. avoid using personal protective equipment whenever possible
   - ☐ d. follow the spill cleanup guidelines on the Material Safety Data Sheet (MSDS)

3. How often must you clean personal protective equipment?
   - ☐ a. at the end of each work day, before using the equipment again
   - ☐ b. at least once per week if the equipment is used more than 2 days
   - ☐ c. at least once per week if the equipment has visible residues on it
   - ☐ d. you do not need to clean personal protective equipment

4. What is one tip to follow when trying to select a pesticide that is less hazardous to waterways, people, and wildlife?
   - ☐ a. choose a pesticide that will kill a broad range of pests
   - ☐ b. avoid low-persistence insecticides such as insecticidal soaps
   - ☐ c. choose a pesticide with the signal words DANGER or WARNING
   - ☐ d. avoid pesticides that say on the label that they are extremely toxic to fish and wildlife

5. When transporting pesticides in a vehicle
   - ☐ a. secure the packages inside the passenger compartment
   - ☐ b. carry them on the floor in the cab of the truck
   - ☐ c. secure the containers in the cargo area of the truck
   - ☐ d. strap the containers to the top of the vehicle

6. Keep pets away from vertebrate pest control materials by
   - ☐ a. putting baits out of their reach such as in bait boxes
   - ☐ b. discarding dead rodents
   - ☐ c. never scattering them on the soil surface
   - ☐ d. all of the above

7. Prevent pesticide drift and other off-site movement by
   - ☐ a. applying when there is little wind
   - ☐ b. using larger droplets
   - ☐ c. leaving a buffer zone between where you treat and the untreated landscape
   - ☐ d. all of the above

8. Recognizing when exposure to pesticides has occurred is important because
   - ☐ a. you must decontaminate immediately
   - ☐ b. symptoms are always easy to detect
   - ☐ c. if you don't have symptoms within 15 minutes, no exposure occurred
   - ☐ d. a small amount of exposure will never cause illness

9. You will find first aid and other emergency information for pesticide accidents
   - ☐ a. in the front section of the local telephone directory
   - ☐ b. in a pesticide manufacturer's informational brochure
   - ☐ c. on the bottom of the pesticide container
   - ☐ d. in the precautionary statements section of the pesticide label

10. When cleaning up a spilled pesticide, contain the spill by
   - ☐ a. using water to wash the spill and any contaminated cleanup material into a storm drain or drainage ditch
   - ☐ b. using paper towels and cat litter to soak up pesticide, and then throwing the contaminated paper towels and cat litter in the trash
   - ☐ c. placing obstacles around spilled area, containing the spill, soaking it up with an absorbent material, and then placing the contaminated absorbent material into a sealable container
   - ☐ d. none of the above

11. If the wrong pesticide has been accidentally applied to a site, you should
   - ☐ a. immediately notify the property owner and the county agricultural commissioner
   - ☐ b. immediately notify your pesticide dealer and the regional water quality control board
   - ☐ c. immediately call 9-1-1 for the Poison Control Center for advice
   - ☐ d. immediately call 9-1-1 for the nearest emergency medical facility for advice

12. Dealing with fires involving pesticides requires
   - ☐ a. large amounts of water to disperse the burning materials
   - ☐ b. professional help that is equipped and trained to fight pesticide fires
   - ☐ c. seeking immediate help from anyone nearby
   - ☐ d. large amounts of sand to smother the flames and contain the blaze

13. As long as you follow some of the pesticide label directions, you are not liable for injury to plants, animals, or people except when you
   - ☐ a. use more than the label allows
   - ☐ b. apply on a site that is not addressed on the label
   - ☐ c. apply a lower rate
   - ☐ d. you are always liable for injury caused by pesticides you apply

(Answer sheet is on pages 206–207.)

6 Selection and Use of Pesticide Application Equipment

Pesticide application equipment used in landscape and turf settings must be suited to the application area. Each type of pesticide application equipment is designed for a specific type of job.

1. Know the benefits of designating separate application equipment for herbicide use only; designate other application equipment for other pesticides.

2. List and describe the uses for the following types of landscape and turf-grass pesticide application equipment: aerosol can, hose-end sprayer, trigger pump sprayer, compressed air sprayer, backpack sprayer, mechanical duster, hand-operated broadcast spreader, and drop spreader.

3. Identify and know the function of the following components of liquid application equipment: tank, hose, pump, wand, control valve, and nozzle (including cone, flat fan, and adjustable nozzles).

4. Know how to clean, service, and maintain pesticide application equipment.

5. Know how to use bait and bait stations for pests.

6. Know proper procedures for mixing pesticide sprays, including how to measure pesticides safely and accurately.

7. Be aware of the hazards involved with using improper measuring and mixing tools.

8. Explain the importance of calibrating pesticide application equipment.

9. Know how to calibrate liquid sprayers and dry applicators for turfgrass and ornamental applications.

10. Know how to calculate the amount of pesticide to apply to a known area.

11. Know why the following are necessary for a successful pesticide application: appropriate equipment, correct application rate and dilution, proper application site, appropriate coverage (broadcast versus spot treatment), vulnerable life stage of the target pest, and personal protective equipment.

12. Know how to determine whether a pesticide application was successful.

PESTICIDE APPLICATION equipment used in landscape and turf settings must be suited to the application area. Equipment used by maintenance gardeners ranges from the simple, such as a small hand-held spray container, to the complex, such as compressed air sprayers or backpack sprayers. Each type of pesticide application equipment is designed for a specific type of job. Pesticides formulated as liquids, dusts, and granules each require different types of application equipment. Select the right equipment for the job and properly maintain it. In addition, pesticides must be properly measured and mixed and equipment correctly calibrated to assure effective control of pests.

■ Selecting and Maintaining Application Equipment

The pesticide application equipment you use must fit the pesticide application method required by the label and the location and condition of the treatment area. Equipment that is too big or too powerful may be as much of a problem as equipment that is too small. Most pesticide application equipment is designed to work efficiently only in a limited number of situations. Consider the size of the area to be treated, convenience, and sturdiness. Read pesticide labels to see if there are specific equipment requirements or suggestions.

Choose application equipment that is comfortable to work with and easy to use and maintain (Figure 6-1). Be sure the equipment is simple to repair and parts are readily available. Hand-held equipment must be lightweight enough to be convenient to use for longer time periods. Before buying equipment, consult with pest control dealers and other applicators who are familiar with application equipment to be sure the equipment will work well in the sites you will be treating.

Invest in pesticide application equipment that is durable. Make sure that caps on spray tanks close and seal well. Hoses and fittings should resist leaks or drips that could cause personal injury, damage to plants, or environmental contamination.

Equipment used for herbicide applications should only be used for weed-killing applications. Herbicide residues in tanks, hoppers, hoses, or nozzles may injure desired plants when you use the same equipment to apply an insecticide or fungicide to foliage (Figure 6-2).

1. Know the benefits of designating separate application equipment for herbicide use only; designate other application equipment for other pesticides.

NILA HINES

Figure 6-1. Pesticide supply stores sell a variety of pesticide application equipment. Learn about the types of equipment.

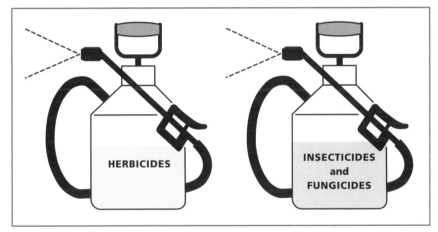

Figure 6-2. Use separate sprayers for herbicides. Don't use herbicide spray equipment to apply fungicides and insecticides. Herbicide application equipment can have small residues that would harm landscape plants.

LIQUID PESTICIDE APPLICATION EQUIPMENT

Selecting the sprayer type for a particular application of a liquid pesticide depends on the application site location and size, as well as the pesticide formulation. Most liquid pesticide applications done by maintenance gardeners are made with compressed air sprayers, backpack sprayers, or trigger pump sprayers. Larger sprayers and stronger pumps are required when greater volume and pressure are needed for the application. Construction materials and the type of pump also affect how well a sprayer will last. Table 6-1 lists common types of liquid application equipment used by maintenance gardeners.

Table 6-1. Selection Guide for Liquid Pesticide Application Equipment.

LIQUID PESTICIDE APPLICATION EQUIPMENT		
	USES	**COMMENTS**
Aerosol can	Insect control on house or patio plants, pets, small areas, cracks and crevices, and confined spaces.	Very convenient. High cost per unit of active ingredient. Wind drift can occur.
Hose-end sprayer	Home garden and small landscape areas. Used for insect, weed, and pathogen control.	Delivery may not give desired rate. Use back flow prevention device to protect water supply.
Trigger pump sprayer	Indoor plants and small home yard areas. Used for insect and pathogen control.	Low cost if you mix your own but expensive if you purchase premade (ready-to-use) products. Easy to use.
Compressed air sprayer	Many commercial and homeowner applications. Can develop high pressures. Used for insect, weed, and pathogen control.	Good overall sprayer for many types of applications. Requires periodic maintenance.
Backpack sprayer	Same uses as compressed air sprayers.	Durable and easy to use. Requires periodic maintenance.

Types of Liquid Pesticide Application Equipment

Aerosol Can Sprayers. Pressurized-can spray applicators expel a fine spray of premixed, ready-to-use pesticide through a nozzle at the top of the can. Aerosol cans have a size of 1 quart or less and are not reusable. Aerosol pesticides are convenient, handy, and do not need mixing, but only a few aerosol products are available or appropriate for use in landscapes.

Aerosol can sprayers give you no control over droplet size. They are best for small spot applications very close to the target since the very fine mist they produce can easily move off-site with the slightest air movement. Some pesticide products in aerosol cans come with a nozzle that produces a solid stream for pinpoint applications.

Hose-End Sprayers. Hose-end sprayers can be easy to use but you must assure that you apply the desired rate of pesticide and do not risk contaminating water supplies. Attach an antisiphoning device (Figure 6-3) such as a hose bibb vacuum breaker to the faucet to

2. List and describe the uses for the following types of landscape and turfgrass pesticide application equipment:

- *aerosol can*
- *hose-end sprayer*
- *trigger pump sprayer*
- *compressed air sprayer*
- *backpack sprayer*

Figure 6-3. Use an antisiphoning device with hose-end sprayers. This prevents pesticides from flowing back into the water supply. Attach the device to the water source (A) and screw the hose (B) into it.

prevent backflow of the pesticide into the water supply. Backflow of pesticide into the water system is illegal and could pollute drinking water.

Common uses for hose-end sprayers are for applying pesticides to lawns, flowers, and shrubs, usually in small areas. The hose-end sprayer combines concentrated pesticides with water from a garden hose and expels it through a high-volume nozzle. Some nozzles adjust for droplet size and to aim the spray. These sprayers generally have a valve to start and stop the flow of pesticide in the stream of water. (If there is no valve, be very careful when starting the flow of water: The pesticide–water mixture will spray out immediately.) Some have another valve to regulate and shut off the water flow from the garden hose. Hose-end sprayers may be difficult to calibrate accurately, so be sure the spray pattern and output are what you intend.

Trigger Pump Sprayers. The trigger pump sprayer (Figure 6-4) is a simple liquid applicator. Squeezing a trigger forces a pesticide mixture through a nozzle, producing a fine spray. Some styles have an adjustable nozzle for controlling droplet size. The pesticide is in a plastic container that ranges in size from 1 pint to 1 gallon. Use this type of applicator to apply pesticides to small areas, such as potted plants, spot-spraying where only small portions of a few plants will be sprayed, and in confined areas. Most premixed ready-to-use pesticides come in trigger pump sprayers that are disposed of when the product is used up.

Compressed Air Sprayers. Use compressed air sprayers (Figure 6-5) to apply pesticides to specific areas or targets. Compressed air sprayers are lightweight enough to be carried by one person. Tanks usually do not have agitators, so they require occasional shaking when you use wettable powder, flowable, or emulsifiable concentrate formulations.

These low-pressure air sprayers hold a diluted pesticide mixture in a small, airtight tank. You use a hand pump to compress air inside the tank. The compressed air forces the liquid through a hose and nozzle when you open a valve. Some models use compressed carbon dioxide cartridges as the propellant, eliminating the need for hand pumping.

Figure 6-4. Trigger pump sprayers are convenient for small jobs.

Figure 6-5. Compressed air sprayers are used for many types of applications.

Metal or plastic tanks hold less than 5 gallons. Conventional tank sizes include 1-, 2-, and 3-gallon capacities.

Backpack Sprayers. Backpack sprayers (Figure 6-6) have a hand-operated pump that forces liquid pesticide through the nozzle. You operate the pump by moving a hand lever up and down. For best results, operate the hand lever with a constant number of pumps per minute to keep the pressure even. Some pumps create pressures more than 100 pounds per square inch (psi). The tanks, usually made of plastic, have a capacity of around 5 gallons. Backpack sprayers are also known as knapsack sprayers.

Parts of Liquid Pesticide Application Equipment

Compressed air and backpack sprayers have up to six parts (Figure 6-7), including a

- tank for mixing and holding the diluted pesticide mixture
- pump and pump lever which creates pressure to move the liquid
- hose
- control valve
- wand
- nozzle that produces small droplets in a spray pattern and directs spray toward the target

Pumps. Compressed air sprayers and backpack sprayers use pumps to move pesticide from the tank to the nozzle. The pump must generate enough pressure to propel spray droplets to the target. Compressed air and backpack sprayers used by maintenance gardeners come equipped with pumps. You generate pressure with these pumps by moving a lever up and down. Hand-held compressed air sprayers have a piston-type air pump, similar to a bicycle tire pump. The pump compresses air in the sealed pesticide tank. When you open the control valve the compressed air forces liquid out of the tank.

Figure 6-6. Backpack (knapsack) sprayer (front and back).

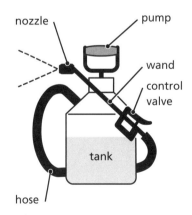

Figure 6-7. Compressed air sprayer parts. Know where each part is located and be sure it works before adding pesticide to the tank.

nozzle   pump

wand

control valve

tank

hose

Tanks. Application equipment sprayer tanks are designed for mixing and holding liquid pesticides. Tanks must be corrosion- and rust- resistant to protect them from reacting with corrosive pesticides. Choose models with large openings for easy filling and cleaning. A tight-fitting cap prevents pesticide from spilling or splashing. Tanks should not leak pesticide mixtures. When filling tanks, be sure there is an air gap separation (Figure 6-8) so that none of the pesticide is able to flow back into the water system.

Hoses. Compressed air sprayers and backpack sprayers use a hose to move the liquid from the tank to the wand.

Control Valves. Most liquid spraying systems have an on/off control valve. The user presses a lever for the spray to be released. Valves allow spray to pass through when they are open.

Wands. The nozzle attaches to the spray wand and the wand attaches to the hose. The purpose of the wand is to aim the nozzle at the target.

Figure 6-8. Don't put the water hose in the tank as you fill it. An air gap separation between the water supply and the tank keeps the pesticide in the tank from contaminating the water supply.

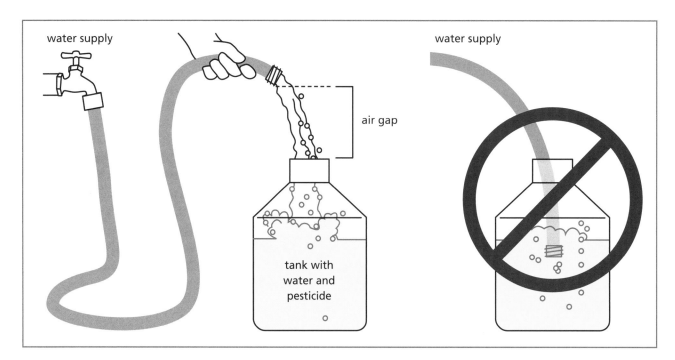

water supply

air gap

tank with water and pesticide

water supply

Nozzles. Nozzles are the most important parts of a sprayer because they control the application rate, droplet size, and spray pattern. They also affect the thoroughness and safety of the pesticide application. Several nozzle types (see Figures 6-9, 6-10, and 6-11) are available, depending on the type of application. If you use the wrong nozzle you may apply too much or too little of the pesticide, get poor coverage on the treated plant, or allow pesticides to drift onto surrounding nontarget plants or areas.

Often, less expensive and less effective adjustable nozzles are sold with application equipment such as backpack sprayers. These nozzles may be made of plastic and will not last as long as metal ones. You can replace them with a sturdier metal nozzle made of brass or stainless steel. Ceramic nozzles are very long-lasting but may be too expensive for incidental pesticide use.

Choose an appropriate nozzle for the application. Ask a salesperson for assistance to select the best nozzle for the type of pesticide application you will be making. Make your nozzle choice based on

- nozzle material

- nozzle design (affects spray pattern)

- nozzle orifice (opening) size

All nozzles will wear. The rate of nozzle wear depends on the design of the nozzle, the kind of material being sprayed, the spray pressure, and the usage. As a nozzle wears, the volume and pattern of spray changes and affects the quality of application. Replace nozzles when they do not deliver an accurate amount during calibration or do not produce the desired spray pattern.

The nozzle size, design, and amount of wear affect the droplet size. Pump pressure also affects droplet size. An ideal spray application results in uniform-sized droplets evenly spread to all treated surfaces. Increase the effectiveness of your spray application by using nozzles designed specifically for the working pressure and volume of your application equipment and by replacing worn or defective nozzles.

Nozzle designs include flat-spray, cone, and adjustable. Each design is best adapted to specific requirements. For instance, nozzles

3. Identify and know the function of the following components of liquid application equipment:

- *tank*
- *hose*
- *pump*
- *wand*
- *control valve*
- *nozzle (including cone, flat fan, and adjustable nozzles)*

Figure 6-9. Flat-spray nozzles.

Figure 6-10. A cone nozzle and its parts.

Figure 6-11. An adjustable nozzle.

used to apply herbicides, such as a flat-spray, may be wrong for applying insecticides or fungicides to foliage where a cone spray is better.

- **Flat-spray nozzles** (Figure 6-9). Use flat-spray nozzles to apply herbicides. Flat-spray nozzles distribute pesticide in a flat fan shape, with fan angles ranging between 50 and 160 degrees. Flat-spray nozzles produce a pattern with more spray droplets in the center of the fan. The pattern tapers off at each end.

- **Cone nozzles** (Figure 6-10). Use cone nozzles to apply insecticides and fungicides to dense foliage. Cone nozzles produce spray in either a hollow cone or solid cone pattern. If using a high-pressure sprayer, the hollow cone may work better.

- **Adjustable nozzles** (Figure 6-11). Adjustable nozzles are commonly found on trigger pump pesticide sprayers and some lower priced pump sprayers. Many backpack sprayers also come with an adjustable nozzle that controls droplet size and spray pattern. These nozzles change their spray angle from a wide cone pattern to a solid stream when the nozzle collar is turned.

Liquid Application Equipment Maintenance

Properly maintained application equipment is essential for the legal and effective use of pesticides. Without regular maintenance, you may apply more pesticide than is safe or legal or not enough to be effective. Regular inspections and maintenance help avoid accidents or spills caused by broken hoses, bad fittings, damaged tanks, or other problems.

Before each application, inspect equipment for wear, corrosion, or damage. Replace or repair any defective parts. Thoroughly clean equipment after every application. Wear protective clothing, rubber gloves, and eye protection when cleaning or repairing equipment. When not in use, store equipment in a way that prevents deterioration or damage. Keep equipment covered inside weatherproof buildings.

Preventing Problems with Liquid Application Equipment

When using equipment, take the following preventive measures to reduce problems due to sprayer malfunction or breakdown and to maintain uniform, effective, and accurate application.

1. **Flush and test sprayer before use when new or coming out of storage.** Clean the equipment. Use clean water to flush new

sprayers and sprayers coming out of storage. This removes foreign particles, dirt, and other debris. The manufacturing process may leave metallic chips, dirt, or other residue in the tank or pump. Improper storage always subjects spraying equipment to contamination with dirt, leaves, rodent debris, and rust.

2. **Use clean water when mixing pesticides.** Water that contains sand or silt causes rapid pump wear and may clog screens and nozzles. Know the pH of your water. Some materials may require adjusting the pH of the water; consult the label or pesticide distributor.

3. **Always keep screens in place during an application.** Filter screens remove foreign particles from the spray liquid. It is a nuisance to remove collected debris from the screens, but debris buildup shows that the screens are working. Make sure screens are the proper size for the type of pesticide being applied.

   If too much plugging does occur, clean the screens and try to determine and eliminate the cause. For example, change the water source, or, before mixing with the pesticide, run the water through coarse filters or screens to reduce debris. Do not use equipment with screens removed because the debris increases wear on the pumps and nozzles.

4. **Clean the filter screens after each use** (Figure 6-12). It is very important to routinely clean filter screens at the end of the day or pesticide application period. This will prevent the buildup of materials that could impair the sprayer accuracy and spray pattern.

5. **Use pesticides that are compatible with the sprayer and pump.** Some pesticides are corrosive to certain metals and deteriorate rubber and plastic components. The pesticide label will tell whether the pesticide is corrosive to metals, rubber, or plastics. Be sure your application equipment is compatible with the specific pesticide product you are using. If you are using equipment that is likely to deteriorate rapidly, inspect it regularly for wear.

4. Know how to clean, service, and maintain pesticide application equipment.

Figure 6-12. Clean nozzle filter screens regularly with a soft brush and clean water or a detergent solution. Wear gloves when cleaning pesticide application equipment and parts.

6. **Properly clean nozzles when necessary.** Spray nozzles are made to precise specifications. Never use any metal object to clean or remove debris, as it may damage the orifice (opening) or change the spray pattern or spray volume. Clean nozzles by flushing them with clean water or a detergent solution. Remove stuck particles with a soft brush or a round wooden toothpick (Figure 6-13). Nozzle suppliers sell special brushes for this purpose. Always wear rubber gloves and eye protection when handling or cleaning spray nozzles. Never blow on nozzles with your mouth, because nozzles contain pesticide residues.

7. **Clean the sprayer tanks and hoses after use.** Spray equipment must be cleaned at the end of each job. Cleaning removes residues that might clog the equipment, contaminate future sprays, or damage other treatment areas.

Avoid leaving pesticide mixtures in a sprayer overnight or for longer periods of time. Prolonged contact increases the risk of corrosion or deterioration of the sprayer's parts. Also, certain pesticides must be used very soon after mixing because they lose their effectiveness if left too long in the sprayer. Some pesticides settle out from the water and, even with agitation, may not return to suspension after sitting in an idle sprayer.

Pesticides left in a sprayer may present a hazard to people, wildlife, or the environment. Apply leftover pesticide spray mixture to an appropriate site listed on the label. Unused pesticide mixtures are hazardous wastes that require special handling and transportation for disposal.

After using the spray mixture, clean the sprayer and flush out the tank at the application site and spray the rinse materials back on the application site. Never drain rinse water onto the ground or into sewers, storm drains, or septic lines. If unused undiluted pesticides need disposal, contact the county agricultural commissioner about the legal and best method to handle them, including future household hazardous waste disposal events in the

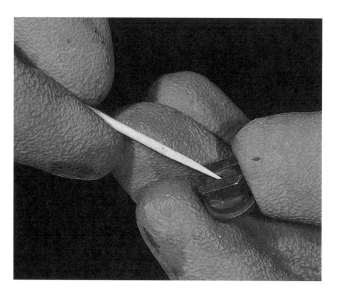

Figure 6-13. A round toothpick is good for removing dirt from a clogged nozzle. Don't use metal tools that could damage equipment.

area or local recycling programs. You may also call the California Environmental Hotline, **1-800-253-2687 (1-800-CLEAN-UP),** or visit the Earth 911 Web site (**www.earth911.org**) to find the closest hazardous waste disposal site.

8. **Regularly inspect and maintain equipment.** Perform regular inspections and periodic maintenance on pesticide application equipment. This keeps it in good operating condition and ready for use. Do simple maintenance, such as greasing bearings, while you inspect the equipment. See Table 6-3 for a sample checklist for equipment maintenance. Always wear gloves and eye protection when repairing, cleaning, or maintaining equipment to protect yourself from pesticide residues. Keep a record of what you did and when for each piece of application equipment. Have a supply of repair parts on hand so you can quickly fix equipment. Check for the following problems with liquid application equipment:

   - weakened, dried, cracked, or leaking hoses (do not fix them by wrapping tape or other hose mender; replace with a new hose)

   - loose or leaking fittings and tank covers

   - damage to the tank or tank protective coating

   - broken parts

   - clogged or worn nozzles

   - clogged or dirty screens

   - other mechanical defects or wear

DUST AND GRANULE APPLICATION EQUIPMENT

Pesticide granules and certain dust formulations are applied dry, and these products need special application equipment (Table 6-2). Dust formulations are highly susceptible to drift, so outdoor uses of dusts are limited, and clients may not like having a dust coating on their plants. Dusts also present inhalation (breathing) hazards for applicators. Their greatest use is for pest control indoors in small cracks and crevices. Granules are generally applied to soil or turf. Some granules must be incorporated (worked in) into the soil.

Table 6-2. Selection Guide for Dust and Granular Pesticide Application Equipment.

DUST AND GRANULAR PESTICIDE APPLICATION EQUIPMENT		
	DESCRIPTION AND USES	**COMMENTS**
Hand-held dust applicator	Used to apply dusts, such as sulfur, in confined spaces.	Avoid breathing dusts.
Hand-operated broadcast sprayer	A manually operated granule spreader that is carried in front of the operator. Used for a pesticide application on turf.	Allows the application of granular pesticides over uneven areas. Effective in landscapes where a machine on wheels would be unusable. Drawbacks include inaccuracy of application and off-site deposition of granules.
Drop spreader	A mechanically driven granule applicator that is pushed in front of the operator. Used on turf and other landscape areas.	Requires accurate calibration but gives even, accurate distribution, since material drops straight out of the spreader. Overlap the wheel marks of each pass to avoid skips.
Rotary spreader	A mechanically driven granule applicator that is pushed in front of the operator. Used on turf and other landscape areas.	Requires accurate calibration. Can scatter too widely, resulting in contamination of nontarget areas. Overlap each pass for even coverage. Better to use a drop spreader to prevent pesticide contamination of surrounding nontarget areas.

Types of Dust and Granule Application Equipment

Dust Applicators. Dust applicators (Figure 6-14) combine the pesticide product dust with moving air and spread it evenly over an area by forcing dust-laden air out of a hopper. The pesticide dust passes through an orifice (opening) or through a hose aimed by the person making the application. Dusters have back or chest straps, though smaller units are hand-carried.

Hand-Operated Broadcast Spreaders. Hand-operated granule applicators (Figure 6-15), also known as belly grinders, usually hang from the operator's chest. Granules pass through an adjustable opening at the bottom of a cloth, metal, or plastic hopper and drop onto a spinning plate operated by a hand crank. The material shoots out in front of the operator, who turns the crank to achieve an even distribution of granules. These spreaders are often used to cover small to medium

2. List and describe uses for:
- *mechanical duster*
- *hand-operated broadcast spreader*
- *drop spreader-push spreader.*

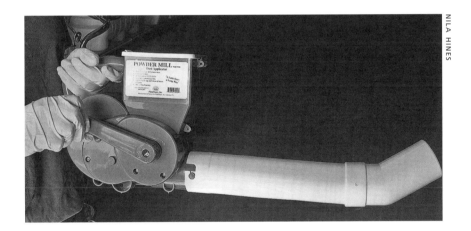

NILA HINES

Figure 6-14. When you use mechanical dust applicators, be very careful to avoid breathing dusts.

NILA HINES

Figure 6-15. Hand-operated granule spreaders are useful for small applications of granular pesticides. (They are also known as "belly grinder applicators.")

areas and areas with uneven terrain, but the swath is often too wide to keep granules off of sidewalks and streets.

Drop Spreaders. Several types of drop spreaders (Figure 6-16), also known as mechanically driven granule applicators, are available. Some have ground-wheel-driven metering devices attached to a hopper. Drop spreaders are the most accurate spreaders available for granules. To control the rate of application, adjust the openings that granules pass through. All the granules fall within the wheelbase, so slight overlapping of the wheels with each pass is necessary for uniform coverage. Read the pesticide label and booklets that come with the spreader so you are familiar with the settings and can determine which setting is best for the specific application you are doing.

Common problems associated with drop spreaders include

- skips from granules not dropping evenly or consistently on certain spots during an application
- too little or too much overlap
- uneven spreading when turning corners
- when conditions are moist, the hopper openings in the bottom may clog due to the granules clumping together

Figure 6-16. Drop spreaders are useful for applications of granular pesticides on lawns. Pesticide labels show spreader settings for various equipment brands.

Rotary Granule Spreaders. Rotary granule spreaders come in different sizes. Granules drop onto a spinning disc that scatters granules over a wide area. Use particular care if using a rotary spreader to leave an untreated border between nontarget areas and the treatment zone. They may be ground-wheel driven, so your walking speed affects the amount of off-site movement. Common problems with rotary granule spreaders include

- wide scatter, including to nontarget areas such as sidewalks, driveways, and patios

- the spinning disc turns faster as you move faster, scattering granules more widely (wider swath width)

- varying granule sizes and weights do not spread uniformly

- turning changes the rotation speed of the plate, causing uneven distribution

Dust and Granule Application Equipment Maintenance

Well-maintained application equipment is essential for the legal and effective use of pesticides. Without regular maintenance, you may apply more pesticide than is safe or legal, or not enough to be effective. Regular inspections and maintenance help avoid accidents and spills caused by broken equipment, bad fittings, damaged hoppers, or other problems.

4. Know how to clean, service, and maintain pesticide application equipment.

Before each application, inspect equipment for wear, corrosion, and damage. Replace or repair any defective parts. Clean equipment after every application. Wear protective clothing, rubber gloves, and eye protection when cleaning or repairing equipment. When not in use, store equipment in a way that prevents deterioration or damage. Keep equipment covered inside weatherproof buildings out of the sunlight.

Preventing Problems with Dust and Granule Application Equipment

Thoroughly clean application equipment after each use. Be sure to remove all pesticide residues. Lubricate moving parts according to the manufacturer's instructions. Inspect equipment and repair if any of the following are found:

- wear and corrosion

- rusted or corroded components

- broken parts

- clogged delivery systems
- other mechanical defects

By spending a few minutes each day inspecting and servicing pesticide application equipment, you increase the length of its useful life, help avoid costly breakdowns, and discover possible leaks. Develop your own checklist (Table 6-3) for inspecting and servicing each piece of equipment regularly to help remember what needs to be done for that particular device.

Table 6-3. Maintenance Checklist for Pesticide Application Equipment. Develop checklists for regularly inspecting and servicing each application device. Keep notes about inspections, repair, and maintenance.

MAINTENANCE CHECKLIST FOR PESTICIDE APPLICATION EQUIPMENT		
Equipment: _____ (backpack sprayer, granule applicator, etc.)	Date of Inspection: _____	
CHECK WHEN INSPECTED	**INSPECT FOR**	**ACTION TAKEN**
☐	Cleanliness of equipment (free from pesticide residues).	
☐	Weakened, dried, cracked, or leaking hoses.	
☐	Loose or leaking fittings and tank covers.	
☐	Damage to the tank or tank protective coating.	
☐	Broken parts.	
☐	Clogged or worn nozzles.	
☐	Clogged or dirty screens.	
☐	Mechanical defects or wear.	
☐	Bearings and all moving parts lubricated and functioning.	
☐	Rust or corrosion.	

Bait Applications

Pesticide baits combine pesticides with food, attractants, or feeding stimulants and require special application methods. Baits are used to control rodent pests as well as invertebrate pests such as ants and snails.

Bait application methods vary, depending on which pest you are controlling. A problem with baits is the risk to nontarget organisms such as children, dogs, and cats. Bait stations and specialized bait boxes can help prevent nontargets from coming into contact with bait pesticides. Bait stations also have the advantage of protecting the bait from rain and irrigation water.

Rodent baits. Baits used for rats, mice, ground squirrels, and other rodent pests are safest when used in bait stations (Figure 6-17) or bait boxes. Enclosed bait stations hold supplies of poisoned food baits, which attract target pests to enter and eat the bait. Use bait stations that prevent children, pets, and nontarget animals from contacting baits. Bait station openings should be the appropriate size for the pest being controlled, and a station should have at least two openings.

Be sure to read the pesticide bait label directions before using. Labels will have information on how to load bait stations. Bait stations should be tamper-resistant and secure so bait cannot be shaken out. Prevent loose bait from spreading outside the station. For example, put any bait scattered by squirrels back in the station.

Some rodent baits kill with a single feeding; others require multiple feedings to kill pests. Prebaiting with untreated grain for 5 or more days encourages squirrels to eat the treated bait when it is put in the station. Be sure to dispose of unused baits properly. Keep bait fresh; do not use moldy bait, as it will not be effective. The application method you use will depend on the bait product and the target pest (Table 6-4).

5. Know how to use bait and bait stations for pests.

Figure 6-17. Rodent bait stations, such as the one shown here, should be labeled with signal word, name of pesticide, and responsible party.

Underground Applications: Gophers. Underground applications are the preferred method for control of gophers. Bait applicator tools (Figure 6-18) are useful for putting bait in tunnels. See *Wildlife Pest Control around Gardens and Homes* (UC ANR Publication 21385) or *Pocket Gophers* (UC IPM Pest Note 7433, available at **www.ipm .ucdavis.edu**), for more information. Underground application may be the only legal method when using certain baits.

Use a probe to locate the main tunnel, which should be about 8 to 12 inches from the plugged side of the gopher's mound (see Figure 2-13) and 6 to 12 inches deep. Place bait underground using a probe

Table 6-4. Bait Placement for Rodent Pests. Combine use of baits with other management practices for best control.

BAIT PLACEMENT FOR RODENT PESTS		
PEST	**PLACEMENT OF BAIT OR STATIONS**	**CONCERNS**
Rats	In runways or next to burrows; next to walls; along travel routes.	Some baits may be used only in and around buildings but not in gardens and landscapes.
Mice	In areas of mouse activity.	Keep fresh bait present for at least 2 weeks.
Ground squirrels	Place stations at 100- to 200-foot intervals near burrows or runways. Prebaiting with untreated bait may be helpful.	Keep pets out of treated areas. Check daily. Keep bait fresh. Put any squirrel-scattered bait back in the station.
Gophers	In underground tunnels.	Do not place bait on soil surface. Remove dead gophers.

(Figure 6-18) in the main tunnel, not in the lateral tunnels. Do not scatter grain on the soil surface. Use a grain bait that lists gophers on the label as a target pest. Be sure to remove dead gophers so that pets and wildlife do not feed on them.

Snail and Slug Bait. Snails and slugs can be killed by scattering baits (Figure 6-19). Snail and slug bait stations reduce hazards and protect baits from moisture, however they reduce effectiveness.

The best timing for control is when snails and slugs are active. Sprinkle baits around sprinklers, close to walls and fences, or in moist, protected locations. Scatter baits along areas where snails travel. Snails and slugs tend to revisit food source sites, so place baits repeatedly in the same area. Never pile bait in mounds or clumps, because this makes bait attractive to pets and children.

Read the label on each bait product to become aware of the risks to nontarget species, such as dogs, cats, children, fish, and other animals. The different active ingredients in baits vary in terms of risk. Metaldehyde baits are quite attractive and toxic to dogs. Iron phosphate products are safe around animals, children, birds, fish, and other animals.

Insect Bait: Ants. Ants (Figure 6-20) are best controlled with baits. Ant baits are insecticides mixed with materials that attract worker ants looking for food. Workers take the bait back to the colony, and the active ingredients eventually kill the colony and queen. Baits may be liquids or solids and usually are prepackaged into ant stakes or small plastic bait stations. However, refillable bait stations are most effective for difficult ant problems. Bait stations protect baits from breakdown caused by sunlight (photodegradation) and keep children from coming into contact with insecticides. Some baits come in gel formulations that can be applied to cracks and crevices.

Figure 6-18. Gopher bait should not be scattered on the ground. Gophers will not come to above-ground bait stations. Use a probe to place gopher bait underground in the main tunnel.

Figure 6-19. Sprinkle snail and slug baits close to walls and fences or in moist, protected locations where snails and slugs travel. Do not pile bait in mounds. Iron phosphate baits are safer for pets than are metaldehyde products.

Figure 6-20. Bait products used for ant management.

FORMS

Ant bait

- solid (in bait station)
- liquid (in station or placed onto card by user)
- granules

Prepackaged

- ant stakes
- small plastic bait stations

PLACEMENT

- Place baits near nests, on ant trails beneath plants, or along edges where ants travel.
- Space every 10 to 20 feet outside building foundation.
- Install in the ground or near outside walls where ants are entering homes.
- Be sure to place out of reach of children and pets.

COMMENTS

- Cultural controls must be part of effective ant control.
- Refillable stations can be opened, checked, and refilled for serious ant problems.

Indoor plastic bait stations

An enclosed pesticide bait (ant stake)

Refillable ant bait stations

Bait effectiveness varies with ant species, availability of alternative food, pesticide active ingredient, type of bait, and time of year. To determine which bait works best, offer small quantities of several baits and watch to see which one the ants prefer. Baits are best placed near ant nests, on ant trails beneath plants, or along places where ants travel. Space bait stations every 10 to 20 feet.

Ants may be found on plants where they eat honeydew that is produced by aphids or soft scales. These ants can be kept out by banding tree trunks with sticky materials, such as Tanglefoot. Ant stakes with bait can also be used around trees. For more information, see *Ants* (UC IPM Pest Note 7411, available at **www.ipm.ucdavis.edu**).

Measuring and Mixing Pesticides

Pesticides are useful pest management tools only if you properly mix and apply them. All pesticides are hazardous chemicals, so they require special handling. This section covers methods of measuring and mixing pesticides, as well as making sure your application equipment puts out the correct amount of material. This way, you will get the greatest benefit from your time and investment.

Calibration is the process of measuring and adjusting the output of pesticide application equipment so that the desired amount of pesticide can be applied to a given area. Properly maintained and calibrated application equipment is key for the legal and effective use of pesticides. Without calibration, you may apply more pesticide than is safe or legal, or not enough to be effective. Regular calibration can help avoid accidents or spills caused by ruptured hoses, faulty fittings, damaged tanks, or other equipment problems.

6. Know proper procedures for mixing pesticide sprays, including how to measure pesticides safely and accurately.

PREPARATIONS FOR MEASURING AND MIXING PESTICIDES

Before you purchase a pesticide you should review the label to assure that it is registered (see Chapter 1) for the application you wish to make. Before you buy, mix, or apply any pesticide, review the label again to assure that you and any handlers have and will wear the required personal protective equipment for each handling task. Determine what type of PPE will be needed for measuring, mixing, and application by reading the PRECAUTIONARY STATEMENTS section of the label. Different types of PPE may be required for mixing than for application.

Before beginning to mix a pesticide, read the DIRECTIONS FOR USE section on the pesticide label. The label may mention the proper order to add the chemicals to the spray tank (Figure 6-21). If adjuvants (additives) are needed, these are usually added before any pesticides go into the tank, unless label instructions give a different order. When combining pesticides of different formulations, note the proper order for their addition, which usually is wettable powders first, then flowables, then water-soluble concentrates, then emulsifiable concentrates. For example, when combining a water-soluble concentrate with a wettable powder, add the wettable powder to the spray tank first; or, when mixing an emulsifiable concentrate with a flowable,

Figure 6-21. Read the mixing directions and precautionary statements on the pesticide label.

For medical emergencies, call a poison control center or doctor. You may also contact the National Pesticide Information Center at 1-800-858-7378

PRECAUTIONARY STATEMENTS
HAZARDS TO HUMANS AND DOMESTIC ANIMALS
CAUTION: Harmful if swallowed, inhaled or absorbed through the skin. Avoid contact with eyes, skin or clothing. Avoid breathing spray mists or vapors. Applicators should wear long-sleeved shirt and long pants, chemical resistant gloves such as Barrier Laminate, Nitrile Rubber, Neoprene Rubber or Viton, and shoes plus socks. Wash thoroughly with soap and water after handling. Remove and wash contaminated clothing before reuse. Avoid contamination of food. Do not ship or store with food, feeds, drugs or clothing.

Environmental Hazards
This pesticide is toxic to fish. Do not apply directly to water, or to areas where surface water is present or to intertidal areas below the mean high water mark. Do not contaminate water by cleaning of equipment or disposal of equipment washwaters.

Physical or Chemical Hazards
Combustible. Do not use or store near heat or open flame. Do not cut or weld container.

add the flowable first. However, if a different order is given on the label, follow the label directions. Be sure not to mix incompatible pesticides, such as sulfur and oils. Mixing order is important because it reduces incompatibility problems, assures a uniform mixture, increases user safety, and improves the effectiveness of the application.

Before adding any pesticides to the spray tank, gather everything you need for the mixing process. Make a safety survey: Check your application equipment to be sure there are no cracked hoses or other leaks and that the filters, screens, and nozzles are clean. Gather any measuring devices and other materials you will need. Have an emergency supply of soap and clean water within 100 feet of the mixing area for washing in case of an exposure. Make sure you have and will wear the required PPE.

The water you use to fill a spray tank should be clean enough to prevent damage to application equipment and be free of sand, dirt, and other foreign matter. Sand or dirt causes excessive wear on pumps and nozzles and clogs filters, screens, and nozzles.

Be sure you have a pH testing kit to check the acidity or alkalinity of the water. Determine whether you will need to adjust the pH of the water in the spray tank with a buffer (which helps keep the pH constant) or acidifier (which makes the water more acidic). Get adjuvants if you may need them and make sure you read their labels. Do not use the water if you detect any chemical odors, since chemicals may react unfavorably with some pesticides. Some herbicides adhere (stick) to soil particles, so if the water is contaminated, the herbicide application might not be effective. If you have any doubts about the water quality, locate another source for filling your spray tank.

Obtain the Right Measuring Devices and Use Them Properly to Avoid Hazards. Measure pesticides carefully, accurately, and safely (Figure 6-22). Inexact measuring can produce large errors in the amount of pesticide being applied and may cause injury to plants, people, or the environment. It may also result in hazardous waste that needs special disposal.

Liquids and some granular pesticides are measured by volume, while dusts, powders, and most dry formulations are usually measured by weight. Pesticide labels use the English system of measurement: liquid volumes are in fluid ounces, pints, quarts, and gallons; dry weights are in pounds and ounces (Table 6-5).

You will need an assortment of glass or plastic measuring utensils and devices (Figure 6-23). DO NOT USE ANY UTENSILS OR DEVICES THAT MIGHT ALSO BE USED FOR MEASURING, HOLDING. OR STORING FOOD. Get measuring utensils, from one cup to one gallon, from pesticide dealers. Some pesticides react with metal, especially aluminum and iron, so don't use metal measuring utensils. Some pesticides will stick to plastic measuring containers. Separate measuring containers should be used for herbicides if staining is noticed.

Figure 6-22. Measure or weigh pesticides carefully.

Table 6-5. Conversions for Fluid Measure and Weight. In this table, each row describes a quantity in 2 or 3 ways. For example, 8 fluid ounces is the same amount as 1 cup or ½ pint.

CONVERSIONS FOR FLUID MEASURE AND WEIGHT		
FLUID MEASURES		
¼ fluid ounce		1½ teaspoons
½ fluid ounce	1 tablespoon	3 teaspoons
1 fluid ounce	2 tablespoons	⅛ cup
8 fluid ounces	1 cup	½ pint
16 fluid ounces	2 cups	1 pint
32 fluid ounces	4 cups	1 quart
128 fluid ounces	16 cups	1 gallon
WEIGHT		
1 ounce		28.35 grams
1 pound	16 ounces	454 grams
1 kilogram	2.2 pounds	1,000 grams

Figure 6-23. Liquid measuring tools come in different sizes. Measuring tools must be calibrated to the smallest unit you will measure. Smaller quantities require smaller measuring devices, such as an eye dropper, for accurate measuring.

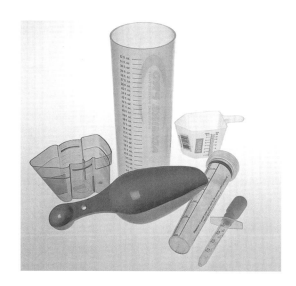

7. Be aware of the hazards involved with using improper measuring and mixing tools.

The measuring device used should be calibrated or marked in the smallest unit in which the pesticide is being measured or weighed. For example, you cannot use a measuring device that is calibrated in 1-cup graduations (markings) to accurately measure 12 ounces of liquid; in this case, you would need a measuring device calibrated in ounces. Use a calibrated eyedropper to measure small quantities of liquid. If measuring by weight, use an accurate scale (Figure 6-24). For measuring dry materials, use marked measuring cups and spoons. Certain pesticide products may remove the painted graduation markings (calibrations) on measuring devices. The painted graduations can be permanently scribed with a knife blade to extend the useful life of the measuring container.

Some measuring equipment that is designated only for pesticide use can be mistaken for kitchen utensils. Identify all your pesticide measuring utensils in a very clear manner and only use them for pesticides. For example, paint handles with brightly colored waterproof paint or attach waterproof labels to each utensil. Keep all measuring and weighing equipment locked when not in use so it cannot be used for other purposes. Clean and wash utensils before they are stored to prevent contaminating future mixtures.

Purchase the Right Size Package. Pesticide products are sold in packages of various sizes with different weights or volumes. Whenever possible, plan a mixture that uses exactly the amount of pesticide in a package. Buy small amounts of pesticides and use them soon after purchasing. It may cost you more per unit to purchase pesticides in smaller packages, but the added convenience and safety of not having to weigh or measure them or dispose of leftover hazardous materials will be worth the investment. Premixed ready-to-use products may be the most convenient and appropriate formulations for spot treatments and very small jobs.

Choose a Safe Mixing Location and Protect Yourself. Refer to the PRECAUTIONARY STATEMENTS section of the pesticide label for the specific PPE you will need for mixing and loading pesticides. Wear proper eye protection when handling all pesticides. If mixing outdoors, stand upwind to reduce the risk of exposure and prevent inhaling (breathing) dusts. Protect your hands and body with chemical-resistant gloves and the other label-required PPE.

Maintenance gardeners should not be using pesticides that require the use of a respirator or dust mask. However, if you are considering using one, be sure to get training and updated regulatory information about how to use respiratory protective equipment safely for the particular product you will use. Poorly fitted respiratory protection can give you a false sense of security about your safety. It is very important to increase your knowledge and understanding before even considering the use of respirators. You may need a respirator if the pesticide label's PRECAUTIONARY STATEMENTS say "Do not breathe vapor or mist" and you are spraying areas above waist high.

Liquids can be spilled and splashed, so wear a rubber apron. A face shield, goggles, or other protective eyewear and chemical-resistant gloves must be worn by any employees who mix pesticides, even if these requirements are not on the pesticide label. (California regulations require eye protection and gloves when mixing and when using hand-held equipment.) Reduce the risk of spills or splashes into your face and eyes by always measuring and pouring pesticides *below* eye level (see Figure 6-22).

Carefully select an appropriate location for mixing pesticides. Choose a spot that can be easily cleaned in case of a spill and that is away from drains or waterways. Measure and weigh chemicals in a clear, open area. Consider the surroundings and the environment of the mixing site to reduce the chance of problems.

Figure 6-24. When measuring by weight, use an accurate scale. The markings on the scale must be as small as the units you are weighing.

Mixing a Pesticide Solution

Begin mixing by filling your spray tank at least half full with clean water (unless directed otherwise by the pesticide label). Don't completely fill the tank. Leave room for the pesticide, adjuvants, and rinsate (wash water) from triple-rinsing containers. Check the water with a pH testing kit (see the section "Preparations for Measuring and Mixing Pesticides") and adjust the pH of the water in the spray tank at this time by using buffer or acidifer, as needed. Add adjuvants and combinations of pesticides to the tank in the correct order as described on the DIRECTIONS FOR USE section of the label and earlier in this chapter.

Open pesticide containers carefully to prevent spilling and to make resealing easier. Cut open paper containers with a sharp knife or scissors. Do not tear. Metal, glass and plastic bottles, and plastic containers may have protective seals that you must break open before use. Most of these containers can be resealed easily.

After measuring or weighing the correct amount of pesticide, carefully pour it into the partially filled spray tank. Drain empty liquid pesticide containers into the spray tank for 30 more seconds after they have been emptied, then add rinse water, swirl it around, and drain back into the spray tank. Do this at least two more times or until the rinsate runs clear. After each draining, fill the container about one-quarter full of water, put the cap back on, and shake or swirl for several seconds to mix the residue with water. Pour the rinse solution into the spray tank. (See Chapter 1 for more information on triple-rinsing containers.) Punch a hole in the container so it cannot be reused and then dispose of it. Rinsed, clean pesticide containers can be taken to the local landfill. Home-use pesticide product containers that are empty may be put with normal household trash, but be sure to follow the product label directions on correct disposal methods.

When you have completed using the measuring cups and spoons, also rinse them and put the rinsate back into the spray tank. Once all of the pesticide has been added, along with the pesticide container rinsate, fill your spray tank to its final volume. Do not allow the tank to overflow during filling. Also, never let the hose, pipe, or other filling device reach below the top of the tank or come in contact with liquid in the tank, to decrease the risk of the pesticide flowing back to contaminate the water source (see Figure 6-8).

Calibration for Pesticide Applications

Benefits of Calibration. Calibration is the process you use and all the adjustments you make to your pesticide application equipment to assure that the correct amount of pesticide is applied to a given area. The rate and dilution of the pesticide must be correct. Improper calibration causes too little or too much pesticide to reach the target site. Accurately calibrated equipment helps deliver the desired amount of pesticide evenly to the target area. Failure to calibrate properly is a common cause of poor pesticide applications. Calibration is required for several reasons. (Figure 6-25)

- **Legal.** If you use pesticides improperly you are subject to criminal and civil charges, resulting in fines and lawsuits. Poor calibration can lead to application of pesticides above label rates. You are liable for injuries or damage to people, the environment, crops, and property caused by improper pesticide application.

- **Pest management.** If you use less pesticide than the label rate you may fail to control the pest and waste your time and money. Inadequate amounts of pesticide can lead to problems such as pesticide resistance and pest resurgence. Using too much pesticide can harm natural pest predators, treated surfaces, and the environment.

8. Explain the importance of calibrating pesticide application equipment.

Figure 6-25. Calibrating pesticide application equipment is important for these reasons.

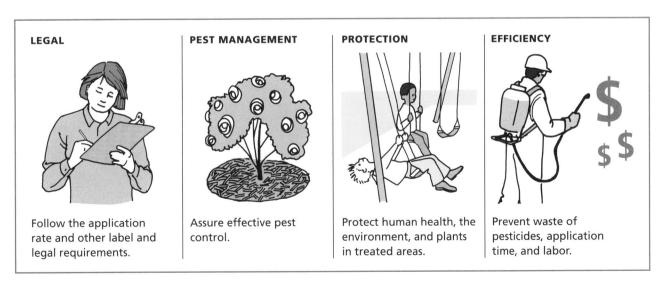

LEGAL

Follow the application rate and other label and legal requirements.

PEST MANAGEMENT

Assure effective pest control.

PROTECTION

Protect human health, the environment, and plants in treated areas.

EFFICIENCY

Prevent waste of pesticides, application time, and labor.

- **Protection of human health.** If you apply pesticides at rates higher than the label recommends, you may harm the health of the applicator, workers, and people contacting the treated areas. Dangerous levels of residue may remain on landscape plants when a pesticide is overapplied.

- **Protection of the environment.** The pesticides you use in a landscape may cause environmental problems if you do not use them properly. Avoid harm to beneficial insects such as honey bees and wildlife by carefully calibrating your equipment to maintain your application rates within rates on the label. Also, correct calibration helps prevent drift and runoff.

- **Protection of treated plants and areas.** Certain pesticides are phytotoxic (harmful to plants) and can damage sensitive plants if you use them at higher than recommended rates due to poor calibration. Manufacturers evaluate phytotoxicity during product testing of pesticides to determine safe concentrations.

- **Efficiency.** Applying too much or too little pesticide wastes not only pesticides but also your time and adds extra costs to the application. Pesticides are expensive, and the extra applications when the first treatment fails are costly since they require more labor and create more wear and tear on your equipment.

9. Know how to calibrate liquid sprayers and dry applicators for turfgrass and ornamental applications.

Calibration Methods. Calibrate your pesticide application equipment regularly (several times a year). Be sure to calibrate at the beginning of the season when you bring the equipment out of storage and when the rate or speed of application changes. Calibrate whenever you are using a new pesticide product and anytime there is a possibility of a change that would affect the output of pesticide to the site.

Regular calibration checking is important even if you always spray the same pesticide at the same rate, because equipment parts wear out, which affects the flow rate. Nozzles and pumps are especially prone to wear, which can decrease or increase output rate. Also, since pesticide formulations vary, anytime you use a different product, review the label directions and determine whether you need to recalibrate for a new application rate. Each piece of equipment used for pesticide applications should be calibrated for each person who uses that equipment.

Calibrating for Liquid Pesticide Applications. Before beginning the calibration process, gather together needed information and equipment.

- Assemble tools needed for calibration (Sidebar 6.1).

- Read the pesticide label to determine the pesticide application rate and any other application information. Rates may be given as the amount of product per square area (for example, 4 ounces per 1,000 square feet), amount of pesticide per gallon of water, or a percentage (for example, a 2% solution).

- Determine how large an area (or the number of plants) you will be treating (Sidebar 6.2).

- Wear personal protective equipment to protect yourself from pesticide residues, including eye protection, chemical-resistant gloves, and appropriate footwear.

- Use clean water for calibrating liquid sprayers.

Most liquid pesticides applied in hand-operated equipment are mixed as a percentage (for example, a 2% solution). Some will specify a rate for a specific area (for example, 1 ounce per 500 square feet). You must apply pesticides as diluted solutions according to label instructions. Figure 6-26 describes steps to follow when calibrating liquid pesticide application equipment for a known area.

10. Know how to calculate the amount of pesticide to apply to a known area.

SIDEBAR 6.2—MEASURING THE AREA TO TREAT

You must make accurate area measurements when applying a pesticide to turf or large beds of ornamentals. Use a tape measure to determine the dimensions of the area to be treated. Use the methods below to calculate the size of the area to be treated.

STEPS TO CALCULATE THE AREA OF A RECTANGLE

1. Measure the length of the area.

2. Measure the width.

3. Multiply the width by the length. This will give you the area of the space to be treated.

AREA = WIDTH × LENGTH

STEPS TO CALCULATE THE AREA OF A TRIANGLE

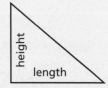

1. Make sure the triangle has one 90-degree angle.

2. Measure the height of the triangular area you are going to treat.

3. Measure the length of the triangular area.

4. Multiply the height by the length, then multiply the result by ½. This will give you the area of the space to be treated.

AREA = HEIGHT × LENGTH × ½

Carry out your calibration process at an appropriate site. A large area of turf may be suitable for some materials. If the equipment is used to apply herbicides, calibrate it on an area free of desirable plants, such as a vacant lot, because herbicide residues may remain in the tank. Even though calibration is carried out with water only, you should wear your PPE since the spray equipment often has pesticide residues.

Walk at a steady pace when you calibrate your equipment, moving your wand evenly across the application area as you would with the actual pesticide. If you slow your pace or change your spraying pattern this will affect the output rate and calibration as well. To assure accurate calibrations and applications, perform the calibration at the desired (operating) pressure for your spray equipment. Perform calibrations three times and then average the figures. Recheck your calculations.

Calibrating for Granule Pesticide Applications. Granule application equipment is calibrated by adjusting the settings on the application equipment to fit the size and volume of the granular pesticide you are using. Follow the instructions on the pesticide label under

Figure 6-26. Steps to calibrate a liquid pesticide sprayer.

Before you start:

- Run the sprayer to flush out the hoses.
- Make sure your tank is properly rinsed.
- Make sure you have clean and nonleaking nozzles and screens.
- Check nozzles to make sure they are spraying properly at the desired pattern and size.

1. Mark off 200 square feet.

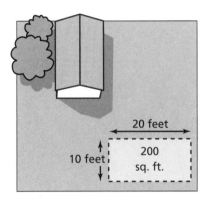

2. Fill the spray tank with clean water and mark the level.

water level

NILA HINES

3. Spray the water on the marked 200-square-foot area, as if you were making an actual pesticide application. Operate at the proper speed.

4. Mark the new water level in the spray tank.

volume of water after spraying the 200-square-foot area

5. Measure the amount of water needed to refill the sprayer to the first marked water level. This measured amount of water equals the volume of pesticide solution needed to cover the 200 square feet.

volume of pesticide needed to cover the 200-square-foot area

6. Use the amount from Step 5 to find out how much liquid you need to cover the area you are treating. For instance, if you are treating 1,000 square feet, you will need 5 times the amount of water needed for 200 square feet (from step 3). You may need multiple tanks.

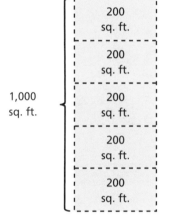

1,000 sq. ft.

200 sq. ft.
200 sq. ft.
200 sq. ft.
200 sq. ft.
200 sq. ft.

7. Read the label and determine the pesticide application rate. Calculate the total amount of pesticide you will need for the entire treatment area and the total amount of liquid mixture. Calculate the amount of pesticide needed for each tank for the desired application rate.

DIRECTIONS FOR USE to properly calibrate your equipment. Granule application equipment must be calibrated for each type of granule pesticide and equipment that you will use. Granules vary in size and shape from one pesticide to the next, affecting their flow rate from the hopper or container. Weather and the surface conditions of the treatment area also may affect granule applications.

Before beginning the calibration process, gather together needed information and equipment.

- Assemble tools needed for calibration.

- Read the pesticide label to determine the pesticide application rate and any other application information. Rates will be given as amount of product per area (for example, 2 pounds per 1,000 square feet). The pesticide should have a booklet with information on the different spreader settings for the desired rate of application.

- Determine the location and size of the test area you will be treating (for example, 100 square feet).

- Wear personal protective equipment to protect yourself from pesticide residues, including eye protection, chemical-resistant gloves, and appropriate footwear.

- Be sure your applicator is clean, rust free, lubricated, and ready to use.

Carry out your calibration process at an appropriate site. A large area of turf is suitable for most granular materials. Once you have read the pesticide label and determined the best application rate, note the setting recommended for your type of spreader for that rate of application. Set your spreader at this number and then test it to be sure you are getting the delivery rate you want. To increase the uniformity of granule applications, apply one-half of the required material in one direction (north to south) and then the other half in the perpendicular direction (east to west).

Calibration of granular materials involves doing an application to a measured test area, determining the weight or volume of the granules applied to the test area, and then calculating whether the rate of application in the test area is within 10% of the desired rate. If not, make adjustments in your travel speed or spreader setting. Once you have the desired spreader setting, you can apply at that setting to the entire treatment area. Sidebar 6.3 gives information on granule applications and assuring an accurate application rate.

SIDEBAR 6.3—GRANULE APPLICATION EQUIPMENT CALIBRATION

Compare the amount of pesticide you actually used with the amount you expected to use. Do the calibration on the treatment site or a similar one labeled for the pesticide.

1. **Determine the desired application rate.**

2. **Check the label for recommended spreader settings.** Set your spreader to the appropriate setting for the rate of application.

3. **Fill the spreader with the appropriate amount of granules for the premeasured area.** Apply the granules over this premeasured area, watching the applicator and the site as you apply.

4. **Note the results:**
   - increase the setting on your spreader if there is still product in the hopper,

     OR

   - if you run out of product before finishing, lower the setting.

Once you determine the right setting for the desired rate, record this setting number.

SPREADER SETTINGS & CALIBRATIONS

Drop spreaders and rotary spreaders should be calibrated for uniform application of this product.

Single Pass — Operate the equipment at intervals corresponding to the width or swath of the spreader. For drop spreaders, overlap the wheel tracks to ensure complete coverage. Close the spreader openings when turning to change directions or when stopping.

Calibrate — For 3.6 pounds of product per 1,000 square feet of turfgrass: Check your spreader on 275 square feet and adjust to apply at the rate of 1 pound of product per 275 square feet.

IMPORTANT - It is important to follow the directions as indicated on this quality lawn care product as over application may cause injury to your lawn. Spreader settings are approximate. Differences may occur due to condition of spreader, speed at which applied and roughness of area treated. Be sure to check spreader before beginning, adjusting if necessary. Consult owner's manual. *Never apply by hand.*
To avoid gaps and streaks, first spread border of lawn and then fill in center with uniform, parallel passes. Walk at a steady pace so as to apply evenly throughout the lawn.

Coverage —To determine how much you need to apply, multiply the length of your lawn by its width. This equals your total square footage. Deduct any non-lawn areas (house, garden, etc.). One bag covers 5,000 sq ft.

Rotary Spreader Settings		Drop Spreader Settings	
Republic EZ	5	Republic EZ	6
Ortho	5	Ortho	6
Republic EZ Grow	10	Precision	4 1/2
Quaker	4	Scotts EvenGreen	6
True Temper	4	Scotts Drop	7
EV-N-Spred	18	Vigoro	5
Precision	4 1/2		
Scotts EasyGreen	28		
Scotts SpeedyGreen	6 1/2		
Vigoro	7 1/2		

Figure 6-27. Soil drench pesticide application. Following label directions, measure the insecticide into a bucket, dilute it with water, and pour it onto soil near the base of the tree trunk or bush.

Calibrating for Soil Drench Applications. Soil drenching (Figure 6-27) beneath infested plants is an effective method to use when applying some systemic insecticides to trees, hedges, shrubs, or clumped groups of plants. Pesticides applied this way are absorbed by plant roots and move to growing points in trees and bushes. This method of application must be shown on the label for the pesticide you are using. Trees growing along city streets and other woody plantings in highly populated areas are suitable for soil drench applications. Drench applications are especially useful because they reduce the risk of spray drift exposure to people or plants.

The timing of soil drench applications depends on the target pest. Pesticides applied by soil drench take time to move through the plant. Be sure that treated trees and shrubs are well watered before doing a soil drench, as soil moisture is critical for plants to take up the systemic pesticide.

Follow the pesticide product label directions to calculate the rate for a soil drench application. Product labels usually indicate the amount of pesticide needed per inch of plant height, or per inch of trunk diameter (distance across the trunk) at breast height (DBH), or per inch of trunk circumference (distance around the trunk) (Sidebar 6.4). It is very important to know whether the label rate is based on tree diameter or circumference. For shrubs in grouped plantings, calculate the amount of pesticide to use based on the total height in feet of the plants. Read the pesticide label to determine the correct amount of pesticide to use for the planted area you will be treating.

The pesticide used in a soil drench application must be diluted with water. Add part of the measured water to a bucket (this bucket should be used only for pesticide mixtures), then add the measured amount of pesticide product, and then fill the bucket with the remainder of the measured water. Pour the mixture onto the soil near tree trunks or the base of the shrubs, as directed on the label. Application measurements for trees and shrubs are discussed in Sidebar 6.4.

The calculation may be different for a soil injection application, depending on label instructions. If you are considering doing a soil injection application, review the product label carefully to be sure you have the correct application equipment.

SIDEBAR 6.4—CALCULATING TRUNK DIAMETER AND APPLICATION RATES

1. **Read the label to find the rate of application.** For instance, the label may say to apply 1.2 teaspoons (tsp) of a systemic pesticide for every inch of the circumference of the trunk. Some rates require you to determine the diameter of the tree.

2. **Measure the tree.** To determine how much pesticide is needed for drench applications, you need to know the circumference or diameter of the tree trunk at chest height. To measure the circumference of the trunk (the distance around it), use a tape measure or string.

   Once you know the circumference, you can find the diameter by multiplying the circumference by 0.32. For example, a trunk that has a circumference of 32 inches would have a diameter of about 10 inches (32 inches × 0.32 = 10.24 inches).

3. **To determine the total pesticide you will need, multiply the tree size by the application rate.** For instance, if your rate is 1.2 teaspoons per inch of circumference and your circumference is 15 inches:

   15 in × 1.2 tsp = 18 tsp

4. **Convert the teaspoons to liquid ounces (oz).** (6 teaspoons = 1 liquid ounce):

   18 tsp ÷ 6 tsp/oz = 3 oz

5. **Multiply by the number of trees to be treated.** If you have two trees:

   3 oz × 2 = 6 oz

   A total of 6 ounces of the pesticide product will need to be applied to the soil surrounding the two trees.

6. **Next, determine how much water to mix with the product by reading the label.** Some labels specify mixing the pesticide with 1 gallon of water for trees less than 40 inches in diameter and 2 gallons of water for trees more the 40 inches in diameter. For applications to multiple trees, calculate the amount of pesticide to use based on the added sizes of the plants. Mix the pesticides, following the label rate instructions, in a bucket containing the measured amount of water.

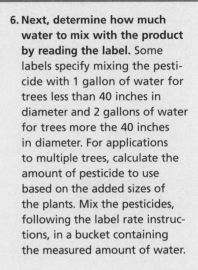

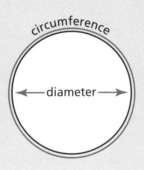

circumference
the distance around the trunk

diameter
a straight distance through a trunk

11. Know why the following are necessary for a successful pesticide application:
- *appropriate equipment*
- *correct application rate and dilution*
- *proper application site*
- *appropriate coverage (broadcast versus spot treatment)*
- *vulnerable life stage of the target pest*
- *personal protective equipment*

■ Applying Pesticides Safely and Effectively

To use pesticides safely and effectively, you have to make sure that the pesticide is only applied to the treatment area and that it is applied in the proper amount. Most applications require even coverage of treated surfaces. For example, both sides of leaf surfaces must be coated with pesticide droplets for adequate control of many plant-feeding insects or mites. Sprays improperly aimed at the foliage may cause the leaves to clump together and prevent spray droplets from reaching some leaf surfaces.

Safe applications require that you use the right equipment, have good application techniques, prevent drift or other off-site movement, and are aware of potential hazards and know how to avoid them. Spills, leaks, and drift may cause pesticides to get into nontarget areas and waste the pesticide product. Successful and safe pesticide applications require the appropriate application equipment (including personal protective equipment), correct application rates and dilution, a proper site, appropriate coverage and timing, and a vulnerable life stage of the target pest (Figure 6-28).

SITE CHARACTERISTICS AND ENVIRONMENTAL HAZARDS

Before beginning a pesticide application, check the landscaped area and nearby areas and note all potential hazards. Check for nontarget organisms or structures that might be damaged by pesticides or water or by the physical movement of equipment through the area. Ditches, embankments, steep slopes, electrical wires, irrigation systems, and electric fences can create hazards to people doing the application or the equipment. Also check to see whether people or pets are around or likely to return to the site. Check for ponds with fish or other pesticide-sensitive sites.

EQUIPMENT OPERATION

Learn how to operate pesticide application equipment effectively and consistently. For example, in turf applications the walking pace of the applicator must remain constant to assure even pesticide coverage.

When using hand-held spray wands, develop a technique that keeps the application uniform on all parts of the surfaces being treated. Make sure the spray reaches the upper foliage or branches of trees or shrubs. Direct the spray to all sides of the plant, but avoid unnecessary runoff and overspray onto nontarget plants. When spraying upwards, be sure

ESSENTIAL ELEMENTS FOR SUCCESSFUL APPLICATION	
	Correct application equipment including personal protective equipment
	Correct pesticide application rate and dilution for the site
	Correct type of coverage (broadcast or spot treatment)
	Life stage of target pest when pesticide is most likely to be effective
	A site where the pesticide can be safely applied without injuring people or the environment

Figure 6-28. Effective and safe pesticide applications require several conditions.

the spray does not drip down onto the applicator's arm or head, or drift to nontarget plants. Walk at a regular pace and avoid uneven steps when operating backpack sprayers. Hold the nozzle steady and keep it at a uniform distance (height) from the target surface.

Maintain even pressure in the spray tank. When the sprayer is running out of mix, be cautious of air in the wand causing fine atomization of the spray mix so that a fine mist drifts off the target area. Return any spray in the wand back into the tank before transporting to prevent accidental discharge. Use a containment device to catch any remaining drips from wand tips during transit.

COVERAGE: SPOT TREATMENTS VERSUS BROADCAST TREATMENTS

You can increase selectivity and reduce the amount of pesticide used by applying pesticides as spot treatments rather than making a broadcast application. Spot treatments are appropriate for many applications by maintenance gardeners. For example, certain weeds may grow in scattered clumps. Spot treatment involves treating just the weed clumps or patches rather than the whole area. At times, insects and mites congregate in a few areas before spreading more widely, especially if the infestation is just beginning. Control these pests by treating only the infested plants or parts of plants where pests are together. In addition, most pests occur only on certain plant species, so spot-treat only the infested plants (Figure 6-29).

TIMING APPLICATIONS FOR EFFECTIVE PEST CONTROL

The timing of an application is important for good control of target pests as well as for protection of pests' natural enemies and beneficial insects. Because some pesticides are more effective than others at controlling different life stages, time your pesticide application for the most susceptible stage of the target pest. Understanding the biology of the pest will help you determine the best life stages for treatment and decide whether a pesticide application will be effective.

Avoid injuring nontarget organisms, such as bees or hummingbirds, by making applications when they are not present in the treatment area. This works well for honey bees because they forage only during warm daylight hours. If you apply pesticides during the early morning, late afternoon, or on cold and cloudy days you will usually reduce hazards to honey bees.

FOLLOW-UP MONITORING

You should monitor every pesticide application right after completion to determine whether it was successful. Compare the amount of pesticide actually used with the anticipated amount. This should vary by no more than 10%. If more or less pesticide was applied,

Figure 6-29. Small scattered pest infestations can be controlled with spot applications. Selective herbicides (such as 2,4-D) to control broadleaf plants may be spot-applied.

12. Know how to determine whether a pesticide application was successful.

determine the cause. Check the sprayer calibration and tank-mixing procedures and recalculate the size of the target area. Look for clogged or worn nozzles and wear or blockage in the sprayer pumping system. Also, check your walking speed.

While wearing the handler PPE, inspect the application site to make sure coverage was adequate and uniform. Look for

- signs of too much runoff of the pesticide applied
- lack of penetration into dense foliage or lack of coverage on plant surfaces that require treatment
- uneven coverage

Make a second follow-up visit a day or so after an application of insecticides or acaricides. Before entering the treatment area, review the label for PPE requirements and be sure to minimize body contact with treated surfaces. Try to assess whether the application was effective at controlling the target pest (Figure 6-30). Remember that broad-spectrum insecticides kill natural enemies, which could lead to outbreaks of other pests. In addition, look for other problems, such as phytotoxicity or spotting of nearby painted surfaces, which would indicate drift.

Follow up fungicide applications with an inspection to verify that the fungicide was effective. Look for new plant growth or other signs that further infection has been prevented. Remember, most fungicides do not suppress or kill a pathogen; they prevent a pathogen from infecting a plant. Often repeat applications are required, especially if conditions such as wet weather favoring fungal growth continue.

After applying herbicides, you might not see anything for days or weeks. Follow up to see which weed species were controlled and which were partially or not controlled. Also look for any damage to nontarget plants. Record this information and use it to determine whether additional management is required. Often, combining chemical and cultural practices gives the best weed control.

Record your follow-up observations in the same notebook in which you record other aspects of the pesticide application and other pest observations and pest management practices. This information will be useful when you plan future applications for the same pest or in similar target locations. Keep records of all pesticides used at each treatment location and remember to report use to the county agricultural commissioner.

Figure 6-30. Monitor the site after pesticide applications to see if the pesticide was effective. Look to see if the pest has been controlled. See if plants have suffered any damage from the treatment.

■ Chapter 6 Review Questions

1. Why is it important to use separate pesticide application equipment for applying herbicides only?
   - ☐ a. to assure that susceptible plants are not injured by herbicide residues when fungicides or insecticides are applied
   - ☐ b. to make the pesticide application more efficient
   - ☐ c. to save time cleaning out the pesticide tank
   - ☐ d. to reduce fire hazard, risk of explosion, or possibility of damage to the equipment

2. What component of liquid pesticide application equipment is used to move the pesticide mixture from the tank to the nozzle?
   - ☐ a. trigger
   - ☐ b. filter
   - ☐ c. pump
   - ☐ d. screens

3. What type of nozzle is used for applying insecticides and fungicides to dense foliage?
   - ☐ a. fan nozzle
   - ☐ b. flat-spray nozzle
   - ☐ c. cone nozzle
   - ☐ d. low-volume

4. Why is it important to conduct regular inspections of pesticide application equipment?
   - ☐ a. to make sure you have adjustable nozzles
   - ☐ b. to prevent accidents or spills caused by ruptured hoses, faulty fittings, damaged tanks, or other problems
   - ☐ c. to prevent theft
   - ☐ d. it is required by law

5. What should be done with unused mixed pesticides in the spray tank?
   - ☐ a. keep in sprayer tank for several days until needed
   - ☐ b. as soon as possible spray on plants according to label directions until empty
   - ☐ c. drain into sanitary sewer
   - ☐ d. spray it onto an industrial drain as soon as possible

6. The best way to clean screens and nozzles is
   - ☐ a. to blow on them
   - ☐ b. use a metal wire
   - ☐ c. with a stick
   - ☐ d. flush with clean water and soft brush

7. Dry granules can be applied using a
   - ☐ a. drop spreader
   - ☐ b. hand-held dust applicator
   - ☐ c. hose-end sprayer
   - ☐ d. trigger pump

8. Bait stations are recommended for use in urban areas because
   - ☐ a. rodents are more likely to take the bait
   - ☐ b. they help protect pets
   - ☐ c. they allow for more targeted applications for some pests and lower the risk of human exposure
   - ☐ d. all of the above

9. Which are important for a successful spot or broadcast pesticide application?
   - ☐ a. vulnerable life stage of the target pest
   - ☐ b. the best equipment for use at the site
   - ☐ c. the label rate and dilution
   - ☐ d. all of the above

10. Frequent calibration of your application equipment will assure that you
    - ☐ a. are using the correct amount of pesticide
    - ☐ b. always use the maximum amount of pesticide allowed by law
    - ☐ c. have fewer mechanical breakdowns and less wear and tear of sprayer parts
    - ☐ d. can make effective pesticide applications during severe weather conditions

11. For liquid calibration, which factors need to be known?
    - ☐ a. tank size
    - ☐ b. size of area to be treated
    - ☐ c. pesticide application rate, tank capacity, and size of area to be treated
    - ☐ d. size of area to be treated, tank capacity, and nozzle type

12. Calibration of granule applicators requires that you know
    ☐ a. the treatment area size
    ☐ b. the applicator setting for the desired rate
    ☐ c. the actual applicator output
    ☐ d. all of the above

13. To most effectively use systemic insecticides as a drench, you must
    ☐ a. measure the height of all trees in the area
    ☐ b. know precisely how many shrubs you wish to treat
    ☐ c. read and follow the label application directions
    ☐ d. be sure to apply to very dry soil

14. One of the methods to determine whether a pesticide application is successful is to
    ☐ a. inspect plants to see if natural enemies have declined
    ☐ b. verify that the amount of product you used matches the amount you estimated
    ☐ c. look for signs of excessive runoff of the pesticide applied
    ☐ d. determine which weed species were controlled immediately after you apply a preemergent herbicide

(Answer sheet is on pages 206–207.)

■ Answer Sheet for Review Questions

CHAPTER 1	CHAPTER 2	CHAPTER 3
1. d	1. b	1. c
2. b and d	2. d	2. a
3. c	3. c	3. d
4. d	4. d	4. a
5. d	5. d	5. d
6. d	6. d	6. b
6. a	7. a	7. b
8. c	8. c	8. A. ladybeetle
9. d	9. a	B. green lacewing
10. c	10. b	C. syrphid fly
11. a	11. A. ant	9. a
12. d	B. lawn grub	10. c
	C. snail	11. d
	D. scale	
	E. mealybug	
	F. whitefly	
	G. mite	
	H. aphid	

CHAPTER 4	CHAPTER 5	CHAPTER 6
1. b	1. d	1. a
2. c	2. b	2. c
3. d	3. a	3. c
4. c	4. d	4. b
5. d	5. c	5. b
6. c	6. d	6. d
7. a	7. d	7. a
8. b	8. a	8. d
9. b	9. d	9. d
10. a	10. c	10. a
11. d	11. a	11. c
12. b	12. b	12. d
13. b	13. d	13. c
14. b		14. b

Glossary

abiotic. Nonliving factors, such as wind, water, temperature, or soil type or texture.

absorb. To soak up or take in a liquid or powder.

acaricide. A pesticide used to control mites.

accidental misapplication. An unintentional incorrect application of a pesticide.

accumulate. To increase in quantity within an area, such as in the soil or tissues of a plant or animal.

acidic. A solution or substance that has a pH lower than 7.0.

acidifier. An adjuvant used to lower the pH (or acidify) the water being mixed with a pesticide. Pesticides often break down more slowly if the spray water is slightly acid.

action threshold. The level of pest damage or pest infestation that warrants some type of control action.

active ingredient (a.i.). The material in the pesticide formulation that actually destroys or affects the target pest or performs the application's desired function.

acute effect, acute illness. An illness or injury that becomes apparent soon after an organism is exposed to a pesticide. Acute illnesses tend to develop quickly after exposure to pesticides, as compared to the slower development of chronic illnesses.

acute onset. Symptoms of pesticide-related illness or injury that appear soon after the exposure incident.

adjuvant. A material added to a pesticide mixture to improve or alter the deposition, toxic effects, mixing ability, persistence, or other qualities of the active ingredient.

aerating. A process used to reduce soil compaction in turf. Two processes are used: one uses metal prongs to create holes in the turf, and the other uses hollow tubes to remove plugs of soil from the turf. Also known as aeration.

aerosol. Very fine liquid droplets, often emitted from a pressurized can.

agricultural commissioner. The official in each county in California who has the responsibility for enforcing state and federal pesticide regulations. County agricultural commissioners and their staff frequently inspect pesticide applications and application sites. All pest control for hire that includes the use of pesticides must be reported monthly to the county agricultural commissioner.

agricultural use (of pesticides). A classification of certain pesticides that limits their use to production agriculture; also includes pesticide applications to landscape, turf, parks, golf courses, cemeteries, and along roadside and railroad rights-of-way.

air gap. A space between the filling hose and the liquid in the pesticide tank that prevents the backflow of pesticide liquids into the water source. The air gap should be a minimum of 2 times the diameter of the filling hose or pipe.

alkaline. A solution or substance that has a pH greater than 7.0.

amending. Adding materials, such as nutrients or organic material, to the soil in order to make up for deficiencies.

annual. A type of plant that passes through its entire life cycle in 1 year or less.

annual weeds. Weed species that have an annual life cycle.

anticoagulant. A type of rodenticide that causes death by preventing normal blood clotting.

application rate. The amount of pesticide that is applied to a known area, such as 1,000 square feet.

aquatic. Pertaining to something that grows or lives in water or is frequently found in water.

attractant. A substance that attracts a particular species of animal. When manufactured to attract pests to traps or poisoned bait, attractants are considered pesticides.

back siphoning. The process of pesticide-contaminated water being sucked from a spray tank back into a well or other water source. To prevent back siphoning, provide an air gap or backflow prevention (antisiphon) device in the pipe or hose used to fill a spray tank.

backflow. *See* back siphoning.

backpack sprayer. A small portable sprayer carried on the back of the person making the pesticide application. Also known as a knapsack sprayer.

bacterium (pl., bacteria). A one-celled microscopic plantlike organism that lives in soil, water, organic matter, or in the bodies of plants and animals. Some bacteria cause plant or animal diseases.

bait. A food or foodlike substance that is used to attract pest animals. Pesticides combined with these substances are also called baits.

bait station. A box or similar device designed to hold poisoned bait for controlling rodents, insects, or other pests. Bait stations usually have baffles or small openings to prevent access to the bait by nontarget animals.

belly grinder. A hand-operated device used to apply pesticide granules. The device straps to the front of the operator, who then turns a crank while walking forward through the treatment area. Also known as a hand-operated broadcast spreader.

beneficial. Helpful in some way to people, such as a beneficial plant or insect.

beneficial organism. An organism that is helpful in some way to people, such as a parasitic wasp, predatory insect, or honey bee.

biennial. A plant that completes part of its life cycle in one year and the remainder of its life cycle the following year.

biological control. The action of parasites, predators, pathogens, or competitors in reducing pest populations. Biological control may occur naturally or it may be the result of the manipulation or introduction of biological control agents by people.

biological control agent. Any living organism that reduces the population of a pest or the severity of its damage, including parasites, predators, pathogens, or competitors.

biology. Knowledge about the life habits of a plant or animal.

biotic. Pertaining to living organisms, such as the influences living organisms have on all pest populations. Also refers to damage caused by pests.

botanical. Derived from plants or plant parts.

brand name. The registered or trade name given to a pesticide by its manufacturer or formulator. A specific pesticide may be sold under several brand names.

breakdown. The process by which chemicals, such as pesticides, decompose into other chemicals.

broad-spectrum pesticide. A pesticide that affects many different species or types of pests. May also injure many nontarget organisms.

broadcast application. A method for applying granular pesticides by dispersing them over a wide area using a spinning disc or other mechanical device.

broadleaves. One of the major plant groups; they have net-veined leaves that usually are broader than grass leaves. Broadleaves include many herbaceous plants, shrubs, and trees.

buds. Newly emerging plant parts that will turn into flowers, leaves, or shoots.

buffer, buffering agent. An adjuvant (additive) that lowers the pH of a spray solution and, depending on its concentration, can maintain the pH within a narrow range even if acidic or alkaline materials are added to the solution.

bulbs. The underground, resting stages of certain perennial plants.

calibration. The procedure used and adjustments made to pesticide application equipment so that the correct amount of pesticide is applied to a given area.

California Department of Pesticide Regulation (DPR). The state department within the California Environmental Protection Agency (CAL/EPA) responsible for regulating the use of pesticides in California. *See* Environmental Protection Agency.

carcinogenic. Having the ability to produce cancer.

cardiopulmonary resuscitation (CPR). A procedure designed to restore normal breathing and heartbeat after breathing and heartbeat have stopped. Rescue breaths and chest compressions are combined to help circulate blood within the victim's body.

carrier. The liquid or powdered inert (other) substance that is combined with the active ingredient in a pesticide formulation. May also apply to the water or oil that a pesticide is mixed with prior to application.

caustic. Quality of a chemical describing its ability to burn or injure the skin, eyes, or mouth and intestinal lining.

CAUTION. The signal word used on labels of the least-toxic pesticides. These pesticides have an oral LD_{50} greater than 500 mg/kg and a dermal LD_{50} greater than 2,000 mg/kg. *Also see* LD_{50} and signal word.

certified pesticide applicator. A person who has demonstrated through an examination process the ability to safely handle and apply pesticides.

chemical name. The official name given to a chemical compound to distinguish it from other chemical compounds.

chemical resistant. A waterproof material, such as personal protective equipment, that allows no movement of pesticide through it.

CHEMTREC. A chemical-industry-supported organization that provides assistance and advice on pesticide emergencies. The telephone number of CHEMTREC is 1-800-424-9300.

chronic. Pertaining to long duration or frequent recurrence.

chronic illness. An illness that lasts for a long period. Cancer, respiratory disorders, and neurological disorders are examples of chronic illnesses that have been associated with exposure to some types of pesticides. Chronic illnesses tend to develop over time, as compared to the sudden onset of acute illnesses.

common name. The recognized nonscientific name given to plants or animals. Many pesticides also have common names, separate from their brand names and chemical names.

compatible. The condition in which two or more pesticides mix without unsatisfactory chemical or physical changes.

compressed air sprayer. A hand-held sprayer that uses a hand-operated air pump to pressurize the liquid pesticide mixture in a sealed tank. The air pressure forces the pesticide out of the tank and through the hose to a nozzle.

cone nozzle. A style of nozzle that produces liquid pesticide sprays in a solid cone pattern or a hollow cone pattern.

conflict with label. Not following the directions, requirements, or prohibitions on the pesticide label. This is an illegal practice. *Also see* deviation.

contact, contact poison. A pesticide that provides control when target pests come into physical contact with it.

contamination, contaminant. Tainted with a substance that is not supposed to be in that location. A pesticide residue off the target area would be a contaminant.

control agent. An organism or chemical, such as a natural enemy or a pesticide, that reduces pest populations.

convulsions. Contortions of the body caused by violent, involuntary muscular contractions. Convulsions can be a symptom of pesticide poisoning.

corrosive materials. Certain chemicals that react with metals or other materials. Some pesticides are corrosive, and special handling requirements are needed when using them.

coverage. The degree to which a pesticide is distributed over a target surface.

coverall. A one- or two-piece garment of closely woven fabric that covers the entire body except for the head, hands, and feet, worn as personal protective equipment. Coveralls differ from, and should not be confused with, work clothing.

CPR. *See* cardiopulmonary resuscitation.

cultural practice. Plant management activity other than the use of a pesticide. Certain cultural practices can prevent a pest from causing damage. Examples include planting pest-resistant varieties, hand-weeding, and irrigation timing.

DANGER. The signal word used on labels of highly hazardous pesticides. These pesticides have an oral LD_{50} of less than 50 mg/kg or a dermal LD_{50} of less than 200 mg/kg. Also, these have specific, serious health or environmental hazards. *Also see* LD_{50} and signal word.

decontamination. The most important step in reducing potential injury when someone has been exposed to a pesticide. Decontamination involves thoroughly washing the exposed skin with soap and water or flushing the exposed eye with a gentle stream of running water.

degradation. The breakdown of a pesticide into an inactive or less-active form. Environmental conditions, impurities, and microorganisms can contribute to the degradation of pesticides.

dermal. Pertaining to the skin. Dermal entry is one of the major ways pesticides can enter the body and possibly cause poisoning.

dermal absorption. *See* skin absorption.

developmental stages. The different forms that animals and plants take as they grow into maturity.

deviations. Circumstances when you do not need to follow the label exactly. *See* conflict with label.

diagnosis. The identity of the cause of the problem.

dilute. To add water or other liquid to lower concentration.

directions for use. The instructions found on a pesticide label indicating the proper procedures for mixing and application.

disease. A condition, caused by biotic or abiotic factors, that impairs some or all of the normal functions of a living organism. Typically characterized by specific signs or symptoms.

disposal site. A site for disposing of materials such as household and commercial waste. Some disposal sites have special provisions for accepting household and other hazardous waste. Disposal sites that accept pesticides and empty pesticide containers must comply with many state and local environmental laws.

dissolve. To pass into solution.

dormant. Inactive during winter or periods of cold weather.

dose. The measured quantity of a pesticide. Often the size of the dose determines the degree of effectiveness, or, in the case of affecting nontarget organisms, the degree of injury or illness.

DPR. *See* California Department of Pesticide Regulation.

drift. The movement of pesticide dust, spray, or vapor through the air away from the application site.

dust. Finely ground pesticide particles, sometimes combined with inert (other) materials. Dusts are applied without being mixed with water or other liquids.

ecological. Related to the interrelationship between living organisms and the environment.

ecosystem. Plants, animals, and microorganisms and the physical environment they live in, interacting and affecting each other.

efficacy. The ability of a pesticide to produce a desired effect on a target organism.

emergence. The appearance of a seeding plant through the surface of the soil or an adult insect from a pupa.

emergency medical care. Arrangements made ahead of time for treatment of pesticide illness or injury.

emulsifiable concentrate. A pesticide formulation consisting of a petroleum-based liquid and emulsifiers that enable it to be mixed with water for application.

emulsifier. An adjuvant that is added to a pesticide formulation to permit petroleum-based pesticides to mix with water.

endangered species. Rare or unusual living organisms whose existence is threatened by people's activities, including the use of some types of pesticide.

entomopathogenic. Having the ability to cause disease in insects.

environment. All of the living organisms and nonliving features of a defined area, including air, soil, and water.

environmental contamination. The spread of pesticides away from the application site into the environment, usually with the potential to cause harm to organisms.

Environmental Protection Agency (EPA). The federal government agency responsible for regulating pesticide use in the United States. *Also see* California Department of Pesticide Regulation.

eradicant. A pesticide that is used to destroy a pest organism such as a fungus.

eradication. The pest management strategy that attempts to eliminate all members of a pest species from a defined area.

evaporate, evaporation. The process by which a liquid turns into a gas or vapor.

exposure. The unwanted contact of pesticides or pesticide residues with people, other organisms, or the environment.

federally restricted. An EPA classification for pesticides that restricts their use to certified pesticide applicators.

fertilization. The addition of plant nutrients to the soil.

fictitious business name. A business operating under a name other than the name of the legal owner. A maintenance gardener business with a fictitious business name is required to include this name as part of the DPR's application for a pest control business license.

first aid. The immediate assistance provided to someone who has been exposed to a pesticide. First aid for pesticide exposure usually involves

removing contaminated clothing and washing the affected area of the body to remove as much of the pesticide material as possible. First aid is not a substitute for competent medical treatment.

flaming. A nonchemical weed control method involving the use of a propane-fueled torch to burn or scorch emerged weeds.

flat-spray (flat fan) nozzle. A nozzle that produces a fan-shaped pattern with more droplets in the center part of the fan than at either edge.

flow rate. The amount of pesticide being expelled by a pesticide sprayer or granule applicator per unit of time.

flowable. A pesticide formulation consisting of finely ground particles of active ingredient mixed with a liquid, along with emulsifiers, to form a concentrated emulsion. These liquids are mixed with water for dilution prior to spraying.

foliage. The leaves of a plant.

formulation. A manufacturer's mixture of pesticide active ingredient with inert (other) materials added to improve the mixing and handling qualities of the pesticide.

fungicide. A pesticide used for control of fungi.

fungus (pl., fungi). A multicellular lower organism such as mold, mildew, rust, or smut. The fungus body normally consists of strands called the mycelium.

germinate. To begin growing, especially plants that have emerged from seeds.

granule, granular formulation. A dry formulation of pesticide active ingredient and inert (other) materials compressed into small, pebble-like shapes.

ground-wheel-driven. Describes a hand-operated granule applicator that uses the rotation of one of its wheels to drive the operation of its dispersal mechanism (often a spinning disc).

habitat. The place where a species of plant or animal lives and grows.

half-life. The time for a pesticide to lose half of its toxicity or effectiveness.

hand-operated backpack sprayer. A backpack sprayer that has a hand-operated hydraulic pump, operated by moving a lever up and down, that forces liquid pesticides through a hose to the nozzle.

hand-operated broadcast spreader. *See* belly grinder.

handler. A person who mixes, loads, transfers, applies, or assists with the application of pesticides; who maintains, services, repairs, adjusts, cleans, or handles equipment used to apply pesticides; or who works with unsealed pesticide containers.

hazard. The degree of danger to people or the environment posed by a pesticide.

hazardous materials. Materials, including many pesticides, that have been classified by regulatory agencies as being harmful to the environment or to people. Hazardous materials require special handling and must be stored and transported in accord with legal requirements.

hazardous waste. A hazardous material for which there is no further use. Remains from a pesticide spill cleanup often are hazardous wastes. Hazardous wastes can be disposed of only through special hazardous material disposal programs and locations.

heat illness. The potentially life-threatening overheating of the body under working conditions. Usually occurs when proper preventive measures are not taken, such as working during the cool parts of the day, drinking plenty of water, taking frequent breaks in the shade to cool down, and removing or loosening personal protective equipment during breaks. California regulations require that pesticide handlers receive training on how to recognize, avoid, and treat heat illness.

herbaceous plant. A plant that is herb-like, usually having little or no woody tissue.

herbicide. A pesticide used for the control of weeds.

honeydew. The sweet, sticky fluid secreted by plant-feeding insects such as aphids and scales. A coating of honeydew on leaf surfaces promotes the buildup of sooty mold fungus. Ants, bees, wasps, and other insects feed on honeydew and may protect and care for the plant-feeding insects from attack by other insects.

hopper. The bin of a granule applicator where the pesticide is placed for application; granules move from the hopper to the metering device for dispersal.

horticulture advisors. University of California specialists in most counties of California who serve as a resource for state residents on pest management, water management, soil management, plant nutrition, and many other issues.

hose bibb. Faucet.

hose-end sprayer. A simple application device for small areas. It consists of a glass or plastic jar holding a pesticide mixture that is sucked up by and diluted in a stream of water from a garden hose and then sprayed out through a nozzle.

host. A plant or animal species that provides sustenance for another organism.

host resistance. The ability of a host plant or animal to ward off or resist attack by pests or to be able to tolerate damage caused by pests.

hygiene. As it applies to pesticide exposure, hygiene involves washing exposed body areas promptly to remove pesticide residues.

illegal. Against the law.

immature. Young. *See* developmental stages.

impermeable. Having the ability to resist penetration by a substance or object.

incidental. Something that is done in conjunction with other activities. In the case of maintenance gardeners, pest control activities are incidental services provided for their clients as part of a landscape maintenance business, as opposed to pesticide application services performed for hire as the primary function of the business.

incompatible. The result when two or more pesticides are combined and they react to make the mixture unusable.

inert. Not having any chemical activity.

inert (other) ingredients. All materials in the pesticide formulation other than the active ingredient. May still be toxic or hazardous to people.

infection. The establishment of a microorganism within the tissues of a host plant or animal.

infestation. A troublesome invasion of pests within an area such as a landscaped location.

ingest. To take into the body through the mouth, as by eating or drinking.

inhalation. The method of entry of pesticides through the nose or mouth into the lungs.

insect. An invertebrate animal with an external skeleton and jointed body parts. Adults have three body parts (head, thorax, and abdomen), with six legs attached to the thorax and two antennae on the head. Many are pests but some are beneficial or predators or parasites of pests.

insecticide. A pesticide used for the control of insects. Some insecticides are also labeled for control of ticks, mites, spiders, and other arthropods.

integrated pest management (IPM). An ecosystem-based strategy for managing pests that focuses on long-term prevention of pests or their damage through a combination of cultural practices, mechanical and physical controls, biological controls, and pesticides. Key components are prevention, regular monitoring, pest and symptom identification, treating only when necessary, and integrating appropriate management methods. The goal is to achieve long-term suppression of target pests with minimal impact on nontarget organisms and the environment.

invertebrate. Any animal without an internal skeleton, such as an insect, spider, mite, worm, nematode, snail, or slug.

irreversible injury. A health condition caused by certain types of exposure to some pesticides, and for which there is no medical treatment or chance of recovery.

irrigation. Applying water for plant growth.

knapsack sprayer. *See* backpack sprayer.

knowledge expectations. The breadth of knowledge about an occupation or procedure, such as pesticide handling, that a person performing this job is expected to have. Regulations establish minimal expectations for pesticide applicators, and certification examinations test whether a person's knowledge meets these expectations.

label, labeling. The pesticide label and all associated materials, including supplemental labels and manufacturer's information. The pesticide label is a legal document.

landscape fabric. A porous synthetic cloth that is placed over the soil to slow growth of weeds.

larva (pl., larvae). The active immature form of insects that undergo metamorphosis to reach adulthood.

LD$_{50}$. The lethal dose of a pesticide that will kill half of the animals in a test population. LD$_{50}$ values are given in milligrams per kilogram of test animal body weight (mg/kg).

leaching. The process by which some pesticides move down through the soil, usually dissolved in water, with the possibility that they will reach groundwater.

lethal. Capable of causing death.

lethal dose. *See* LD$_{50}$.

liable. Legally responsible.

life cycle. The series of stages that an organism goes through during its life.

life stage. Any one of the development stages that a living organism passes through over time. Plants and animals (especially insects) pass through several life stages during which their susceptibility or tolerance to pesticides varies.

long-term health problem. A pesticide-related illness or disease that may extend over months, years, or a lifetime.

management. *See* pest management.

Material Safety Data Sheet (MSDS). An information sheet provided by a pesticide manufacturer that describes the chemical qualities, hazards, safety precautions, and emergency procedures to be followed in case of a spill, fire, or other emergency.

mechanical duster. A device designed to apply pesticide dusts, which are finely ground pesticide particles sometimes combined with inert (other) materials and applied without mixing with water or other liquids.

medical facility. A clinic, hospital, or physician's office where immediate medical care for pesticide-related illness or injury can be obtained.

metamorphosis. The changes that take place in certain types of living organisms, such as insects, as they develop from eggs through adults. Some families of insects undergo "complete metamorphosis," meaning that their young do not resemble their adults.

microorganism. An organism of microscopic size, such as a bacterium, virus, fungus, etc.

misapplication. The improper use of a pesticide, such as exceeding the label rate or applying the material to a site not listed on the label.

mite. A very small invertebrate animal with an external skeleton and jointed body parts. Adults have two body parts (head and abdomen) and no antennae. Adults usually have eight legs attached to the abdomen, and immatures have six. Many are pests but some are beneficial or predators of pests.

mixing. The process of opening pesticide containers, weighing or measuring specified amounts, and transferring these materials into application equipment

mode of action. The mechanism by which a pesticide kills or controls the target organism.

molluscicide. A pesticide used to control slugs and snails.

monitoring, pest monitoring. The process of carefully watching the activities, growth, and development of pest organisms over time.

Monthly Pesticide Use Report. A form that in California must be completed and submitted to the county agricultural commissioner's office by the tenth of the month following any month in which pesticides are applied to landscapes, turf, or interiorscapes.

MSDS. *See* Material Safety Data Sheet.

mulch. A layer of material applied to cover the soil surface in planting beds and other areas to control weeds and reduce soil moisture loss.

mycelium (pl., mycelia). The vegetative body of a fungus, consisting of a mass of slender, threadlike strands.

natural areas. Locations where plants grow without being cultivated or planted.

natural enemy. An organism that can kill a pest organism; includes predators, pathogens, parasites, and competitors.

negligent application. A pesticide application in which the applicator fails to exercise proper care or to follow label instructions, with the potential result of injury or illness to people, property, or the environment.

nematode. An elongated, cylindrical, nonsegmented worm. Most nematodes are microscopic; some are parasites of plants or animals.

neoprene. A synthetic rubber material used to make gloves, boots, and clothing for protection against pesticide exposure.

nonselective. A pesticide having action against many pest species rather than just a few.

nontarget organism. An animal or plant that lies within a pesticide-treated area but is not the intended target of the pesticide application.

notification. Informing homeowners or residents about pesticide applications that take place on their property.

nozzle. The mechanical device at the tip of a liquid pesticide application device from which the pesticide is discharged. The type and size of the nozzle determine the application rate, droplet size, and spray pattern.

nutritional deficiency. Lacking minerals that are essential for growth.

nymph. Immature stage of an insect that has incomplete or gradual metamorphosis, or the immature stage of a mite. Insect nymphs resemble the adult insects except they are smaller and lack wings.

off-site movement. Any movement of a pesticide from the location where it was applied. Off-site movement occurs through drift, volatilization, water runoff, sediment movement, erosion, pruning, and blowing dust, and transportation on organisms or equipment.

oral. Pertaining to the mouth. This is one of the routes by which pesticides can enter the body.

organic matter. Material in soil that has come from a living organism such as leaves, stems, bark, and other plant material that breaks down and contributes to the fertility and structure of soil. Organic matter has a higher number of microorganisms than does soil with less organic matter.

organism. Any living thing.

orifice. The opening of a nozzle, which affects the spray droplet size and spray pattern.

ornamentals. Cultivated plants that are grown for purposes other than production of food or fiber.

parasite. An organism (animal, plant, or microorganism) that lives and feeds in or on a larger host. Unlike predators, parasitic organisms have a prolonged and specialized relationship with their hosts, usually parasitizing only one host individual in their lifetime.

pathogen. A microorganism that causes a disease.

pellet. A pesticide formulation consisting of the dry active ingredient and various inert (other) materials pressed into uniform-sized granules.

percentage. One of the ways a pesticide can be diluted for application: solutions are made that contain a certain percentage of the pesticide formulation or its active ingredient.

perennial. A plant that lives longer than 2 years, or in some cases, indefinitely. Some perennial plants lose their leaves and become dormant during winter; others may die back and resprout from underground root or stem structures each year. Evergreens are perennial plants that do not die back or become dormant.

persistent, persistence. Pesticides that remain active in the environment for long periods because they are not easily broken down by microorganisms or environmental factors.

personal hygiene. *See* hygiene.

personal protective equipment (PPE). Devices and garments that protect handlers from exposure to pesticides. These include coveralls, eye protection, and chemical-resistant gloves, boots, aprons, and hats.

pest. An organism that interferes with the availability, quality, or value of a plant, other managed resource, or the environment.

Pest Control Business License. The license that a business must obtain from the California Department of Pesticide Regulation before it can engage in pest control for hire.

pest management. Lowering pest populations or reducing pest damage using a variety of methods so that pests are kept at tolerable levels and plant damage is minimized.

Pest Notes. A resource on the Internet developed by the UC Statewide Integrated Pest Management Program that provides up-to-date information on managing pests in landscape, turf, interiorscape, and other settings. Pest Notes can be viewed at **http://www.ipm.ucdavis .edu/PMG/selectnewpest .home.html.**

pest resistant varieties. *See* host resistance.

pest resurgence. *See* resurgence.

pesticide. Any substance or mixture of substances intended for preventing, destroying, repelling, or mitigating any insect, rodent, nematode, fungus, plant, or any other living thing that is recognized as a pest; also, any substance or mixture of substances intended for use as a plant growth regulator, defoliant, or desiccant.

pesticide container. A pesticide material's original packaging, including the pesticide label.

pesticide fate. What happens to a pesticide after it has been released into the environment.

pesticide formulation. The pesticide material as it comes in its original container, consisting of the active ingredient blended with inert (other) materials.

pesticide handler. *See* handler.

pesticide resistance. Genetic qualities of a pest population that enable individuals to resist the effects of certain types of pesticide that are toxic to other, less-resistant members of that species.

Pesticide Safety Information Series (PSIS). A series of informational sheets developed and distributed by the California Department of Pesticide Regulation that pertains to pesticide handling, personal protective equipment, emergency first aid, medical supervision, and other pesticide-related topics. The N series are for pesticide users in nonproduction agriculture settings such as landscapes.

pesticide use hazard. The potential for a pesticide to cause injury or damage during handling or application.

pesticide use record. A record of the pesticide applications made to a specific location.

pesticide use report. Pesticide application information made during one month, on an official DPR form, submitted to the county agricultural commissioner.

pH. A measure of the concentration of hydrogen ions in a solution. As the number of hydrogen ions increases, the pH reading gets lower and the solution becomes more acidic.

phytotoxic. Injurious to plants.

plant disease. *See* disease.

plant growth regulator (PGR). A pesticide used to regulate or alter the normal growth of plants or the development of plant parts.

poison. A substance, such as certain pesticides, that causes serious injury or death if small amounts are ingested, inhaled, or absorbed through the skin or eyes.

postemergent. An herbicide applied after emergence of a specified weed.

posting. The placing of signs around an area to inform residents and the public that the area has been treated with a pesticide.

powder. A finely ground dust containing pesticide active ingredient and inert (other) materials. This powder is mixed with water and then applied as a liquid spray.

PPE. *See* personal protective equipment.

precautionary statements. The section on a pesticide label that lists human and environmental hazards. Personal protective equipment requirements are also listed there, along with first aid instructions and information for physicians.

predaceous. Having the habit of hunting and eating other animals.

predator. An animal that attacks, kills, and eats other animals.

preemergent. An herbicide applied before weed emergence to control the weeds as they sprout from seeds and before they push through the soil surface.

pressure. The amount of force that an application equipment pump applies to the liquid pesticide mixture in order to force it through the nozzle.

preventive pest control. Steps taken to prevent pest damage or infestation, including such methods as planting pest-resistant plant varieties.

propellant. A material such as compressed air or gas used to propel a spray liquid or dust onto target surfaces.

protectant. A pesticide that provides a chemical barrier against pest attack.

protective clothing. Garments of personal protective equipment that cover the body, including the arms and legs.

pump. Part of a liquid pesticide application system that causes the movement of the liquid from the tank to the nozzle.

pupa (pl., pupae). In insects having complete metamorphosis, an individual in the resting life stage between larval and adult forms.

pyrethroid. A synthetic pesticide that mimics pyrethrin, a botanical pesticide derived from certain species of chrysanthemum flowers. Pyrethroids are much more persistent and more toxic to pests and natural enemies than natural pyrethrins are.

Qualified Applicator Certificate (QAC). The credential required for individuals applying or supervising the incidental application of any pesticides as part of a maintenance gardening business. To obtain a QAC, an individual must pass the required examination administered by the California Department of Pesticide Regulation.

Qualified Applicator License (QAL). The credential required for individuals applying or supervising the pesticide application operations of a landscape maintenance pest control business. To obtain a QAL, an individual must pass the required examinations administered by the California Department of Pesticide Regulation.

rate. The quantity or volume of liquid spray, dust, or granules that is applied to an area over a specified period.

ready-to-use (RTU). A special pesticide formulation type that requires no dilution or other mixing before use. RTU pesticides are often packaged in aerosol or trigger pump containers for home and garden use.

reentry interval. A period of time that must elapse after the application of a pesticide before it is safe to allow people into the treated area without requiring that they wear personal protective equipment.

registered pesticide. A pesticide that has been reviewed and approved for specific uses by the EPA. It may be applied only to sites or plants listed on the label. California registered pesticides are reviewed and approved by the California Department of Pesticide Regulation.

regulations. The guidelines or working rules that a regulatory agency uses to carry out and enforce laws.

repellent. A pesticide used to keep target pests away from a treated area by saturating the area with an odor that is disagreeable to the pest.

rescue breathing. Also known as artificial respiration. Mouth-to-mouth breathing of air into a person who is not breathing to restore breathing. Rescue breathing is administered if the victim has a pulse. *Also see* cardiopulmonary resuscitation.

residue. Traces of pesticide that remain on treated surfaces after a pesticide application.

resistance. *See* pesticide resistance or host resistance.

resistant varieties. *See* pest-resistant varieties.

respirator or respiratory protection equipment. A device that filters out pesticide dusts, mists, and vapors to protect the wearer from respiratory exposure during mixing, loading, and application of pesticides.

restricted-use. *See* restricted-use pesticide.

restricted-use permit. A permit issued by a county agricultural commissioner office that enables an individual to possess and apply a restricted-use pesticide.

restricted-use pesticide. A pesticide that can only be possessed or used by a certified applicator who has a restricted-use permit from the county agricultural commissioner.

resurgence. The sudden increase of a pest population after some event, such as a pesticide application.

reversible injury. A pesticide-related injury or illness that can be reversed through medical intervention or the body's healing process.

rhizome. An underground stem of certain types of plants, often capable of growing roots at its nodes to sprout new plants.

rinsate. Liquid that has been used for rinsing pesticide containers or spray equipment.

rodenticide. A pesticide used to control rats, mice, gophers, squirrels, and other rodents.

route of exposure. The path by which a pesticide gets onto or into the body. The four routes of exposure are dermal (on or through the skin), ocular (on or in the eyes), respiratory (into the lungs), and oral (through the mouth or by swallowing).

RTU. *See* ready-to-use.

runoff. The liquid spray material that drips from the foliage of treated plants or from other treated surfaces. Also, the rainwater or irrigation water that leaves an area; this water may contain trace amounts of pesticide.

secondary pest. An organism that becomes a serious pest only after a natural enemy, competitor, or primary pest has been eliminated through some type of pest control method.

selective pesticide. A pesticide that has a mode of action against only a single pest species or a small number of pest species.

selectivity. The degree to which a particular pesticide will kill some organisms without harming others. Phenoxy herbicides, for example, exhibit selectivity in that they control broadleaf plants but not grasses.

service container. Any container other than the original pesticide container that holds concentrated or diluted pesticide mixtures, including the sprayer tank.

shelf life. The maximum period of time that a pesticide can remain in storage before it loses some of its effectiveness.

shingling. The clumping or sticking together of plant foliage caused by the force of a liquid spray. Shingling prevents spray droplets from reaching all surfaces of the foliage and may result in poor pest control.

shoot. New plant stem growth.

signal word. One of three words (DANGER, WARNING, or CAUTION) found on every pesticide label to indicate the relative hazard of the chemical. *Also see* toxicity category.

site. The area where pesticides are applied for control of a pest.

skin absorption. The passage of pesticides through the skin into the bloodstream or other organs of the body. Also called dermal absorption.

skull and crossbones. The symbol on the label of a pesticide that is highly poisonous. This symbol is always accompanied by the signal word DANGER and the word POISON.

soil profile. The characteristics and differences of a soil at a particular depth.

solarization. A control method for weeds, weed seeds, soil pathogens, nematodes, and other soil-inhabiting pests that does not use pesticides. Moist soil is covered with clear plastic film during periods of hot weather. Heat from the sun is trapped beneath the film, raising the soil temperature high enough to destroy seeds and kill living organisms.

soluble. Able to dissolve completely in a liquid.

solution. A liquid that contains dissolved substances, such as a soluble pesticide.

solvent. A liquid capable of dissolving certain chemicals.

spore. A reproductive structure produced by some plants, fungi, and microorganisms that is resistant to environmental influences.

spot treatment. A method for applying pesticides only in small, localized areas where pests congregate, rather to a larger, general area.

spray nozzle. *See* nozzle.

spreader. A device used to apply granular pesticides, usually on a lawn.

statement of practical treatment. A section of the pesticide label that provides information on treating people who have been exposed to the pesticide. This includes emergency first aid information.

stolon. An aboveground runner stem found in some plant species.

stomach poison. A pesticide that kills target animals that ingest it.

summer annuals. Plants whose seeds sprout in the spring, grow and produce seeds, and then die during the summer or fall.

supplemental label. Additional instructions and information not found on the pesticide label because the physical label on the container is too small, but legally considered to be part of the pesticide's labeling.

surface water. Water contained in lakes or ponds or flowing in streams, rivers, and canals.

susceptible life stage. The life stage of a pest organism that is most susceptible to the pesticide used to control it. In general, insects are most susceptible during the larval or juvenile stage, and weeds are most susceptible during the seedling stage.

symptom. Any abnormal condition that is caused by exposure to a pesticide and can be seen or felt or can be detected by examination or laboratory testing.

systemic, systemic pesticide. A pesticide that is taken up by a plant and moves, after application, to other tissues in the plant.

tank. The part of the pesticide application system that stores the pesticide or mixture that will be applied.

tank capacity. The largest volume of liquid that can be put into the tank of pesticide application equipment.

tank mix. A mixture of pesticides or of fertilizers and pesticides that are applied together in a single application.

target. Either the pest that is being controlled or surfaces within an infested area that the pest will contact.

target pest. *See* target.

target plant. *See* target.

toxicant. A substance that, at a sufficient dose, will cause harm to a living organism.

toxicity. A pesticide's potential for poisoning an exposed organism.

toxicity category. The three classifications of pesticides that indicate the approximate level of hazard. The three categories are indicated by the signal words DANGER, WARNING, and CAUTION.

toxicity testing. A process in which known dosages of a pesticide are given to groups of test animals and the animals' responses are observed.

toxicology. The study of toxic substances and their effects on living organisms.

training record. A document signed by the trainer, employer, and trainee and used to record the dates and types of pesticide safety training that a trainee receives.

translocate, translocation. The movement of pesticides from one location to another within the tissues of a plant.

treated surface. The surface of plants, soil, or other items that were contacted with pesticide spray, dust, or granules for control of pests.

treatment area. *See* site.

trigger pump sprayer. A simple plastic container that holds a pesticide mixture, in which the applicator expels the pesticide by squeezing a lever (trigger) while pointing the nozzle at the target plant.

triple rinse. The process of partially filling an empty pesticide container, replacing the lid, swirling or shaking the container, then emptying its contents into the spray tank. This procedure is performed three times to ensure that most of the pesticide residue is removed.

tuber. An enlarged, fleshy underground stem with buds that are capable of producing new plants.

vaporize. To transform from a spray of droplets to a foglike vapor or gas.

vegetative reproductive structure. Part of a plant that allows it to regrow or produce a new plant without flowers or seeds; includes rootstocks, rhizomes, stolons, bulbs, and tubers.

vertebrate. An animal that has an internal skeleton and segmented spine, such as a fish, bird, reptile, or mammal.

virus. A very small organism that multiplies in living cells and is often capable of producing disease symptoms in plants and animals.

volatile. Able to pass readily from liquid or solid form into a gaseous form at low temperatures.

volatilization. The process by which a pesticide liquid or solid passes into a gaseous form.

WARNING. The signal word used on labels of pesticides considered moderately toxic or hazardous. Pesticides that are assigned the signal word WARNING based on toxicity usually have an oral LD_{50} between 50 and 500 mg/kg and a dermal LD_{50} between 200 and 2,000 mg/kg. *Also see* LD_{50} and signal word.

water soluble. Of a liquid or solid, having the ability to dissolve completely in water.

water-soluble concentrate. A liquid pesticide formulation that dissolves in water to form a true solution.

waterproof. *See* chemical-resistant.

weed. A nondesired plant.

wettable powder. A type of pesticide formulation consisting of an active ingredient that will not dissolve in water, combined with mineral clay and inert (other) ingredients and ground into a fine powder.

wildlife. Vertebrate animals such as gophers, moles, squirrels, and other animals that occur in nature. Pesticide applications need to be done with care so they do not harm naturally occurring wildlife that are not target pests.

winter annuals. Plants whose seeds sprout in the fall, grow over the winter, and produce seeds and die before summer.

woody plant. A plant that retains some living woody material at or above ground level through the nongrowing season.

work clothing. Garments such as long-sleeved shirts, short-sleeved shirts, long pants, short pants, shoes, and socks. Work clothing is not considered to be personal protective equipment, although pesticide product labeling or regulations may require that specific work clothing be worn during some activities. Work clothing differs from and should not be confused with a coverall.

◼ Further Reading

Abiotic Disorders of Landscape Plants. 2003. L. R. Costello. Oakland: Univ. Calif. Agric. Nat. Res. Publ. 3420.

IPM in Practice: Principles and Methods of Integrated Pest Management. 2001. M. L. Flint and P. Gouveia. Oakland: Univ. Calif. Agric. Nat. Res. Publ. 3418.

Landscape Maintenance Pest Control. 2006. P. O'Connor-Marer. UC Statewide Integrated Pest Management Program. Oakland: Univ. Calif. Agric. Nat. Res. Publ. 3493.

Landscape Pest Identification Cards. 2009. L.L. Strand (editor). UC Statewide Integrated Pest Management Program. Oakland: Univ. Calif. Agric. Nat. Res. Publ. 3513.

Laws and Regulations Study Guide. 2001. Sacramento: State of California Department of Pesticide Regulation. Publication Number PML LRSG 1.

Natural Enemies Handbook: The Illustrated Guide to Biological Pest Control. 1998. M. L. Flint and S. H. Dreistadt. UC Statewide Integrated Pest Management Project. Oakland: Univ. Calif. Agric. Nat. Res. Publ. 3386.

Pests of Landscape Trees and Shrubs. 2nd ed. 2004. S. H. Dreistadt. UC Statewide Integrated Pest Management Program. Oakland: Univ. Calif. Agric. Nat. Res. Publ. 3359.

Pests of the Garden and Small Farm. 2nd ed. 1998. M. L. Flint. UC Statewide Integrated Pest Management Program. Oakland: Univ. Calif. Agric. Nat. Res. Publ. 3332.

The Safe and Effective Use of Pesticides. 2nd ed. 2006. P. O'Connor-Marer. UC Statewide Integrated Pest Management Program. Oakland: Univ. Calif. Agric. Nat. Res. Publ. 3324.

UC Guide to Healthy Lawns. Available at the UC IPM Web site, http://www.ipm.ucdavis.edu/TOOLS/TURF/

Weeds of California and Other Western States. 2007. J. M. Ditomaso and E. A. Healy. Oakland: Univ. Calif. Agric. Nat. Res. Publ. 3488.

Weeds of the West. 2002. L. Burrill, D. Cudney, S. Dewey, R. Lee, B. Nelson, R. Parker, and R. Whitson, Oakland: Univ. Calif. Agric. Nat. Res. Publ. 3350.

Wildlife Pest Control around Gardens and Homes. 2nd ed. 2006. T. P. Salmon, T. A. Whisson, and R. A. Marsh. Oakland: Univ. Calif. Agric. Nat. Res. Publ. 21385.

University of California, Statewide Integrated Pest Management Program Web site **www.ipm.ucdavis.edu** includes much information of interest to maintenance gardeners including:

- The *Pest Notes* publication series, which are short-answer publications describing management solutions for over 140 insect, weed, pathogen, and vertebrate landscape and garden pests.

- The *UC Guide to Healthy Lawns,* a comprehensive, interactive source for all lawn management information.

- *Pests in Gardens and Landscapes* database that allows you to choose a plant to find the most likely source of your pest problem.

- Information on home and landscape pesticides.